Routledge Studies in Leadership Research

Researching Leadership-As-Practice
The Reappearing Act of Leadership
Vasilisa Takoeva

Adaptive Leadership in a Global Economy
Perspective for Application and Scholarship
Edited by Mohammed Raei and Harriette Thurber Rasmussen

Women Business Leaders
Identity, Resistance, and Alternative Forms of Knowledge in Saudi Arabia
Liela A. Jamjoom

Responsible Leadership in Corporate Governance
An Integrative Approach
Monique Cikaliuk, Ljiljana Eraković, Brad Jackson, Chris Noonan and Susan Watson

Leadership and China
Philosophy, Place and Practice
Edited by Ralph J. Bathurst and Michelle Sitong Chen

Leadership and Narcissism in the Organization
Mateusz Grzesiak

Public Sector Leadership
A Human-Centred Approach
Petri Virtanen, Marika Tammeaid and Harri Jalonen

Toxic Leadership
Research and Cases
Steven Walker and Daryl Watkins

For more information about this series please visit: https://www.routledge.com/Routledge-Studies-in-Leadership-Research/book-series/RSLR

Leadership and China

Philosophy, Place and Practice

Edited by Ralph J. Bathurst and Michelle Sitong Chen

Routledge
Taylor & Francis Group
NEW YORK AND LONDON

First published 2023
by Routledge
605 Third Avenue, New York, NY 10158

and by Routledge
4 Park Square, Milton Park, Abingdon, Oxon, OX14 4RN

Routledge is an imprint of the Taylor & Francis Group, an informa business

Library of Congress Cataloguing-in-Publication Data
Names: Bathurst, Ralph, editor. | Chen, Michelle Sitong, editor.
Title: Leadership and China : philosophy, place and practice / edited by Ralph J Bathurst and Michelle Sitong Chen.
Description: New York, NY : Routledge, 2023. | Series: Routledge studies in leadership research | Includes bibliographical references and index.
Identifiers: LCCN 2022022951 | ISBN 9781032100920 (hbk) | ISBN 9781032100937 (pbk) | ISBN 9781003213604 (ebk)
Subjects: LCSH: Leadership--China. | International trade. | China--Economic conditions.
Classification: LCC HD57.7 .L43136 2023 | DDC 658.4/0920951--dc23/eng/20220610
LC record available at https://lccn.loc.gov/2022022951

ISBN: 978-1-032-10092-0 (hbk)
ISBN: 978-1-032-10093-7 (pbk)
ISBN: 978-1-003-21360-4 (ebk)

DOI: 10.4324/9781003213604

Typeset in Bembo
by MPS Limited, Dehradun

Contents

About the Authors

Ralph J. Bathurst is a lecturer in Management and Leadership at Massey University's Albany Campus. His research in the aesthetics of leadership focuses on music performance and composition. This and other arts inform his interests in sustainability and corporate social responsibility, as well as Chinese philosophy and what we can learn from ancient texts today.

Simon Burgess is a lecturer in Ethical Leadership within the University of New England Business School in Armidale, New South Wales. He has a BCom (Economics) and BA (Philosophy) from the University of Melbourne, and a PhD in ethical theory from Monash University. After completing his PhD, he worked in social policy design, management, academia, and management consultancy. Simon nourishes his interest in Confucius mainly via the written word, and almost entirely in translation. Having happily married into a Chinese family, however, he also appreciates the more personal insights and reflections that his wife and certain in-laws can provide. Simon especially enjoys the robust and generous-spirited discussions about Chinese politics that he has with his Chinese-born father-in-law.

Michelle Sitong Chen is a Professional Teaching Fellow at the University of Auckland Business School. She worked as a lecturer and senior tutor over the past 6 years across New Zealand Tertiary institutions, such as Massey University, Unitec Institute of Technology, and Whitireia and Wellington Institute of Technology. Her PhD research is about helping Chinese and New Zealand organizations in managing tensions arising from sustainability.

Ling Ding is the International Officer at the School of Digital Creativity and Performing Arts, the University of York, UK, and is a graduate teaching assistant for the courses in MA Music Education and MA Community Music. Her work focuses on international cooperation between the UK and Chinese higher education institutions in the arts. She was the director or coordinator in multiple international conferences and music festivals and has been awarded *Top 30 Global Characters 2020* by

Chinese Central Television. She completed two Masterates in Community Music and Music by research and holds a Ph. from the University of York.

Ambrose Field is dean of Arts and Humanities at the University of York, UK and is a member of the executive board of the university. His work has focused on creating new international relationships within the arts, looking for creative solutions to some of today's pressing issues within the education sector. Field was awarded an honorary professorship with the Beijing Institute for Advanced Innovation in 2017 and presents regularly at international interdisciplinary conferences on creativity and technologies. He studied education at the University of Cambridge (Robinson College), UK and holds a PhD from City, University of London. He has acted as a consultant to two multinational technology companies and has a research training in high performance computing. Field was an international research fellow at Massey University, Aotearoa New Zealand in 2019. His own creative musical work is recorded by ECM records and distributed by Universal.

Stephen A. Linstead is professor of Management Humanities and Co-Lead of the Management and Humanities Research Theme in the School of Business and Society at the University of York. A Fellow of the Academy of the Social Sciences with a higher doctorate from the University of Durham, his previous Chairs include the Universities of Durham, Essex, and Wollongong, and a visiting scholarship at Hong Kong University of Science and Technology. He has also been a visiting professor at the University of Business and Economics, Beijing. He has served on validation panels for the Hong Kong Council for Academic Awards, and consulted to organizations including Cathay Pacific, Hong Kong Mass Transit Railway Corporation, Hong Kong Hospital Authority, and the University of Macau. He has published on China in journals including the *Asia Pacific Journal of Management*, *Culture and Organization*, and *Gender, Work and Organization*. He is a former member of Silk Roots, a band performing Celtic-Chinese crossover music.

Theresa McNichol is an award-winning artist, curator, and Senior Associate Adjunct Professor of Asian Art History and studio for 30 years at both community college and university levels. She holds a Master's degree in Chinese art, Asian art history, Chinese language, and area studies. A former museum director, her research, international conference presentations, and publications highlight both wise pedagogy and wise management. McNichol has been a sponsored presenter at international management conferences in the UK, Taiwan, Beijing (PRC) and the wise management conference held in Shanghai China (PRC). Her chapter "Appreciative Inquiry Case Study: Executive MBA Candidates" is in the recent second printing of *The Sustainable Enterprise Fieldbook: Building New Bridges* (Routledge, 2019); her chapter "The Art Museum as Laboratory for Re-Imagining a Sustainable

Future" is based on her students' introspective museum essays in *Positive Design and Appreciative Construction: From Sustainable Development to Sustainable Value* (Vol. 3). She is President, Ren Associates and developer of *imaginement*® a tool for assessing wise thinking processes in college student first-report essays written on an art object in the museum that highlight reverent attention, awe, *seeing* reflexively, insightful moral imagination and *becoming* proper stewards.

Hunter Meng Qingyu was raised in Luoyang and studied at the University of International Business and Economics (UIBE) in Beijing. He is currently completing post graduate studies at Massey University, exploring the *Tao Te Ching* and its potential contributions to leadership theory.

Selina Yang Xiaona was raised in Dalian and studied at Liaoning University of International Business and Economics in China. She is currently completing post graduate studies at Massey University, studying how Chinese business leaders establish and sustain trusting partnerships within the New Zealand context.

Yue Feng has a PhD in Management from Massey University, New Zealand, and his work orients toward critical management and leadership studies. Many years of training and developing leadership in businesses provide him with the awareness of and sensitivity towards business-related needs and expectations. Dr Yue's academic work is based on the work of French philosopher François Jullien, and was the first PhD thesis of its kind in organizational studies. In today's world where China takes a significant role in the global economy, learning about a Chinese perspective is essential. His work casts Chinese thought as a system that is in tune with the energetic dimension of reality. This Chinese lens provides refreshing new angles to help understand existing management and leadership issues, critique current thinking and practices, decolonize organizational knowledge, and resolve enduring issues in organizational studies.

Forward: Why Leadership and China?

Ralph J. Bathurst and Michelle Chen Sitong

China has held fascination for Westerners for generations. Her stunning landscapes, multiplicity of foods, varieties of languages, and long history of human settlement have attracted travellers along its winding and sometimes treacherous roads from Europe to Xi'an, the center of ancient Chinese civilization. China's ability to manage its large population over centuries, with its changing dynasties and sophisticated bureaucracies has caused much admiration. Further, her ability to master technologies in support of her people has inspired artists, inventors, and engineers throughout the ages. Indeed, long before its global technology giants were conceived, the Great Wall, once a defensive technological device to resist marauding invaders, is now a compulsory stopover for tourists of all kind, world leaders included. For several millennia now, China has shown pathways to civilization.

For much of the 20th-century China was absorbed in a quest to redefine its sense of nationhood. First, it overthrew the Qing dynasty in a more-or-less bloodless revolution in 1911. The rise of the Republic of China, under the initial leadership of Sun Yat-sen came with a struggle for political control where the larger party of the Kuomintang (KMT) sought dominance over the Communist Party of China (CCP). China was divided with the Kuomintang ascendant in urban districts while the Communist Party's influence was in rural areas.

The Japanese invasion beginning in 1931 also brought with it a struggle between the two rival Chinese parties. This was a very troubled time, and much blood was shed. The Japanese invasion ended in 1945, but the civil war continued until 1949 when the leader of the Kuomintang, Chiang Kai-shek left with his supporters to re-establish his base in Taiwan. On October 1, 1949 the leader of the Communist Party of China, Mao Zedong (1893–1976) announced the formation of the People's Republic of China.

And so began several decades of a fortress nation. During this time China established itself as a Communist state, with an alliance formed with the Soviet Union.

Several significant events moved to China from a closed country to one that was more open for Western business development. First, on February 21, 1972, the then US President Richard Nixon visited the nation to assist efforts in building diplomatic ties. Second, in December 1978, leader Deng Xiaoping announced the Open Door Policy that was to encourage Western business investment in Chinese companies, especially those in the coastal cities. Third, to reinforce the earlier diplomatic efforts, in January 1979 Deng Xiaoping visited the USA, to be hosted by President Jimmy Carter. Perhaps as a sign of divisions which would surface in the 21st-century Deng's visit was met with some protest, including an assassination attempt in Houston Texas by a member of the Ku Klux Klan.

Since that time China has experienced exponential growth. Businesses have thrived and megacities have sprouted to accommodate urbanization and the growing middle class. She has managed to embody Deng Xiaoping's famous aphorism: "It doesn't matter if a cat is black or white, so long as it catches mice" by walking a fine line between capitalist expansion and Communist communitarianism.

Of course, this balancing act where business freedom is set against political control has come with much faltering. The so-called Tiananmen incident of 1989 where student protesters were killed by army compatriots reveals a cadre of nervous leaders worried about political change driven by popular movements. Yet despite its totalitarian gestures, China carries on with its business developments and trading patterns across the world.

These contradictions between business expansion and State control have inspired us to bring together this collection of essays under the broad umbrella of leadership.

Leadership is of prime importance because it opens conversations beyond crude managerialism and bureaucratic creep, toward exploring how people move within political and business worlds. The combination of leadership and China, therefore, makes for a compelling enquiry because of the complexities of the Chinese story. Her rich history and current contradictions are intriguing leadership scholars who try to make sense of China's place in the world today.

There is no escaping that today China is a significant actor on the world stage. She is an economic powerhouse with a reach into every corner of the globe. The Belt and Road Initiative formed as part of Xi Jingping's presidency is an ambitious plan that confirms the nation's prominence, facilitating business diplomacy among countries that would otherwise have little in common.

China has her critics, perhaps the most strident coming from other global powers such as the USA and the UK. Much of the criticisms are founded on differences in political leadership, especially the perceptions that China is a totalitarian State. Absent from these denunciations are examinations of authoritarian creep within Western democracies and an accompanying unwillingness to examine the controlling forces at work that stifle open debate. To be sure, the abuse of human rights issues must be examined, and leaders held to account wherever they occur, be they in Xinjiang or Guantanamo Bay.

The 21st century is seeing the rise and rise of China both in business and scholarship. Some even advocate that this is the Chinese century, with Kirby (2014) noting the number of recent publications which suggest a changing world order. But can Chinese leaders chart a course that avoids the negative impacts of empires of bygone ages, including as Lachmann (2020) suggests, the USA?

Perhaps in defence of China, the long history of philosophical enquiry may provide guidance for today's leaders seeking to act good faith. Two names stand aloft the plethora of several millennia of Chinese scholars: Lau Tzu and Confucius. Throughout history, Chinese leaders have both drawn on, and rejected these two lodestars. Their works have been adapted and appropriated for both sacred and secular purposes and yet their influence remains potent.

It is not surprising, then, that Lao Tzu and Confucius play prominent guiding roles in this collection. Their works and ideas have endured, and we seek here to know them within our social and political context. We set our compass through Confucius who begins and ends this book. To start, Ling, Linstead, and Field explore the larger West East convergences through a smaller examination of Confucian *guanxi* and Foucauldian dispositive. They operationalize their study through a case study of cross-cultural collaboration. Burgess ends by looking forward to what he terms Confucian liberalism, noting that an accurate reading of the texts, would lead us toward an open, dialogic political environment.

Yue takes a China-centric approach through his study of the *dao* and *shi*. He establishes the differences between Chinese and Western viewpoints which, he argues, are a necessary beginning when studying leadership. Meng and Yang strengthen these ideas by taking selected passages from the Tao De Jing and overlaying them with an empirical study of Chinese leaders working in a non Chinese context.

McNicol takes an innovative approach to West East constructs by examining landscape paintings by Chinese literati and Hudson River School of Art painters, the first major art movement in the USA. Her study amplifies the need by leaders to develop an environmental consciousness, a necessary precursor to exercising wise leadership.

Chen and Bathurst's essays are empirical in that they focus on conundrums that occupy today's leaders. Paradox and tensions are hallmarks of Chinese and Western business partnerships, and Chen's analyses demonstrate the necessity of embracing both to achieve sustainability. Bathurst takes a cultural approach in his study of indigenous Māori leaders in Aotearoa New Zealand and their fruitful relationships with Chinese counterparts.

Despite efforts by some Western leaders to cast aspersions on China, as does former US Vice President Mike Pence declaring China to be an "evil empire" and "the greatest threat on the face of the Earth" (Fink, 2021), the challenges facing planet Earth today call for collaborative efforts by leaders of all countries. The climate crisis cannot be mitigated by one nation or locale alone. This concerted effort to address this global problem takes leadership, but not of the kinds we have relied on in the past.

We are called to a different form of leadership in the 21st century, and current leaders need to shift their orientation toward future needs rather than defensive postures based on past modalities. Take for example President Xi Jinping's (2021) speech to mark the 100th anniversary of the Communist Party of China, and his affirmation of the strength of the economy and military prowess in maintaining the country's status as an active player on the world stage. His speech was a celebration of the Party's history. However, he warns citizens that they must obey Party objectives and not seek to upset the status quo, saying, "Any attempt to divide the Party from the Chinese people or to set the people against the Party is bound to fail." To other nations, he was also strident in his position:

We Chinese are a people who uphold justice and are not intimidated by threats of force. As a nation, we have a strong sense of pride and confidence. We have never bullied, oppressed, or subjugated the people of any other country, and we never will. By the same token, we will never allow any foreign force to bully, oppress, or subjugate us. Anyone who would attempt to do so will find themselves on a collision course with a great wall of steel forged by over 1.4 billion Chinese people. (Xi, 2021)

Rhetoric of this nature has served leaders well in the past, but it does not invite the kinds of collaboration and partnership necessary to take radical steps necessary to mitigate climate change and the growing divide between the rich and poor.

The future calls for leaders who can reach out and embrace differences of opinion and multiplicities of perspectives. Leadership of tomorrow needs a generous spirit and willingness to learn from the past, especially the philosophers who have helped form our cultural values. China has a vital role to play, and leaders of both the East and West must join hands to strive for the betterment of all humanity.

References

Fink, J. (2021, 14 July). *Mike pence says China seizing on Biden admin 'weakness' to become 'evil empire'*. Retrieved November 3 from https://www.newsweek.com/mike-pence-says-china-seizing-biden-admin-weakness-become-evil-empire-1609794

Kirby, W. C. (2014). The Chinese century? The challenges of higher education. *Daedalus*, *143*(2), 145–156.

Lachmann, R. (2020). *First class passengers on a sinking ship: Elite politics and the decline of great powers*. Verso.

Xi, J. (2021, 1 July). *Speech by Xi Jinping at a ceremony marking the centenary of the CPC*. Retrieved 24 August from http://www.xinhuanet.com/english/special/2021-07/01/c_1310038244.htm

1 Confucian connections: Foucault and guanxi

Ling Ding, Stephen A. Linstead, and Ambrose Field

Introduction

Confucian dynamism as a concept is familiar to students of cross-cultural management, popularized in Geert Hofstede's inventory of work-related values drawing on research by psychologist Michael Harris Bond (Hofstede & Bond, 1988). It represents the ability of Confucian cultures to move quickly and uniformly to implement decisions due to shared implicit cultural imperatives and has been found to be characteristic of many entrepreneurial overseas Chinese economies (Kim & Park, 2003; Kim, 2009). Some commentators have given more attention to components of the Confucian code, such as hierarchy, and how they are applied in international business, such as Westwood, Chan, & Linstead (2004) on employment relations. Westwood (1997; Westwood & Chan 1992) suggests that such is the collective importance of this family of characteristics, the term *leadership* is less appropriate than that of *headship* for such cultures. While in the past such work has tended to focus on facilitating entry into internal Chinese markets or understanding the rapid growth of overseas Chinese-driven Asian tiger economies, more recently it has begun to focus on developing effective partnerships. Here, two concepts seem to offer themselves as fruitful ground for comparison – the Eastern concept of connections, or *guanxi*, as it is found in Confucianism and practiced culturally; and the Western concept of *dispositif*, or dispositive, a specific form of disposition as found in the work of Michel Foucault in particular. In this chapter, we discuss the development of the East-West hybrid concept of *guanxi dispositive* (Ding, 2021; Ding, Linstead, & Field, 2019) and its relevance to relational leadership (Fulop, Linstead, & Lilley, 2009). We explore through discourse analysis examples from empirical work on international cooperation and collaboration between institutions from the People's Republic of China (PRC) and the United Kingdom (UK) on arts initiatives, to illustrate the importance of mutual understanding of the relationships between governmentality, culture, power, and knowledge.

DOI: 10.4324/9781003213604-1

Confucianism and *guanxi*

Confucianism, still arguably the most important value system in China, remains foundational to most accounts of modern Chinese history and social culture and more recently workplace meaning and values (Luo, 1997; Davies, et al., 1995; Hui & Graen, 1997; Hwang, 2015; Nie & Lämsä, 2015; Westwood & Lok 2003). Confucianism is a social ideology, an ethical system rather than a philosophy per se although it has philosophical elements, touching on metaphysics and centering on lifelong learning; neither is it a typical religion having no godhead, and a heaven (*tiān* 天) that exists more as an abstract principle. Indeed, Confucianism is sometimes called a secular religion that blurs the boundary between religion and humanism, considering that ordinary human activities and relationships of human life are at their best a transcendent manifestation of the abstract sacred. This allows it to sit alongside a variety of religious systems across Asia and accommodate their diversity. As a form of sociopolitical governance, it rests on the twin core values of maintaining social order and establishing and reproducing social harmony (Westwood, 1992, pp. 50–55). *Guanxi* (the concept of connection) derives from this system and its five principles or *wu lun* (King, 1991; Hui, & Graen, 1997; Luo, 1997; Nie, & Lämsä, 2015).

Wu lun (五 伦: *wu* 五 means five, *lun* 伦 means ethics) is a hierarchical system, demarcating the roles and relations of emperor–courtier, father–son, husband–wife, elder–younger siblings, and friend–friend, that enables order and harmony to be preserved (Chen & Chen, 2004). In these five interpersonal relationships, with the exception of friend–friend equity, the former term occupies a higher status position that must be fully respected by the latter from their lower status position (Yang, 1994).

As a result of being embedded in this Confucian hierarchy, Chinese people are sensitive to authority in its different forms and seek to read this with some nuance from situation to situation. Organizationally, Chen et al. (2013) argue, the more positional power a person presents, the more compliance or even obedience their employees will show.

In the *guanxi* research literature, there are both broad typologies of *guanxi* ties and theories of dyadic *guanxi* (Chen, Chen, & Huang, 2013; Lee & Zhong, 2021). *Guanxi* ties include family-non-family *guanxi* (King, 1991; Tsang, 1998), affective-instrumental *guanxi* (Hwang, 1987; Yang, 1999), personal/informal-impersonal/contractual *guanxi* (Yang, 1999; Davies, Leung, Luk, & Wong, 1995), and mixed *guanxi* (Hwang, 1987; Yang, 1994). In analyzing characteristics of relationships more specifically, dyadic *guanxi* research has identified three aspects: *guanxi* bases (Tsui & Farh, 1997; Chen & Chen, 2004), *guanxi* quality (Hwang, 1987; Yang, 1999; Peng & Yang, 1999), and *guanxi* dynamics – strategy, practices, and processes (Luo, Huang, & Wang, 2012; Chen & Chen 2004; Su et al., 2007). *Guanxi* bases are twofold: family and society (Tsang, 1998; Hui & Graen, 1997). Chinese families are patrimonial, in that the male is the head and authority of the household, but not patrilineal, in that inheritance does not pass entirely to the eldest son, but is split between the children, which frequently means that large family companies are subdivided even before the necessity of probate (Westwood, 1992, p. 105; Westwood & Chan, 1992, pp. 123–128). This generates structures that, in contrast to Western organizations, are highly centralized yet low on formality and complexity, with roles often loosely defined and flexible (Westwood, 1992, pp. 112–113). Family-based *guanxi* is built up through immediate familial and wider kinship relations, extending to ancestral connections. More encompassing than the Western nuclear family, where the strength of ties dissipates dramatically as one moves outside the core, Chinese kinship ties may remain compelling to a much greater extent before weakening. This is the strongest and most exclusive form of *guanxi*. In contrast society-based *guanxi* is formulated by friendship and business, which is more open-access, and weaker than the family-based type (Tsang, 1998). In both types, however, *guanxi* has a clear pattern of obligations and benefits associated with its connections (Ambler, et al., 1999; Wang, 2007; Chen, Chang, & Lee, 2015).

Guanxi, can have significant positive implications for a business or public department (Luo, 2008; Davies, et al., 1995). In the modern Chinese business environment, transactions need to be approached via individual *guanxi* networks, with *guanxi* argued to be the most significant element in setting up a new business in China (Ambler, Styles, & Wang, 1999). In the supervisor-subordinate relationship, understanding *guanxi* provides critical guidance for Western managers, highlighting the importance of "personal feelings" and "face" in Chinese leader–member relationships (Nie & Lämsä, 2015; Zhang, Li, & Harris, 2015). China has historically lacked a strong contract system, legal review and enforcement processes, and formal regulations – it has begun to move on these issues recently but slowly as there would need to be a veritable army of lawyers trained and recruited to establish robust regulations and oversee their application. Hence informal obligations have emerged to fill the trust vacuum and enable confidence in commercial, economic, and social relations (Davies, 1995, pp. 158–162). *Guangxi*, or connections, are essential for maintaining what has been described as Confucian dynamism, especially in what have been termed "Overseas Chinese" rapidly growing economies elsewhere in Asia. These connections come with obligations of reciprocity, a principle that is essential for maintaining social harmony, through ties that may be expressive, instrumental, or mixed (Hwang, 1998). *Expressive ties* are those that adhere to familial, extended kinship relations, and friendships, and here *guanxi* is rarely important as issues are kept "in the family" and determined on a needs basis. While the patriarch is the head of the family, and has authority, this needs to be exercised responsibly with care, respect, and consideration, in mutuality, to avoid conflict (Westwood & Chan, 1992, p. 125). *Instrumental ties* are more regulated and objective, often related to bottom line issues in which everyone is treated the same. *Mixed* or *particularistic ties* are where *guanxi* becomes most important, however, in managing an appropriate balance of influence (Davies, 1995, p. 157). On the other hand, *guanxi* can also cause problems within wider society. For example, it is frequently criticized for crossing the boundary into corruption, bribery, or nepotism (Luo, 2008; Fan, 2002; Dunfee & Warren, 2001; Davies, 1995, pp. 163–165) or self-suppressing rather than resolving conflict (Hwang, 1998). In this chapter, nevertheless, we explore the use of the simplified – elementary level of *guanxi* to understand processes of building trust between different institutions.

Dispositive and discourse

Foucault (1977) explains that a *dispositif* (in English "dispositive" from here on) is a sociocultural mechanism that includes discursive and non-discursive practices, which has structural similarities to *guanxi*. This is consistent with Foucault's wider theory of "discourse" (Fairclough, 1992; Wodak & Meyer, 2015; Johnstone, 2017; Gumperz, 1982; Graesser, Millis, & Zwaan, 1997), a useful analytical tool for interpreting the networked and layered nature of knowledge. For Foucault (1971), discourse is knowledge, information, text, and languages as they are used for generating interpreted *truth* in history.

Accordingly, Hall (1997) asserted that Foucault's definition of discourse was as much about *ways of thinking and practices* as it was about language. Hall argues that for Foucault, meaning and meaningful actions are only made meaningful "within the constitutive abstract space of a discourse" (cited in Hobbs, 2008, p. 7). Discourse has different sources that consist of what Foucault called "principles," such as the principle of discipline; the will to truth (will to knowledge, a certain system of exclusion in the process of development) in its continuity, as well as its discontinuity; principles of *specificity* (that a particular discourse cannot be resolved by a prior system of significations) and *exteriority* (we should look for its external conditions of existence to determine its limits).

Foucault (1971) stresses the importance of the discontinuity and exteriority of discourse, as he insists that discourse has its own limitations and that we need to think about the knowledge that surrounds discourse to break the limits of discourse. Foucault's approach to discourse is complemented by his treatment of the related concept of a dispositive, which was influenced by Althusser and by Canguilhem's temporalization of the concept of the norm – the idea that norms are not abstract and universal even in a single culture, but relative as they shift over time (Lambert, 2015a, b). The shaping principles of discontinuity and exteriority of discourse do not determine the discourse itself, but they are rather a series of activities, events and practices that have been done around discourse and lend themselves to its formation, while themselves being affected by it. Such phenomena are located in the theoretical area of the dispositive.

Deleuze (1992) indicates that dispositive is often recognized as an analytical tool. Nevertheless, it is more than merely technical, as Raffnsøe Marius Gudmand-Høyer and Thaning (2016) argue, agreeing with Rabinow and Rose (2003, p xv) that it is "one of the most powerful conceptual tools introduced by Foucault." Basu (2011, p. 34)) explains that "the term dispositive usually refers to a constellation of heterogeneous elements within a system, and the relationships between them, which produce a particular tendency" (p. 34). He articulated first that a dispositive is a system of relations between a particular *arrangement of elements,* which are relations of power, knowledge, and constituted subjectivities. Second, Basu understands a dispositive as a historical formation that has a strategic function, though the strategy itself is not restricted to any one subject.

There are three perspectives on understanding dispositive. First, it encompasses discourse and its related activities, measures, physical forms, and scientific understanding of the world (from the interpretive perspective). Second, it also includes the relations and practices evolving between these discursive elements. Third, the most important point is that a dispositive is a formation, apparatus (*appareil*), and strategic integrator that functions as a matrix within real-world relations that controls, or sets boundaries upon subjection (the process of constructing individual and collective subjects as identities in relation to each other). In summary, a dispositive is a broader phenomenon than discourse, not a subset of it. Discourse is located within the domain of epistemology, the rules of knowledge generation operating via spoken, written textual and non-textual representations. However, Foucault was interested in a wider range of phenomena for studying practice and abstraction, by which he meant "historically specific totalities of discourses *and* practices" and the institutional power relations they form (Peltonen, 2004, p. 206).

In *guanxi* studies, discourse analysis presents a *prima facie* suitable research approach to explain the phenomenon, as the dominant methods employed in existing studies, such as questionnaires and interviews, are linguistic tools. However, *guanxi* itself is not only about cultural and moral roles but also includes practices and actions. Moreover, as *guanxi* is process embedded in Chinese culture, it informs behavior in a way that is often implicit and complex. In relying on the unsaid, *guanxi* lacks the symbolic representational richness of explicit discourse. Therefore, when we attempt to gain a more adequate understanding of how *guanxi* underpins social relations, thinking of it in terms of a dispositive can open new dimensions.

For example, MacInnis (1993 cited in Davies 1995, p. 156) gives a series of examples of *guanxi* discourse, without using the term. Some *active guanxi* expressions include:

> To *la guanxi* (literally to 'pull' *guanxi*) means to get on the good side of someone, to store political capital with them, and carries no pejorative overtones. To *gua guanxi* (literally to 'work on' *guanxi*) means roughly

> the same but with a more general, less intense feeling and usually carries negative overtones … *Lisun guanxi* ('straighten out' *guanxi*) means to put a guanxi back into proper or normal order, usually after a period of difficulty or awkwardness.
>
> (MacInnis 1993)

Different *states of guanxi* are also observed:

> *Meiyou guanxi* ('without' *guanxi*) has become an idiom meaning 'it doesn't matter'. *Guanxi gao jiang* (*guanxi* made ruined) means the relationship has gone bad, usually because of a lack of flexibility of those involved. *You guanxi* (to 'have *guanxi*') means to have access to needed influence. *Youde shi guanxi* ('what one does have' or 'the one thing one does have' is *guanxi*) is sometimes negative, meaning that one has all the *guanxi* one needs, but something else essential is lacking.
>
> (MacInnis 1993)

And different *guanxi situations* are also demarcated:

> *Guanxi wang* ('*guanxi* net') means the whole network of *guanxi* through which influence is brokered. *Guanxi hu* ('*guanxi* family') means a person, organization, even a government department, occupying a focal point in one's *guanxi* network.
>
> (MacInnis 1993)

From the above, we can see how the idea of a dispositive can map onto that of *guanxi* in several ways. First, *guanxi* is a formation or a system where relationships and related elements function through power, knowledge, and subjectivities, and produces and reproduces a particular *tendency*. *Guanxi* predisposes subjects to a particular kind of action without necessarily predetermining it. Second, *guanxi* is also a historical formation that changes demographically by generation. Both of these features allow us to consider *guanxi* as a particular form of social dispositive typically found in China and Chinese communities, and possibly others as well.

Van Fraassen (1970) argues that a dispositive is an objective reality where the relations of elements change with time and space. Although a dispositive involves subjectivity, its nature as a concept does not change according to individual subjects: subjectivity is merely the vehicle, its existence and changes do not rely on it. We would wish to qualify this: while it is important not to reduce disposition to the level of individual psychology, simply dichotomizing subject and object is unnecessarily crude, and at odds with Foucault's obsession with the constructed nature of reality and its often subtle contingencies. *Guanxi* certainly displays exteriority, but this does not constitute objectivity, and *guanxi* is in a constant state of flux that requires attention and maintenance.

As we have noted, it has been frequently observed in Chinese culture in relation to *guanxi* that things left unsaid are just important as those directly said. For example, seemingly non-communicative speaking behavior and empathy – important elements of *guanxi* – all require explicit non-discursive practices to break into a *guanxi* network or to improve *guanxi* relationships.

Nevertheless, it is inadvisable to see these as silent mechanisms operating in the background. Canguilhem (2008, p. 76) cautions that "with the exception of vertebrates, living beings and their forms rarely display to the scrupulous observer devices [*dispositifs*] that could evoke the idea of a mechanism, in the sense given to this term by scientists." Basu (2011) offers an alternative perspective in claiming that dispositive analysis allows us to examine the wide range of phenomena and their relations that constitute a *cultural memory* rather than a mechanism. As Foucault uses it, the term discourse is far more than language or text as conventionally understood, because it implies the poststructuralist understanding of text as any symbolic set of relations despite the continuance of debates as to what is and is not a "text" and how it is distinct from practice. Such analysis involves identifying the constituent elements of cultural memory within a given dispositive, the relations between them, and the subject positions they bring about – which may traverse more than one specific discourse.

Developing this line of analysis, Foucault identifies three prototypical modalities of disposition, particularly associated with his concerns with sovereignty and governmentality (Villadsen, 2021, pp. 478–479). The first is the *juridical* dispositive of the *law*; the second the dispositive of *discipline*; the third the dispositive of *security* (biopolitics and governmentality). If the same concept is approached from each different disposition the distinctions are clearer to see. Foucault (2004b, pp. 6–8; 2007, pp. 4–6) gives the hypothetical example of theft. The juridical disposition focuses on identifying what is prohibited, and what is permitted, lays down a law and specifies penalties for breaking it – matching a type of crime to a type of punishment. The disciplinary disposition is more about prevention, in that by identifying a number of supervisions, checks, inspections, and controls it makes it possible to identify potential thieves before they steal, and monitor them and their situations as a means of correction. The security dispositive is more calculative and risk-oriented, considering how to predict statistically the number of thefts at any point in time, place, or social stratum, and calculate the balance between risk/cost of the theft and the inconveniences of its repression (Foucault cited in Raffensøe et al., 2016, pp. 280–281). We think that this leaves room for a fourth form: the *guanxi* or *connection* dispositive. From this perspective, the informal and formal relations at play in the setting that might make offending or reoffending, prevention or detection more likely, would be paramount. In a society where the juridical dispositive was weak, as it is in China, discipline and security would themselves be dependent on relationships, trust, and networks to maintain order. Therefore, the idea of a *guanxi dispositive* can fit comfortably with Foucault's exemplar (Raffensøe et al., 2016, p. 282).

From both functionalist and interpretivist Western researchers' points of view, *guanxi* has been studied as a knowledge-based, cultural, and communication practice primarily through language, with knowledge being gained from sharing subjective perspectives and interpretations. However, Chinese researchers would tend to approach *guanxi* as a construction or assemblage that can exist in the society with a variety of different layouts, connections, and re-combinations encompassing both discursive and non-discursive practice which renders it amenable to a more Foucauldian post-structuralist approach. In the rest of this chapter, we apply dispositive analysis to help develop the concept we have called the "*guanxi dispositive.*"

The *guanxi dispositive*

The *guanxi* dispositive, here based on UK–China cooperation in higher education institutions in the arts, can be thought to include four stages of benefits and two dimensions of development. These benefits range from the surface level to those which are apparent only after continued development: stabilization, ranking, magnification, and concentration, respectively. The two dimensions represent the quality and quantity of cooperation. These benefits and dimensions formulate the frame of the model, and dimensions of *guanxi* identify roles important in helping institutions to achieve their goals and enjoy strategic benefits.

Stabilization is the first stage of every relationship, which provides an effective communication channel for collaborations. With positive conditions of communication, such as frequent visits, and infrequent staff changes in key positions, collaborations could be initiated. ***Ranks*** and rankings, however contested or controversial, are the dominant symbolic power representing the perceived quality of institutions. They function as an index of the institution's cultural capital. Simultaneously, high standards of stable relationships and cooperation might increase prospective partners' positions in ranking systems like league tables, as internationalization is one of the main criteria in such systems. These rankings further influence the ***magnification*** of institutions in two ways: establishing more practical and quality cooperation, and the possibility of upgrading institutional resources, both physical infrastructure and staff, such as recruiting more staff with overseas backgrounds (software) and purchasing better quality digital media systems in classrooms and laboratories. It is where symbolic power starts to transform into material capital, as institutions with high-ranking positions could potentially locate more funding for research and teaching purposes in the UK, and well-reputed institutions with branches in China will receive more support from central or local government. ***Concentration*** is the final stage of the loop, in which institutions actualize their propositions for international cooperation.

Ding (2021) found that elements of *guanxi* correlated positively with strengthening partnerships between UK and Chinese higher education institutions. Therefore, stabilizing cooperation not only requires people to have a working knowledge of *guanxi*, but also an understanding of how the actions they triggered would benefit relationships. For example, the more that is known about one of the *guanxi* elements, reciprocity, the more favor exchanges are undertaken. The more credit is earned for one's institution, the more it helps build trusting partnerships, the more knowledge that Western institutions have about reciprocity, the more understanding they could have about how the system works in setting up relationships with Chinese partners, but this is difficult to measure empirically. Institutions need to begin implementing actions based on *guanxi* roles to solidify relationships. Therefore, we can infer that a *guanxi dispositive* helps increase the success rate of international cooperation and increases the efficiency of individual collaborations.

Dimensions of the guanxi dispositive

There are two dimensions within the *guanxi dispositive*, namely the quantity and quality of international relationships. Quantity denotes the numbers of relationships that one institution has, whereas quality means the depth of relationships that one institution can maintain with their partner institutions. Combining these dimensions with the important *guanxi* elements (credit, reciprocity, and empathy) from the questionnaire devised by Ding, 2021, we propose the following model (see Figure 1.1).

Credit (*xinyong* 信用) is one of the fundamental elements of *guanxi*, and institutions could begin their relationships by referring to this model. Higher rankings mean the quantity of institutional relationships will be boosted, partners will be motivated to maintain the relationship and reduce

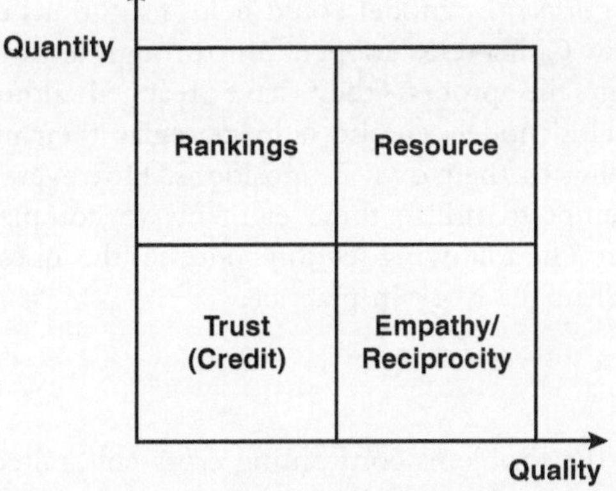

Figure 1.1 Theoretical framework of *Guanxi Dispositive* after Ding (2021).

further environmental search activity, and receive the benefits of stabilization in this direction. Therefore, by prioritizing quantity, institutions can obtain multiple stabilized relationships bolstered by *guanxi*-related trust and rankings (symbolic power), but nevertheless lack deep engagement. By focusing on credit (*xinyong*) as well as the other two elements of *guanxi* – empathy (*ganqing* 感情) and reciprocity (*renqing* 人情) – relationships will be able to provide deeper engagement between partner institutions. With this increased depth of relationships, institutions would achieve the benefit of ***Magnification***.

As a result of the increasing combination of quantity and quality through stabilization, ranking, and sustained magnification, institutions would reach the fourth stage of benefit, ***Concentration***. This requires a higher level of investment into both depth and quantity of relationships, which can be difficult for one institution to manage, especially in terms of time and human resources. From the *guanxi dispositive* model, the elements of *guanxi* play their catalytic action in both directions, but do not play a significant role in this combination phase. Therefore, *guanxi* provides solid conditions and foundations for the combination phase but does not influence it directly. To reach this phase, the investment of time, resource, for instance, must be measured and balanced, and this is a long-term process. However, institutions do not necessarily have a wide range of relationships with multiple institutions, as well as deep collaborations in every individual relationship.

The model does not denote any specific timespan, as the two dimensions represent only the quantity and quality of relationships. Relationships may improve over time, sour, then fail or be repaired as guanxi discourse mentioned earlier recognizes. On the other hand, this model helps institutions save time in accelerating relationship setup and lubricating maintenance. Also, when one institution plans to achieve the combination phase in this model, they find it more time-consuming than the others. However, there is no way to calculate a specific time for how long an institution needs to spend in any phase.

In summation, this *guanxi dispositive* model could help institutions evaluate their current position in China–UK cooperation through an understanding of which stage in the process they have reached although boundaries are permeable. This model can also help strategize their international cooperation according to their own propositions. However, is it possible or desirable to attempt to utilize these elements to complete a specific plan for cooperation? The following section addresses this question by exploring how the model might work in practice.

Discourse

Following Foucault (1997), the problems confronting cross-cultural collaborations are filtered through a variety of discourses, a complex field of both spoken and written statements, considered in their totality, dispersed at a distance, in events, and through time. Discourse denotes the knowledge base that helps understanding the international cooperation between the UK and China, and alerts us with ways of improving it from the perspective of human behavior.

Foucault (1982) defines discourse as, "any group of statements which belongs to a single system of formation; thus, there could be a clinical discourse, an economic discourse, a discourse of natural history, a psychiatric discourse" (p. 141). At the same time, "it is made up of a limited number of statements for which a group of conditions of existence can be defined" (p. 153). In this sense, some criticisms are possible, as the scope of thematic discourses is complex throughout groups of statements. How do we define statements and limit their conditions in a single discourse; and how do we identify a discourse from related groups of statements?

These are the problems that emerge as the discontinuity of history, to which the discursive formation (group of statements) is the key to explanation. Foucault (1997) argues that the relationship between statements in different kinds of technical, economic, social, and political circumstances gives us freedom to underpin or unpin the interplay of the relations within and outside it. We can accordingly analyze discourse from two sets of statements: governmentality/culture and power/knowledge.

Governmentality and culture

Governmentality

Governmentality concerns three ideas that Foucault first outlined in his lectures at the Collège de France in 1978. First, the ensemble of governmentality formed by:

> Institutions, procedures, analyses and reflections, calculations, and tactics that allow the exercise of this very specific, albeit very complex, power that has the population as its target, political economy as its major form of knowledge, and apparatuses of security as its essential technical instrument.
>
> (Foucault, 2007, p. 108)

Second, Foucault understands:

> The tendency, the line of force, that for a long time, and throughout the West, has constantly led towards the pre-eminence over all other types of power – sovereignty, discipline, and so on – of the type of power that we can call 'government' and which has led to the development of a series of specific governmental apparatuses on the one hand, [and, on the other] to the development of a series of knowledges.
>
> (Foucault, 2007, p. 108)

Third, Foucault thinks that this is how we should understand the process:

> Or rather, the result of the process by which the state of justice of the Middle Ages became the administrative state in the fifteenth and sixteenth centuries and was gradually 'governmentalized'.
>
> (Foucault, 2007, pp. 108–109)

For the UK and China, these governmental processes and histories are very different. China has become a one-party state, whereas the UK has several competing parties who may succeed each other or combine to form a coalition in government, and an independent Civil Service to administer policy. The principle is tripartite – the legislative (Parliament) is elected/representative and makes the laws; the executive (Cabinet, other ministers) makes decisions about the laws to propose and their intended application in which it is advised and supported by the Civil Service; and the judiciary (various courts headed by the Supreme Court which judges constitutional issues) determines whether the executives have acted in accordance with the legislation passed (which may then be returned to Parliament for revision). The power of governmentality in a one-party state tends to be different compared to multiple-party states, and there are different requirements of its citizens. Governmentality over time in China is rooted in Confucianism, with Chinese people more likely to accede to government requirements than contest or resist, but historically Chinese governments have not always welcomed Confucianism. Most recently under Mao Zedong, who felt that Confucianism was one reason that revolution had become necessary, it was the subject of ineffective purges, but more recent governments have seen that Confucian dynamism might be selectively and pragmatically exploited to accelerate economic growth (Roberts 2014). Therefore, understanding governmental power, influence, and political changes are a priority for UK and China cooperation.

Barnett (1999) explains that government is understood broadly as "techniques and procedures for directing human behavior" (Foucault, 1997, p. 81, cited in Barnett, 1999). Barnett further explains that the administration of culture can be understood through various agencies and routinized practices of daily lives. In Barnett's view, government is the overall leading force in a broad sense, whereas culture is more individualized via different agencies, or as they are more commonly referred to, communities. There is a significant difference between the two countries in terms of the approaches taken by their respective governments when it comes to the arts, but also in terms of the ignorance and absence of protections for international cooperation regarding art in the higher education sector, especially in the West, which creates discontinuity for the history of international relations in the arts.

According to Foucault (1997),

> 'governmentality' implies the relationship of the self to itself, and I intend this concept of 'governmentality' to cover the whole range of practice that constitute, define, organize, and instrumentalize the strategies that individuals in their freedom can use in dealing with each other. (p. 300)

Power is predicated on freedom: "power relations are only possible in so far as the subject is free" (p. 292 cited in Barnett, 1999, p. 383). Therefore, governmentality formulizes strategies that individuals can employ in dealing with each other within the scope of their freedom. At present, the arts are an established field in most higher education sectors even though they may be treated with some hostility by right-wing governments.

The arts are promoted highly in China within current governmental policies. For example, since 2016, the Chinese Scholarship Council (CSC) has offered a special initiative for artistic talent. The CSC supplies full scholarships for candidates in the arts for Masters', PhD studies, and visiting projects. Candidates (current students and staff) can choose overseas universities and countries by themselves and apply for the scholarship via their universities. Students are well supported,[1] and there are hundreds of thousands of arts students funded by CSC every year.

In China, policies transmit quickly through the institutional framework. In other words, the Chinese government provides a broad goal (in this case promoting the arts) and the funding bodies and institutions respond to the policies accordingly. There is room for a degree of individual development, but all must aim toward the same specified goal. For example, the Global Music Education League was founded in Beijing in 2017 and received financial support from the local government. Vice President Liu Yandong met with Heads of Music from all over the world and stressed the perceived importance of music in China, as well as an appreciation for the development of music education (Wang, 2017). Those promotional initiatives in the arts world were the result of autonomous actions from educational institutions stemming from government policies, and in turn the government supported projects by participating in meetings, which indicates that political power is linked to arts-related policies in China and is a demonstration of policy interpretation from educational perspectives for the rest of China.

In the UK, governmentality has resulted in a marginalization of the arts in higher education sectors. In 2019, BBC News indicated that the number of A-level entries in arts subjects had reduced by 13,000, a reduction of 17% since 2014, which might have been caused by the reduction of arts subjects in the General Certificate of Secondary Education. Jon Andrews, deputy head of research at the Education Policy Institute, stated that students have been pushed away from arts subjects to prioritize the ones that the government prefers, according to the changes in school performance measures.

These prioritized subjects include Progress 8 and the linked English Baccalaureate (EBass) established by the Department of Education (2010). Harvey (2016) indicates that there was a significant funding reduction for arts and culture since 2008, and that every year has seen a decrease in funding for the arts. "According to the Institute for Fiscal Studies, there was a 20 per cent reduction in spending by local authorities in England between 2009/10 and 2014/15" (p. 7). These changes to exams and funding bodies have direct consequences in the education and development of the arts in the UK, which has been guided by successive government policies (see Hall, 2001) and are reviewed and critiqued by bodies including the Cultural Learning Alliance (2022) and the Centre for Cultural Value (2022).

According to the research from Tencent Research Institute, digital media and the arts are parts of Chinese culture that have been promoted globally. Since the past decade, China has stressed methods of increasing soft power promotion. Haneş & Andrei (2015) explains that this soft power[2] consists of three sets: political, cultural and educational, and diplomatic. With the guidance of political power, the arts in the higher education sector represent cultural and educational power, a type of soft power directed at enhancing international prestige of Chinese national identity. For example, Global Music Education League represents the Chinese government under the "One Belt, One Road" scheme to discuss cooperation with institutions from more than 30 countries, including South Korea, Russia, and Italy (China Conservatory of Music, 2017). The promotion of the arts in China provides a free-will space for arts institutions to grow, and the status held by the arts also bestows value on the contributions they make toward China's main political strategies. This interpretation, in terms of power relationships, seeks to promote the arts as a method of public diplomacy to enhance and strengthen relations with other countries. Therefore, international cooperation in the higher education arts sector also illustrates political, cultural, educational, and diplomatic power, cementing the arts as an excellent channel for spreading and promoting China's soft power.

However, Alves (2015) suggests that higher education institutions, "as a set of epistemic communities with a broad range of interests and disciplines … should focus on a single path (usually, based on economic parameters for the measurement of well-being and wealth) endangers this pluralism" (p. 75), the outcomes of academic research usually expressed as patents and involvement in commercial ventures. With a marketing-oriented approach, some disciplines, such as philosophy, art, literature, and language studies are less able to be quantitatively marked in terms of knowledge production. Especially with the COVID-19 pandemic, the UK government and private funding bodies have invested huge amounts of money into the life and natural sciences, and Prime Minister Boris Johnson stated that the UK is facing the worst recession in 300 years (BBC, 2020).

Therefore, from an economic perspective the arts in institutions do not provide enough incentive for UK higher education institutions and the government to use the arts as a strategic tool for internationalization. Traditional art forms, such as voice and instrument tuition, require small-group instruction, or one-to-one teaching methods, as the arts are individualized and involve personalized creations. By virtue of this specific need, teaching in the arts cannot have what are traditionally seen as "cost-effective" lectures, with hundreds of students at one time, in the same vein as subjects like management or economics – it is difficult to achieve the same level of teaching efficiency. Moreover, there is little possibility for research results in the arts to transfer into material capital in the short term, unlike how STEM subjects (science, technology, engineering, and mathematics) can transform patents into immediately viable commercial products (Alves, 2015).

Therefore, for these financial reasons, the arts are not promoted as strongly as they are in China. This is a huge difference in attitudes and policymaking toward the arts from a government level. Art does not seem to factor into government policymaking in the UK, and the government, therefore, shows little enthusiasm for promoting the social importance of the arts. This is the current situation of governmentality toward the arts in these two countries.

Culture

The relationship between culture, politics, and morality generates governmentality. Culture is the system that forms through various agencies, politics are objective activities, and morality is formed through subjective natural behaviors toward rules (culture and policies). How *guanxi* exists in different agencies influences both policymaking and consequent human behavior. Therefore, it is important to develop the theoretical construct of *guanxi* within the given circumstances of Chinese society and intercultural communications.

There is a distinction between the perception and understanding of cultures. Without in-depth knowledge of Chinese culture and language and social moral behaviors, perception as a response to appearance is usually the starting point for international cooperation, such as when a Western delegation goes to China or hosts Chinese guests in the UK for collaborative purposes. It is the necessary knowledge that someone must acquire, and also a part of discourse that someone can learn and experience from historical analysis. UK delegations might have different perceptions toward their Chinese partners depending on what they do, such as politically focused partner institutions in Beijing or business-dominated partner institutions in the Yangtze River Delta Economic Zone.

Varela, Thompson, and Rosch (2016) indicate that perception and cognition has a significant influence on human behaviors and experiences. The differences between perception and cognition are key to understanding cross-cultural behaviors. With regards to the data from Ding (2021), UK institutions stated that Chinese partners will "disappear" or go silent for long periods during collaboration without informing them what has happened. Therefore, their perception of Chinese people is that they might disappear at any given time during collaboration, but this does not denote the end of the relationship. Patience was the only method that UK participants used to deal with these disappearances. Therefore, in this form, the UK institutions generally wait to reflect to these disappearances and silences.

From the Chinese point of view, it is generally considered inappropriate to directly reject people, and silence rather than direct negation is generally seen as a more polite way of rejection (Chen, 2007; Gao, Ting-Toomey & Gudykunst, 1996; Gu, 2004; Hall & Xu, 1990; Kim & Markus, 2002; Li, 2020; Yuan, 2015). As Gu (2004, pp. 65–66) observes:

> those involved are blissfully unaware of structural differences in their beliefs about debate, let alone complex intervening socio-structural, sociopsychological and sociolinguistic processes, often in flux, which determine their quite different styles of discourse over time.

Gu attributes this to a combination of Confucian and Taoist legacies that render speaking in public awkward and unnecessary. Different opinions are rarely ventured in debate in the interests of harmony and the preservation of friendships above the expression of personal inner thoughts. In the West, however, there is a tradition of public speaking and a discipline of rhetoric that extends back to the Ancient Greeks and debate is seen as indispensable to democracy. Silence, on the other hand, is awkward and embarrassing and maybe interpreted as a lack of interest or, competence in verbal skills. In the United States of America (USA), there is almost a compulsion to speak to fill the spaces of silence – freedom of speech must be asserted or lost.

Yuan (2015) denotes a variety of functions of silence where communication can go awry. First, it can be a marker of social or hierarchical relationship between communicators. Social status can be inferred by the deference given by others when a person is speaking. Silence also has a role in organizing discourse. It provides an interval in an ongoing interaction providing time to think, reflect, check or suppress an emotion, prepare a lengthier and considered response, or if necessary, introduce another line of thought or change the topic altogether. Silence is also a semantic marker. Speakers need time to organize their ideas to express themselves and convey information, while hearers need time to infer the other's meaning or intention. As Yuan points out, a silent response to the proposal "Will you marry me?" in English would connote rejection; in Chinese might indicate acceptance. At an affective level, silence has many possible resonances. Silence could be interpreted as lack of interest, hurt feelings, offence given, or contempt for what has been said or the speaker. It may express agreement or disagreement, infer praise (an audience so impressed they are speechless), or be a sign of respect. In the UK and the USA, feedback loops need to be explicit, or speakers will feel that they are "losing" their audience, baffling or boring them. Chinese listeners are often reluctant to ask questions to avoid either the speaker (for lack of clarity) or the hearer (for lack of intelligence) losing face.

If UK institutions understood this cultural context, they might, for example, realize that when Chinese partners go silent, this could denote that the collaboration proposal itself likely does not align with the interests or expectations of their Chinese partner or might contravene Chinese regulations, policies, or custom and practice. They could then interpret information from this silence and explore more valid communications to maintain their co-operation. Sociopsychologically, the role of culture can shape individual perception, which in turn affects the processing of information from the surrounding environment. Demonstrating differences in perception can drive differences in cognition, both of which shape behavior and open avenues for change (Kastanakis & Voyer, 2014).

Shavitt et al. (2008, p. 1103) assert that culture includes "shared elements that provide standards for perceiving, believing, evaluating, communicating, and acting among those who share a language, a historical period, and a geographical location." Markus and Kitayama (2010, p. 422) further contend that:

> The word culture is a stand-in for a similarly untidy and expansive set of material and symbolic concepts … that give form and direction to behavior [and that] culture is located in the world, in patterns of ideas, practices, institutions, products, and artifacts.

Cultures associated with Confucian dynamism, as became clear during the Japanization of British industry in the 1980s, often take longer to commit to decisions but then achieve rapid implementation. The UK and USA approaches tend to press for early commitment then work out the details and iron out problems – which are often quite substantial – along the way. On the other hand, in Ding's (2021) research, UK institutions indicated that Chinese partners wanted things to happen "overnight," in a way that was not possible for UK institutions. From a cultural perspective, Chinese people might interpret resulting delays and slow progress as a sign that UK partners are not really interested in cooperation. These two-way misunderstandings are based on cultural perceptions. Therefore, some deeper cognition of both cultures is necessary in facilitating UK–China cooperation, as these initial perceptions might cause misunderstanding and communication bias, thus misdirecting behavior.

Dirks, Eley, and Ortner (1994 pp. 74–75) state that:

> culture [may be seen] as multiple discourses, occasionally coming together in large systemic configurations, but more often coexisting within dynamic fields of interaction and conflict … This contested nature of 'culture' often gets lost in homogenizing views of 'culture as

> nationality' where dominant cultural voices are often the only ones heard, where the 'preferred' reading of 'culture' is the only reading.

Chinese culture does not just represent the Chinese nationality – Confucian culture includes not only the identification of a social hierarchy but is also imbricated with different configurations of local and Confucian culture. There are different sets of cultural configurations, which require different methods and approaches in terms of intercultural communications. For example, Westerners have long understood the necessity of using *guanxi* in China to conduct business, with Hall and Xu (1990) and Leung and Yeung (1995) establishing that *guanxi* is endemic to Chinese management. However, according to recent data (Ding, 2021), *guanxi* has been perceived as being abandoned in contemporary Chinese society, or merely denotes functional or technical connections and an efficient-communications channel for cooperation, rather than any additional complexities.

Field-level experience is, therefore, needed to distinguish the level of *guanxi* usage and existence in different regions (Ma, 2004). Also, from the model formulated by Ding, *guanxi* could contribute toward the setup of relationships in both dimensions of quantity and quality, but functions less well in the concentration stage, when Western institutions achieve high quality and quantity of relationships with Chinese institutions. Therefore, an understanding of different cultural configurations is required for successful UK-China cooperation.

Shuter (1990) explains that "without a sense of how communication is patterned within groups, we can have little understanding of how that communication differs from or resembles communication between groups" (p. 76) and taking communication *within* cultural groups as a primary focus, can allow us to "gain insight into *inter*cultural communication" (p. 77, emphasis added).

Language plays an important role in how culture affects self-versus-other perceptions. Whorf (2012) argues that the way people perceive themselves and make sense of the world is dependent on the language spoken. Briley, Morris, and Simonson (2005) and Ross et al. (2002) similarly find that language can trigger culture-bound self-perceptions, with English-speaking bi-cultural people reporting a perception of the self as independent of others and Chinese-speaking bi-cultural people[3] reporting a more interdependent perception of the self. Kastanakis and Voyer (2014) further explain that:

> Bi-cultural Chinese-born people describe themselves in terms of their own internal traits and attributes when using English but describe themselves in relation to others when using Chinese. These results suggest that East Asian and Western identities are stored in separate knowledge structures in bi-cultural people, with each structure activated by associated language and language triggers a culture-bound representation of the self. (p. 427)

The language that UK–China cooperation uses is English. English-speaking bi-cultural circumstances represent a Western cultural bind, which results in the potential issue that Chinese delegations are never able to fully express what they really want to emphasize. The *guanxi* concept in the Asian cultural self-construal (Yamada & Singelis, 1999) is more interdependently dominated (Aaker & Lee, 2001; Brewer & Gardner, 1996; Singelis, 1994), which makes a significant difference compared to the independent self-construal dominant in the West (Markus & Kitayama, 1991). Using this Western independent self-construal as the dominant modality represents the interdependent cultural cognition that results in communication being sometimes stifled or misconstrued, which will likely lead to misunderstandings or communication bias. In other words, using independent language styles to represent the meaning of collectivized (in *guanxi* terms, "within the *guanxi* tie, you are one of us"), and interdependent cultural context is difficult. Additionally, the intricate levels of politeness, deference, respect, and status denoted by honorifics in Chinese are difficult to represent in English. Therefore, UK–China cooperation requires bilingual people who can speak both English and Chinese and express the independence and interdependency with its attached cultural context.

In summary, the understanding of cultural perception and cognition is important in understanding human behaviors. Perception and cognition both have the power to guide human reflections and how they process information from their surrounding environment. Cultural configuration is a further step to choosing the most effective communication methods in cross-cultural relations. Practitioners need to become aware of regional-cultural content to locate appropriate communication patterns in their business. The language (the discourse statement) that has been chosen for cross-cultural communication is the trigger for the fluency and success of cooperation. In this current case, English-dominated communication creates biases of understanding in terms of cultural cognitions. Therefore, bilingual communication is required for UK–China cooperation, so as when Western delegations express their ideas in a Chinese-speaking cultural form, their ideas will be much better accepted or understood culturally by their Chinese partners. The prerequisite for successful negotiation is a nuanced understanding of both cultures in language, linguistic registers in play, and practice.

Morality

Within governmentality, morality represents the subjective values guiding a cultural system and its related political activities, communicated through discourse (Xiao & Chen 2009). Foucault (1981) states that:

> The true discourse likewise the manner in which economic practices, codified as precepts or recipes and ultimately as morality, have sought

> since the sixteenth century to ground themselves, rationalize themselves, and justify themselves in a theory of wealth and production. (p. 55)

In other words, discourse is not only about knowledge, but also exists within practices that are based on wealth and production. The concept of morality provides an important link between culture and governmentality in determining how effective actions play out concerning the foundation of international relationships.

Rivera Vicencio (2012) stresses that in Foucault's words, "morality is the link between discursive and non-discursive formation" (p. 746). He further explains that morality means:

> a set of values and rules of action that are recommended to individuals through the intermediary of various prescriptive agencies, such as the family (in one of its roles), educational institution, churches, and so forth.
> (Foucault, cited in Rivera Vicencio, 2012, p. 746)

Morality differs from culture in that it is not guidance or a concept that needs to be interpreted or understood by human beings – it concerns actions and things based on common values and rules. These values and rules could come from governmental policies or cultural groups. In other words, morality is the evidence for or manifestation of identity, which informs the details of how cultures or policies exist and function in practice. The concept of "a middleman" exists in Chinese culture as well as Western culture (Chinese language [Putonghua] uses the term '中间人' or middle *person*) and it is a well-established *guanxi* method for helping friends or business partners to establish new *guanxi* ties, or introduce someone into an exclusive *guanxi* tie. Therefore, despite their best attempts to blur their cultural identity and be more international in their cognition, behaviors and preferences toward their work are revealed by the extent to which traditional actions based on the rules of *guanxi* influence them, consciously or not.

However, there would be a culturally different understanding, as the word "middleman" in English usually has negative connotations, with them now being cut out to avoid any increased costs or commissions. In other words, the middleman in English implies expensive costs, whereas in in China today there is a possibility that these "middle people" have now been professionalized as service providers in their own right. The trust dynamic might change in the future because of this.

Foucault further explains that:

> morality also refers to the real behavior of individuals in relation to the rules and values that are recommended to them; the word thus designates the manner in which they comply more or less fully with a standard of conduct, the manner in which they obey or resist an

> interdiction or a prescription; the manner in which they respect or disregard a set of values. In studying this aspect of morality, one must determine how and with what margins of variation or transgression individuals or groups conduct themselves in reference to a prescriptive system that is explicitly or implicitly operative in their culture, and of which they are more or less aware. We can call this level of phenomena 'the morality of behaviors.'
>
> (Foucault, cited in Rivera Vicencio, 2012, p. 747)

Therefore, morality is the prime part of human lives in its circumstantial integration, which occupies in a pattern of conduct. There is a significant difference between the perception of morality in the West and in China. In the West, morality tends to focus on ethics (Mattingly & Throop, 2018; Schloss, 2004; Dorff & Newman, 1995), whereas in China, morality is more focused on manners in accordance with Confucian ideals (Liu & Xu, 2001; An, 1995; Jia, 2001). In this circumstance, the actions and human behavior that people will take in UK–China cooperation are from different focuses, which might cause cognitive bias.

When conducting collaborative work like this it is essential to find a "middle ground" of morality, and for both parties to consider its related actions and patterns of manners to be acceptable, which could, to a large extent, facilitate bias-free communication when determining how to act. In other words, we could start to create a basic "common sense" within the specific field of international cooperation. This type of common sense is linked to the *guanxi* element of empathy, which is to say, "we understand your preference, your culture and working style without saying anything out loud." With this sense of empathy, relationships would be able to grow in depth according to the *guanxi dispositive model*. However, it is important that the assumption of a common sense does not lead to taking things for granted – common-sense thinking refers to those elements that can *safely*, *reliably*, and *unproblematically* be taken for granted, to allow interaction to focus on the more significant or potentially problematic elements, and sometimes there is a need gently to check understanding of the common ground at the beginning of a negotiation.

Moore (1925) indicates that common sense is a belief commonly entertained by human beings, and that it is a matter of faith, rather than knowledge. Geertz (1975) argues that an analysis of common sense,

> as opposed to the exercise of it, must then begin by redrawing this erased distinction between the mere matter-of-fact apprehension of reality – or whatever it is you want to call what we apprehend merely and matter-of-factly – and down-to-earth, colloquial wisdom, judgments or assessments of it. When we say someone shows common sense, we mean to suggest more than that he is just using his eyes and

> ears, but is, as we say, keeping them open, using them judiciously, intelligently, perceptively, reflectively, or trying to, and that he is capable of coping with everyday problems in an everyday way with some effectiveness. (p. 8)

In other words, common sense is based on using the experience of daily lives and wisdom to solve problems. Common sense is a pragmatic epistemological cultural system. The cognitive dimensions of culture are usually expressed as shared knowledge, that is a body of knowledge that members of a community could be expected to be able to access, incorporate into decisions made, and act upon. It also may be regarded as "common sense," a set of implicit and largely inferred rules that members of that community take for granted. While several philosophers have debated aspects of common sense, Wittgenstein (1953, p. 187) defined it for social science as knowing "how to go on" or proceed within a form of life – in other words what is expected by others and *what to do next,* rather than how to respond in a specific moment. It is not just a matter of passively recognizing the obvious but has a dynamic aspect. This is consistent with Foucault's understanding of discourse, and power as creative.

Anthropologists such as Marshall Sahlins (1976), have observed and categorized culture as practical reason, and in sociology Alfred Schutz (1962) following the philosophy of A. N. Whitehead, and Harold Garfinkel (1967) have theorized it in terms of a collective stock of knowledge used indexically in creating "definitions of the situation" and the rules for subsequent action. These rules are also deployed retrospectively in reflexive sense-making – that is, in making sense of action that just happened. We know what is "common" because we are inducted, formally or informally, into a culture that transmits its values and guiding principles in a variety of symbolic forms, implicitly or explicitly, and we know how to read the signs that tell us whether someone knows how to behave as a competent, trustworthy member of our community – or knows "how to go on." In low context cultures that will be largely absorbed slowly, implicitly, over time, by listening, observation, and mimesis. In high-context cultures, this will be transmitted and communicated explicitly, for example through education and instruction, conveyed rather than absorbed.

There is a "common sense" way of dealing with international cooperation that has formulated over time in both cultures, and these are often at odds with each other. It is dangerous to assume that such common sense is universal within cross-cultural business. A new common sense for UK–China cooperation must take both cultures and working experiences into consideration. Further, the emergence of common sense enhances empathy within relationships. The idea of empathy is to understand what the other party means even without them having to say anything. Common sense would allow people to follow the rules or system in accordance with the situation at hand, and facilitate project completion in a more appropriate way, that would be accepted by both parties without anyone needing to draw attention to the rules. It further enhances the depth of relationships, as empathy is in the second stage of the quality dimension in *guanxi dispositive* model.

There are obvious potential problems here, as notably exposed by Harvey (1988) as the Abilene Paradox, in which a whole family goes to visit other family members entailing a long and difficult journey. None of the family members wanted to go; and the family in Abilene did not want them there either. But everyone assumed that it was expected and did not question it. Empathy does imply an awareness of the other but in contexts that require each to know what the other is saying, we might argue that there needs to be another layer of communication that does not presume common sense but rather checks to understand the sense of the other. But as Hall and Hall (1960) would point out, this is to make the error of reading Chinese psychology – in a high-context culture – through the lens of a low-context culture (the USA/Abilene, but the UK almost equally). In a *high* context culture, everyone can more or less safely assume that others know how to go on because they in fact do – they know what is expected of them and behave accordingly (Wurtz, 2006). In a *low* context culture, we assume nothing and press for answers. The Abilene paradox is not the Guangdong paradox for good reason. Of course, where cultures mix there is a need for some accommodation, and especially where managers have been educated in the West or work for Western companies, but this is not without its frictions.

The relevant Hofstede category would be *Long Term v Short Term orientation*, which was originally coded as Confucian dynamism. What this should mean is that Confucianism allows for such surface turbulence that it can survive periods of suppression and discredit and even oppression – and it has endured such periods, as well as those of flourishing and institutionalization from its inception to the present. For most of the 20th century it was blamed for China's decline by different political groups from all sides, both nationalist and communist. A particular political intent of the state is not to be confused with national culture, as Hofstede emphasises – power distance is about the level of acceptance of steep hierarchical levels in society, not styles of domination. Hofstede (1980, pp. 83–84) borrowed the concept from the Dutch sociologist Mauk Mulder, and notes Mulder's key empirical point about social dynamics – that those on the lower levels seek to minimise the distance to those above (either by rising or pulling them down), while those above seek to maximise the distance to those below (by rising, or by holding others back). Those in the middle are active on both fronts, which is exhausting. The Confucian acceptance of authority need not be linked to class or socioeconomic status, and it certainly does not involve accepting greater extremes of wealth and poverty, but it does reduce the energy expended on managing interlevel tensions.

Power and knowledge

Foucault (1971) indicates that production of discourse is selected, controlled, organized, and redistributed according to a certain number of procedures in every society; a person's speech should form at least part of the common discourse (common sense), and in the past few centuries, words from a madman were either totally ignored or taken as a form of truth in Europe, which indicates that discourse is linked to the exercise of power. Also, Foucault (2019; 1971) expresses that the will to knowledge is the generalization of truth (will to truth) that has been a part of discourse throughout many centuries of history. The will to truth governs the will to knowledge, then formulates a system for development.

Constructing new statements on international relations combines knowledge from different disciplines that are defined by "groups of objects. Methods, their corpus of propositions considered to be true, the interplay of rules and definitions, of techniques and tools" (Foucault, 1971, p. 15). UK–China cooperation needs to be set within the history of international relations in formulating formulated guidelines for its future development. An integration of our discussion up to this point with a generalized understanding of power and knowledge is therefore now necessary.

Power

Neumann (2014) indicates that there are three types of power based on Foucault's insights, namely game power, disciplinary power, and governmentality. There is a difference between disciplinary power (the power of force) and governmentality (the power of guidance) in the West, but there is not much difference between these two powers in China. Governmentality in China is traditionally more forceful, and this is combined with the disciplinary power of peoples' reactions. Therefore, before discussing Foucault's originary concept of power/knowledge in general terms, this section focuses on disciplinary power, to provide an explanation of the working style in Chinese society.

According to Foucault (1997) disciplinary power has three elements: hierarchical observation, normalizing judgment, and examination, which show how individuals can be supervised and controlled. There are two critical points to be made about the standard account of disciplinary power. First, outside of locales of sequestration, the activities of individuals are less prone to detailed regulation and monitoring. "Total institutions" like prisons and asylums epitomize disciplinary power for Foucault. However, although schools, factories, or offices do not operate like prisons and asylums, they share some characteristics. Disciplinary power is likely to be less all-embracing in sites like this – employees are not inmates, even if they are residents. "This opens up the possibility of considering disciplinary power in other locales as less secure and effective, and of considering the possibility of contradictions between the forms of power exercised in different locales" (Barnett, 1999, p. 379). This is generally true when it comes to Western society. In countries influenced by Confucian ideals the social hierarchy is the moral law that governs subjects. This power, to a large extent, is rooted in an innate or encultured sense of self-discipline and hierarchical obligation operating differently from "discipline."

Second, there is the question of how different disciplinary spaces and locales are connected to each other, and how individuals move through them. A prison is different from a school, and a school from a university, and they are all governed by differing forms of disciplinary power, but how are these different institutions, regimes, and their effects articulated together? Barnett (1999) argues that:

> One need not presume some single underlying logic linking all possible sites of subject-formation to raise as a legitimate question the issues of just how the effectiveness of particular disciplinary regimes in specific institutions is supported, subverted or transformed by the movement of 'subject' into other locales and other institutions subject to other modes of discipline. (p. 380)

Disciplinary power takes different forms and effects dependent on its locale, and is inevitably less secure outside of restricted places – total institutions such as prisons and asylums. The specificity of practices with their own regulatory regimes and distributions of effect mean that singular disciplinary power cannot be generated for subject-formation to arise as a legitimate question of effectiveness in other locales, institutions, and modes. Therefore, disciplinary power is loosely correlated with higher education sectors from a Western point of view. However, the Chinese social hierarchy might provide space for it to grow within a framework that is still deferential, which means that disciplinary power might be more strongly applied within Chinese higher education institutions. That would provide guidance for approaching relationship setup and formation.

For example, if one Western institution has direct relationships with the presidents of their Chinese partner institutions, these types of relationships would be more efficient (from a disciplinary standpoint) as Chinese people will always defer to orders from their presidents. Alternatively, if a Western institution has relationships with one of the staff or heads of department, this type of relationship would be more governmental in nature, as the staff or the heads of department need to follow guidance from the presidents before being able to improvise and enact their own ideas.

Therefore, a regulatory, rather than disciplinary, understanding of the practice and methods of power is also important, and might be more appropriate in locales outside of prison, not least because it opens up a reconsideration of issues of agency that is largely absent from the cultural-policy studies literature as Barnett (1999) suggested earlier. Therefore, disciplinary power and regulatory practice, and methods of power, are both important cultural circumstances for international cooperation in China, especially considering that there are significantly different cultural regions within the country.

When it comes to subjective power, Foucault describes pastoral power (1994d), as opposed to political and legal power and it is defined as the power of individualization. In other words, pastoral power would be represented by power relations at the subjective level. Self-interpretation of policies and regulations would be represented as pastoral power, which on the one hand might publicly observe hierarchy and disciplinary power, but on the other hand secretly contradict or subvert authorized power. In this sense, it is reasonable to understand that conflicts of self-interest are a subjective restriction for international cooperation, or from an opposing view, it would expend the significance of authorized (disciplinary, political, and legal) power. Balancing these two powers is critical.

Knowledge

For Foucault, knowledge is not capable of being entirely contained within those forms that explicitly express it. According to Foucault (1997), "positivities do not characterize forms of knowledge – whether they are a priori, necessary conditions or forms of rationality that have, in turn, been put into operation by history" (p. 181). Foucault (1997) defines knowledge as that of which one can speak in a discursive practice, but also as the space in which a subject may take up a position and speak of the "objects with which he heals" in his discourse. For knowledge in specific disciplines, Foucault (1971, p.15) explains that:

> The principles of discourse involved in the formation of disciplines are equally opposed to that of commentary. In a discipline, unlike in commentary, what is supposed at the point of departure is not some meaning which must be rediscovered, nor an identity to be reiterated; it is that which is required for the construction of new statements. For a discipline to exist, there must be the possibility of formulating – and of doing so ad infinitum – fresh propositions.

He continues to define knowledge as the field of coordination and subordination of statements in which concepts appear and are defined, applied, and transformed. He differentiates knowledge and discourse by positing that knowledge is defined by the possibilities of use and appropriation offered by discourse, concluding that there is no knowledge possible without a particular discursive practice, and that any discursive practice may be defined by the knowledge that it forms. In this case this is knowledge about Chinese culture, and its related perceptions and cognitions, as well as the discourses on policies, morality, and plain common sense.

The knowledge of power and its related governmentality would help us understand the biopolitical positioning and exteriority of the force that creates certainty or uncertainty in the environment of international cooperation. The understanding of cultures and their differences delineates some aspects of the social formation and semiotic systematics of Western (UK) and Eastern (China) societies. Furthermore, knowledge of morality helps indicate the value-based behavior of subjects, which from Foucault's epistemology would be the key to accessing ethics and truth-effects discourse.

These sets of knowledges are significant points of discourse to understand how the whole system works within UK–China cooperation, the key to which is the *guanxi dispositive* model and the importance of the model in these relationships. But Foucault never intended his work to be complete:

> The day when all the lecture courses which Foucault gave at the Collège de France are published, the dimensions and importance of his work will receive their due recognition. His 'will to knowledge' has not produced a system – a feature which will be a source of reproach to some and will be seen as a sign of merit by others
>
> (Pasquino, 2013, pp. 66–67).

Similarly, the *guanxi dispositive* model combines Western philosophical insights with Asian cultural concepts, which could be seen as a step forward for the development of Sino–British (and East–West) relationships, but one that is inspirational, non-doxic, flexible, yet robust enough to respond to the continuing dynamic test of day-to-day practice.

Notes

1 One student received 3,820,000 RMB (equals 429,213 GBP) for his Masters and PhD study in 2017.

2 Nanse (2015) follows Nye's summary of soft power as "a country's ability to attract others through ideas, and values and ideologies. This kind of power resembles to formless power, such as culture, ideology and the social system" (p. 32).

3 Most generally, biculturalism represents comfort and proficiency with both one's heritage culture and the culture of the country or region in which one has settled. It is applicable not only to immigrants who have come from other countries, but also to children of immigrants who – although they are born and raised in the receiving society – are likely deeply embedded in the heritage culture at home with their families (Schwartz & Unger 2010).

References

Aaker, J. L., & Lee, A. Y. (2001). "I" seek pleasures and "we" avoid pains: The role of self-regulatory goals in information processing and persuasion. *Journal of Consumer Research, 28*(1), 33–49.

An, M. Y. (1995). Mental nutrition should be absorbed from Confucian culture. *Modern Industry, 2005*(5), 46–47.

Ambler, T., Styles, C., & Wang, X. C. (1999). The effect of channel relationships and *guanxi* on the performance of inter-province export ventures in the People's Republic of China. *International Journal of Research in Marketing, 16*(1), 75–87.

Alves, A. M. (2015). Thinking beyond instrumentality: What if dangerous ideas were the future of academia. In E. Westergaard, & J. S. Wiewiura (Eds.), *On the facilitation of the academy* (pp. 71–86). Springer.

Barnett, C. (1999). Culture, government and spatiality: Reassessing the 'Foucault effect' in cultural-policy studies. *International Journal of Cultural Studies, 2*(3), 369–397.

Basu, L. (2011). Memory dispositifs and national identities: The case of Ned Kelly. *Memory Studies, 4*(1), 33–41.

BBC News. (2019, August 15). *A-levels: What subjects are students dropping and why?* Retrieved from https://www.bbc.com/news/uk-45171371

BBC (2020). Coronavirus: PM 'will not return to austerity of 10 years ago'. *BBC News* 28 June. https://www.bbc.co.uk/news/uk-53207700

Bedford, O. (2011). Guanxi-building in the workplace: A dynamic process model of working and backdoor guanxi. *Journal of Business Ethics, 104*(1), 149–158.

Brewer, M. B., & Gardner, W. (1996). Who is this "We"? Levels of collective identity and self representations. *Journal of Personality and Social Psychology, 71*(1), 83–93.

Briley, D. A., Morris, M. W., & Simonson, I. (2005). Cultural chameleons: Biculturals, conformity motives, and decision making. *Journal of Consumer Psychology, 15*(4), 351–362.

Canguilhem, G. (2008). *Knowledge of life*, trans. Geroulanos, S., & Ginsburg, D. Fordham University Press.

Centre for Cultural Value. (2022). *Understanding the difference culture makes.* https://www.culturalvalue.org.uk/

Chen, C. C., Chen, X. P., & Huang, S. (2013). Chinese *Guanxi*: An integrative review and new directions for future research. *Management and Organization Review, 9*(1), 167–207.

Chen, G-M. (2007). A review of the concept of intercultural effectiveness. In M. Hinner (Ed.), *The influence of culture in the world of business* (pp. 95–116). Peter Lang.

Chen, M. H., Chang, Y. Y., & Lee, C. Y. (2015). Creative entrepreneurs' *guanxi* networks and success: Information and resource. *Journal of Business Research, 68*(4), 900–905.

Chen, X. P., & Chen, C. C. (2004). On the intricacies of the Chinese *guanxi*: A process model of *guanxi* development. *Asia Pacific Journal of Management, 21*(3), 305–324.

China Conservatory of Music. (2017). *Global leadership network on higher music education to be launched in Beijing in September.* https://en.ccmusic.edu.cn/COLLABORATION/NEWS/aafaed7bf9c54034b37339a5f74beb67.htm

Cultural Learning Alliance. (2022). *News.* Retrieved from https://www.culturallearningalliance.org.uk/2022/

Davies, H. (1995). Interpreting *Guanxi*: the role of personal connections in a high context transitional economy. In H. Davies (Ed.) *China Business: Context and Issues* (pp. 155–169). Longman.

Davies, H., Leung, T. K., Luk, S. T., & Wong, Y. H. (1995). The benefits of "*Guanxi*": The value of relationships in developing the Chinese market. *Industrial Marketing Management, 24*(3), 207–214.

Deleuze, G. (1992). What is a dispositif? In T. J. Armstrong (Ed.), *Michel Foucault Philosopher* (pp. 159–168). Harvester Wheatsheaf.

Department of Education. (2010). *The importance of teaching: The schools white paper 2010.* Retrieved from https://assets.publishing.service.gov.uk/government/uploads/system/uploads/attachment_data/file/175429/CM-7980.pdf

Ding, L. (2021). *International co-operation between Chinese and UK higher education institutions in the arts*. PhD Dissertation, University of York.

Ding, L., Linstead, S. A., & Field, A. (2019). *Dispositif* and discourse analysis in guanxi studies. Paper presented at ISER 590th *International Conference of Education and Social Science* (ICESS) Milan, Italy, 26–27 April.

Dirks, N. B., Eley, G., & Ortner, S. B. (1994). *Culture/power/history: A reader in contemporary social theory*. Princeton University Press.

Dorff, E. N., & Newman, L. E. (1995). *Contemporary Jewish ethics and morality: A reader*. Oxford University Press.

Dunfee, T. W., & Warren, D. E. (2001). Is *guanxi* ethical? A normative analysis of doing business in China. *Journal of Business Ethics*, *32*(3), 191–204.

Fairclough, N. (1992). *Discourse and social change*, Vol. 10. Polity Press.

Fan, Y. (2002). Questioning *guanxi*: Definition, classification and implications. *International Business Review*, *11*(5), 543–561.

Foucault, M. (1971). Orders of discourse. *Social Science Information*, *10*(2), 7–30.

Foucault, M. (1977). *Discipline and punish: The birth of the prison*. Penguin.

Foucault, M. (1981). The order of discourse. In R. Young (Ed.), *Untying the text: A post-structuralist reader* (pp. 48–78). Routledge & Kegan Paul.

Foucault, M. (1982). *The archaeology of knowledge* (A. M., Sheridan Smith, Trans.). Routledge.

Foucault, M. (1994). *Dits et ecrits 1980–1988*, Vol. 4. Gallimard.

Foucault, M. (1997). *The archaeology of knowledge*. Tavistock Publications.

Foucault, M. (2004) *Securite, territoire, population. Cours au College de France. 1977–1978*. Gallimard/Le Seuil.

Foucault, M. (2007). *Security, territory, population: Lectures at the Collège de France, 1977–78*. Trans. Graham Burchell. Palgrave MacMillan.

Foucault, M. (2019). *The history of sexuality: 1: the will to knowledge*. Penguin.

Fulop, L., Linstead, S. A., & Lilley, S. (2009). Motivation and meaning. In S. A. Linstead, L. Fulop & S. Lilley (Eds.), *Management and organization: A critical text* (pp. 411–472). Palgrave McMillan.

Gao, G., Ting-Toomey, S., & Gudykunst, W. B. (1996). Chinese communication processes. In M. H. Bond (Ed.), *The handbook of Chinese psychology* (pp. 280–293). Oxford University Press.

Garfinkel, H. (1967) *Studies in Ethnomethodology*. Prentice-Hall.

Geertz, C. (1975). Common sense as a cultural system. *The Antioch Review*, *33*(1), 5–26.

Graesser, A. C., Millis, K. K., & Zwaan, R. A. (1997). Discourse comprehension. *Annual Review of Psychology*, *48*(1), 163–189.

Gu, X. (2004). Contrastive analysis of Chinese and American views about silence and debate. *Intercultural Communication Studies*, *13*(1), 55–67.

Gumperz, J. J. (1982). *Discourse strategies*, Vol. 1. Cambridge University Press.

Hall, S. (ed.). (1997). *Representation: Cultural representations and signifying practices*. Sage Publications.

Hall E. T., & Hall M. R. (1960). *Understanding cultural differences*. Intercultural Press.

Hall, P. (2001). *The necessary theatre*. Nick Hern Books.

Hall, R. H., & Xu, W. (1990). Run silent, run deep: Cultural influences on organizations in the Far East. *Organization Studies*, *11*(4), 569–576.

Haneş, N., & Andrei, A. (2015). Culture As Soft Power In International Relations. *Sciendo*, *21*(1), 32–37. https://doi.org/10.1515/kbo-2015-0005

Harvey, J. B. (1988). The Abilene paradox and other meditations on management. San Diego, CA: Lexington Books.

Harvey, A. (2016). Funding the Arts and Culture in a Time of Austerity London: NLGN (New Local Government Network/Arts Council).

Hobbs, M. (2008). On Discourse and Representation: Reflections on Michel Foucault's Contribution to the Study of the Mass Media Annual Conference of the Australian Sociological Association. Accessed at https://www.academia.edu/2569229/On_Discourse_and_Representation_Reflections_on_Michel_Foucaults_Contribution_to_the_Study_of_the_Mass_Media 7/7/22

Hofstede, G. (1980). *Culture's consequences: International differences in work-related values*. Sage.

Hofstede, G., & Bond, M. H. (1988). The Confucian connection: From cultural roots to economic growth. *Organizational Dynamics, 16*, 4–21

Hui, C., & Graen, G. (1997). *Guanxi* and professional leadership in contemporary Sino-American joint ventures in Mainland China. *The Leadership Quarterly, 8*(4), 451–465.

Hwang, K. K. (1987). Face and favour: The Chinese power game. *American Journal of Sociology, 92*(4), 944–974.

Hwang, K. K. (1998). Guanxi and mientze: Conflict resolution in Chinese society. *Intercultural Communication Studies*, 7(1), 17–40.

Hwang, K-K (2015). Morality'East'and 'West': Cultural Concerns. In Wright, J. D. (ed), International Encyclopedia of the Social & Behavioral Sciences, 2nd ed. Vol 15, 806–810. Elsevier.

Jia, P. R. (2001). The development process of pre-Qin Confucian culture and its moral code. *Magazine of Literature and History* (文史杂志), *2001*(3), 18–21.

Johnstone, B. (2017). *Discourse analysis*. John Wiley & Sons.

Kastanakis, M. N., & Voyer, B. G. (2014). The effect of culture on perception and cognition: A conceptual framework. *Journal of Business Research, 67*(4), 425–433.

Kim, A. E., & Park, G. S. (2003). Nationalism, Confucianism, work ethic and industrialization in South Korea. *Journal of Contemporary Asia, 33*(1), 37–49.

Kim, H. S., & Markus, H. R. (2002). Freedom of speech and freedom of silence: An Analysis of talking as a cultural practice. In R. Shweder, M. Minow, & H. R. Markus (Eds.), *Engaging cultural differences: The multicultural challenge in liberal democracies* (pp. 432–452) Russell Sage Foundation.

Kim, T. (2009). Confucianism, modernities and knowledge: China, South Korea and Japan. In R. Cowen & A. M. Kazamias (Eds.), *International Handbook of Comparative Education* (pp. 857–872). Springer.

King, A. Y. C. (1991). *Kuan-hsi* and network building: A sociological interpretation. *Daedalus, 20*, 63–84.

Lambert, G. (2015a). What is a dispositif? Part 1. Lecture given to *The Society for the Study of Biopolitical Futures* UNSW, Sydney, 2013. Retrieved from https://www.academia.edu/25507473/What_is_a_Dispositif

Lambert, G. (2015b). What is a dispositive? Part II. The category of the subject and its functioning. Retrieved from https://www.academia.edu/28865809/What_is_a_dispositif_II_The_Category_of_the_Subject_and_its_Functioning

Lee, L. S., & Zhong, W. (2021). Guanxi orientation, value creation and value capture in buyer-supplier relationships: A dyadic perspective. *Chinese Management Studies, 15*(1), 44–67.

Leung, T., & Yeung, L. L. (1995). Negotiation in the People's Republic of China: Results of *Journal of Small Business Management, 33*(1), 70–77.

Li, L. (2020). Teaching beyond words: 'Silence' and its pedagogical implications discoursed in the early classical texts of Confucianism, Daoism and Zen Buddhism. *Educational Philosophy & Theory, 52*(7), 759–768.

Liu, W., & Xu, Y. J. (2001). The concept of loyalty and filial piety in traditional culture and its practical implications. *Journal of Liaoning Technical University (辽宁工程技术大学学报：社会科学版), 2001*(02), 11–12.

Liu, S. M., & Wu, H. X. (2017). Explaining Western culture immersion on the basis of colonial history. *Journal of Harbin University, 38*(3), 7–10.

Lovett, S., Simmons, L. C., & Kali, R. (1999). *Guanxi* versus the market: Ethics and efficiency. *Journal of International Business Studies, 30*(2), 231–247.

Luo, Y. (1997). *Guanxi*: Principles, philosophies, and implications. *Human Systems Management, 16*(1), 43–51.

Luo, Y. (2008). The changing Chinese culture and business behavior: The perspective of intertwinement between *guanxi* and corruption. *International Business Review, 17*(2), 188–193.

Luo, Y., Huang, Y., & Wang, S. L. (2012). *Guanxi* and organizational performance: A meta-analysis. *Management and Organization Review, 8*(1), 139–172.

Ma, R. (2004). Guanxi and Chinese communication behaviors. In G. M. Chen (Ed.), *Theories and principles of Chinese communication* (pp. 363–377). WuNan.

MacInnis, P. (1993). Guanxi or contract? A wayto understand and prevent conflict between Chinese and Western managersin China-based joint ventures. In McCarry, D., & Hille, S. (Eds.), *Research on international business management and internationalization of Chinese enterprises* (pp. 345–351). Nanjing University Press.

Markus, H. R., & Kitayama, S. (1991). Culture and the self: Implications for cognition, emotion, and motivation. *Psychological Review, 98*(2), 224–253.

Markus, H. R., & Kitayama, S. (2010). Cultures and selves: A cycle of mutual constitution. *Perspectives on Psychological Science, 5*(4), 420–430. https://doi.org/10.1177/1745691610375557

Mattingly, C., & Throop, J. (2018). The anthropology of ethics and morality. *Annual Review of Anthropology, 47*, 475–492.

Moore, G. E. (1925). A defence of common sense. In J. H. Muirhead (Ed.), *Contemporary British philosophy second series* (pp. 193–223). Allen & Unwin.

Neumann, I. (2014). Governmentality: International Relations 6/7 Open University Retrieved July 7th 2022 from https://www.youtube.com/watch?v=UBpI7PxwjzU

Nie, D., & Lämsä, A. M. (2015). The leader-member exchange theory in the Chinese context and the ethical challenge of *guanxi*. *Journal of Business Ethics, 128*(4), 851–861.

Pasquino, P. (2013). Michel Foucault (1926–84): The will to knowledge. In M. Gane & T. Johnson (Eds.), *Foucault's new domains* (pp. 44–56). Routledge.

Peltonen, M. (2004). From discourse to "dispositif": Michel Foucault's two histories. *Historical Reflections/Réflexions Historiques, 30*(2), 205–219.

Peng, S. O., & Yang, C. F. (1999). Impact factors and development process of interpersonal relationship. *Indigenous Psychological Research* (本土心理学研), *12*, 291–312.

Rabinow, P., & Rose, N. (2003). Foucault today. In P. Rabinow, & J. Faubion (Eds.), *The essential Foucault: Selections from the Essential Works of Foucault, 1954–1984* (pp. vii–xxxv). New Press.

Raffnsøe, S., Marius Gudmand-Høyer, M., & Thaning, M. S. (2016). Foucault's dispositive: The perspicacity of dispositive analytics in organizational research. *Organization, 23*(2), 272–298.

Rivera Vicencio, E. (2012). Foucault: His influence over accounting and management research. Building of a map of Foucault's approach. *International Journal of Critical Accounting, 4*(5–6), 728–756.

Roberts, R. (2014). The Confucian moral foundations of socialist model man: LeiFeng and the twenty four exemplars of filial behaviour. *New Zealand Journal of Asian Studies, 16*(1), 23–38.

Ross, M., Xun, W. E., & Wilson, A. E. (2002). Language and the bicultural self. *Personality and Social Psychology Bulletin, 28*(8), 1040–1050.

Ryan, J., & Louie, K. (2007). False dichotomy? 'Western' and 'Confucian' concepts of scholarship and learning. *Educational Philosophy and Theory, 39*(4), 404–417.

Sahlins, M. (1976). *Culture and practical reason.* University of Chicago Press.

Schloss, P. C. J. (2004). *Evolution and ethics: Human morality in biological and religious perspective* (No. 61). Wm. B. Eerdmans Publishing.

Schutz, A. (1962). Common-sense and scientific interpretation of human action. In M. Natanson (Ed.), *Collected papers I* (pp. 3–47). Springer.

Schwartz, S. J., & Unger, J. B. (2010). Biculturalism and context: What is biculturalism, and when is it adaptive? *Human Development, 53*(1), 26–32.

Shavitt, S., Lee, A. Y., & Johnson, T. P. (2008). Cross-cultural consumer psychology. In P. M. Herr, & Kardes, F. R. (Eds.), *Handbook of consumer psychology* (pp. 1103–1132). Ohio State University.

Shuter, R. (1990). The centrality of culture. *Southern Journal of Communication, 55*(3), 237–249.

Singelis, T. M. (1994). The measurement of independent and interdependent self-construals. *Personality and Social Psychology Bulletin, 20*(5), 580–591.

Storry, M., & Childs, P. (Eds.), (2016). *British cultural identities.* Taylor & Francis.

Su, C., Mitchell, R. K., & Sirgy, M. J. (2007). Enabling *guanxi* management in China: A hierarchical stakeholder model of effective *guanxi. Journal of Business Ethics, 71*(3), 301–319.

Tencent Research Institute (2019), Report of Chinese digital culture overseas annual observation. Retrieved from https://tisi.org/10906

Tsang, E. W. (1998). Can *guanxi* be a source of sustained competitive advantage for doing business in China? *The Academy of Management Executive, 12*(2), 64–73.

Tsui, A. S., & Farh, J. L. L. (1997). Where *guanxi* matters: Relational demography and *guanxi* in the Chinese context. *Work and Occupations, 24*(1), 56–79.

Van Fraassen, B. C. (1970). *An introduction to the philosophy of time and space.* Columbia University Press.

Varela, F. J., Thompson, E., & Rosch, E. (2016). *The embodied mind: Cognitive science and human experience.* MIT press.

Villadsen, K. (2021) 'The dispositive': Foucault's concept for organizational analysis? *Organization Studies 42*(3), 473–494.

Wang, C. L. (2007). *Guanxi* vs. relationship marketing: Exploring underlying differences. *Industrial Marketing Management, 36*(1), 81–86.

Wang, Z. (2017). Liu Yandong meets with Chinese and foreign principals attending the global music school principals exchange season. *Renmin News (Xinhua)* Retrieved from People's Daily Online – *People's Daily* Sept 12 http://cpc.people.com.cn/n1/2017/0912/c64094-29528945.html

Westwood, R. I. (1997). Harmony and patriarchy: The cultural basis for 'paternalistic headship' among the overseas Chinese. *Organization Studies, 18*(3), 445–480.

Westwood, R. I. ed (1992). *Organizational Behaviour: Southeast Asian Perspectives.* Longmans.

Westwood, R. I., & Chan, A. (1992). Leadership and headship. In Westwood, R. I., ed *Organizational Behaviour: Southeast Asian Perspectives*, 118–143. Longmans.

Westwood, R., Chan, A., & Linstead S. A. (2004). Theorizing Chinese employment relations comparatively: Exchange, reciprocity and the moral economy. *Asia-Pacific Journal of Management, 21*(3), 365–389.

Westwood, R. I., & Lok, P. (2003). The meaning of work in Chinese contexts: A comparative study. *International Journal of Cross Cultural Management, 3*(2), 139–165.

Whorf, B. L. (2012). *Language, thought, and reality: Selected writings of Benjamin Lee Whorf.* MIT press.

Wittgenstein, L. (1953). *Philosophical Investigations.* Macmillan.

Wodak, R., & Meyer, M. (Eds.), (2015). *Methods of critical discourse studies.* Sage.

Wurtz, E. (2006). Intercultural communication on web sites: A cross-cultural analysis of web sites from high-context cultures and low-context. *Journal of Computer-Mediated Communication, 11*(1), 274–299.

Xiao X., & Chen, G-M. (2009). Communication competence and moral competence: a Confucian perspective. *Journal of Multicultural Discourses, 4*(1), 61–74.

Yamada, A. M., & Singelis, T. M. (1999). Biculturalism and self-construal. *International Journal of Intercultural Relations, 23*(5), 697–709.

Yang, M. M. H. (1994). *Gifts, favours, and banquets: The art of social relationships in China.* Cornell University Press.

Yang, C. F. (1999). Conceptualization of interpersonal guanxi and interpersonal affect. *Indigenous Psychological Research* (本土心理学研究), *12*, 105–179.

Yuan, Y. Q. (2015). Analysis of silence in intercultural communication. In (Eds.), International Conference on Economy, Management and Education Technology (ICEMET 2015) – *Advances in Social Science, Education and Humanities Research* Volume 29, (pp. 155–159). Atlantis Press.X. YangQ. Xu

Zhang, X. A., Li, N., & Harris, T. B. (2015). Putting non-work ties to work: The case of guanxi in supervisor–subordinate relationships. *The Leadership Quarterly, 26*(1), 37–54.

2 Leadership lessons from landscape painting East & West: Cultivating a spiritual eco-imagination

Terri McNichol

Introduction

Leadership, both in the East and in the West, has deep roots in the ancient world. Despite the abundance of leadership research on the last two millennia, Keith Grint et al. (2016) and his colleagues had to conclude that there is yet not a single consensus on its meaning, much less how its moral effects can be measured or what that even entails (p. 3). In the face of a looming global humanitarian crisis brought about by climate change, we need to *look back to the future* by heeding the call of courageous leaders who can draw on ancient wisdom and chart a sustainable future for the Planet. We need to look to the future informed by the Yale global study of nearly 4,000 graduate students at 29 prestigious business schools, who are turning down jobs in corporations that are unwilling to act on environmental issues (Cort, Franceschini, & Wang, 2015). With 44% willing to accept a lower salary to work where they can find meaning and contribute to a better world, the study's authors predict corporations will be punished by the very men and women they want to recruit.

In his book *Regeneration: Ending the Climate Crisis in One Generation*, environmentalist Paul Hawken (2021) makes clear that this is a watershed moment in history with a heating planet that supports every manner of life on earth (p. 9). He offers a self-regenerative system as a leadership model; one that would not only reverse the climate crisis in the most compelling, prosperous, and inclusive way, but also would result in the "regeneration of life in all its manifestations, human and biological" (p. 9). In this chapter, I argue that to the degree countries and corporations take into consideration their reawakening to nature to address the earth's ecological imbalance may well be the real litmus test for 21st-century leadership.

Yale's rising leaders' survey may provide an indicator of an emerging attitude grounded in what David Orr (1992) sees as *ecoliteracy* – the ability to "observe nature with insight resulting in a merger of landscape and mindscape" (pp. 85–87). To foreground an emerging guiding idea, here I provide a blank canvas for an East-West regenerative leadership landscape through paintings, specifically landscape paintings from 13th-century China

DOI: 10.4324/9781003213604-2

and 19th-century United States of America, to demonstrate the ways in which the painter's brush indelibly marked the national consciousness of both with a birthright and kinship with the natural landscape. A more in-depth consideration of the former will foreground how 13th-century Chinese scholar bureaucrats (hereafter literati) turned to landscape painting at a time of extreme crisis. In nature, they saw a regenerative source mirrored in paintings as both *method* and *measure* of the exemplary individual (*junzi*) who could *awaken* viewers to the laws of nature that govern all of existence. Far from an escapism, the self-cultivation practice of landscape painting provided a mindscape to meet the crises of the time. In foregrounding the essential roles of the self-conscious painter and observer/viewer, philosopher Paul Crowther (2016) writes that both are endowed with powers of memory, imagination, and symbolization, thus demonstrating the way in which the universe can be qualitatively changed by human beings (p. 144). Before exploring painters and their works in more detail I first place this study in its global context.

Taking the global temperature

Speaking ahead of the September 2021 annual United Nations gathering of world leaders, UN Secretary General Antonio Guterres expressed his disappointment at the lack of cooperation between countries to confront global warming and the inequity of global COVID vaccination distribution.

With the meeting of world cultures together in real time, the wealthier segments cannot continue to ignore the current trend of increasing inequality contributing to the dilemma of globalization; that of the operating dynamic that is rewarding a few while holding the majority in poverty, inequality, social dislocation, and ecological degradation (Hug, 2000, p. 16). Guterres also expressed deep concern that rather than cooperating on climate and trade there is a "growing rivalry and foundering relationship between China and the United States and that it must be repaired" (Lederer, 2021, p. 1).

China's present rise on the global stage is marked by its signature 2013 Belt and Road Initiative (BRI), reminiscent of its ancient Silk Route trade networks. Yet more than silk and goods were transported along the trade route – what Yo Yo Ma, world-renowned cellist, refers to as "the internet of the ancient world." Ma reignited a renewed flow of ideas by assembling and collaborating with Central Asian musicians as *The Silk Road Ensemble* to create *A Playlist Without Borders* (2013).

The ancient Silk Route also saw the exchange of cultural influences, religions, as well as ideas and techniques. When British biochemist, historian, and Sinologist, Joseph Needham and his research team, set out to amend what at the time were wholly Eurocentric attributions for technology and science, he could not have imagined that a history on the *Science and Civilisation in China,* would come close to its final count of 28 volumes. China's invention of gunpowder centuries earlier ignited a chain of discoveries and inventions over time in Europe. According to historian James J. Hoffman (2019), Needham establishes that gunpowder not only ushered in inventions, such as firearms and the steam engine, but was the precursor to modern science, permanently revolutionizing European life.

The connecting of points on a contemporary *Sage Green Network* could ignite climate change initiatives bringing a contemporary Axial Age to bear. Visionary leadership would provide criteria toward measures that address both quality-of-life issues, such as the United States of America President Biden plan to alleviate climate change and level social and economic disparities brought into clearer focus by COVID-19. Biden's 2021 *Build Back Better* plan could readily dovetail with China's plan to address both quality-of-life issues and climate change by reducing coal-fired and fossil-fueled plants to "make skies blue again" (AP Press: NBC News, 2017). To meet the challenge requires courageous leadership, for at no other time in the history of the world have human beings impacted the natural environment to the degree that we have at this time. The new Anthropocene epoch, according to scientist Vittorino Ingegnoli (2001) calls for a *reformulation of ecology* that makes space for *Landscape Ecology* (p. 504). For interdisciplinarity with its reductionistic and mechanistic bases can no longer render complex adaptive systems effective; instead, going forward calls for following what Ingegnoli sees as a hierarchic methodology with an open spatial web that is *holistic, integrative,* and *transdisciplinary* (p. 504, emphases added).

Thinking the twenty-first century

This section takes for its heading the title of Malcolm McIntosh's (2015) book that calls for a commitment to sustainable development for seeing "globality and Earth awareness as an idea of shared space" (p. 37). "Globality" he writes, "is simply an emotional, spiritual, aesthetic sense of the globe: that we share one livable space, one planet, one home. Planethome. Earth." (p. 37). Earth's fragility is captured beautifully in astronaut Neil Armstrong's 1969 images of planethome taken from the surface of the moon on July 21, 1969, which was a game-changing day for the astronauts, seeing the blue, delicate, fragile place in space floating, floating among the stars. It was then that we began to appreciate where we are in the universe – no longer the center of it but one small speck, ourselves as individuals just a smaller pinprick on the surface of a hot cosmic body (pp. 204–205).

Although human beings are neither geographically nor culturally bound, we share in one space, as well as in the *inability to see* the nature of our reality (McIntosh, 2015, p. 31). Daniel Kahneman, economist, psychologist, and 2002 Nobel laureate, notes a similar inability he sees as endemic. He attributes this inability to the *failure of the imagination*, that is an over-confidence in one's own ability (Tippett, 2017).

Tom Friedman (2009), opinion writer for *The New York Times*, writes that "for far too long, there has been less than visionary or suboptimal solutions applied to complex problems." Such overconfidence and short-sightedness not only shut down the inquiry process, but also circumvent cooperation and collaboration, and any possibility of what Fritjof Capra refers to as "interconnected solutions" (2014; as cited in McIntosh, 2015, p. 34). Hawken, too, counsels that the interconnectedness of "nature and humanity are composed of exquisitely complex networks of relationships, without which forests, lands, oceans, peoples, countries, and cultures perish" (p. 9). Still, Hawken remains hopeful for solutions that can still replenish nature.

An ecological conversion

In a 2020 meeting with a group of French environmental activists, Pope Francis went off script, telling them the inside story of his own journey of having an "ecological conversion." It was through his meetings between 2007 and 2015 with the First Peoples of Puerto Maldonado in the Peruvian region of Amazonia that Pope Francis came to see in them the *harmony of wisdom*. It is to those conversations with several chieftains from different indigenous cultures that Francis attributes the impetus that led to his writing the acclaimed encyclical *Laudato Si* (*On Care for Our Common Home*). At the urging of the French minister of the environment, Ségolène Royal, Francis completed his encyclical ahead of the 2015 United Nations-sponsored Paris Conference on Climate Change. Francis told the activists that, seeing on display before him the very *harmony of indigenous wisdom*, he came to the realization of the poverty of the "heirs of liberalism and the Enlightenment in that we have lost the harmony of the three languages: the language of the head – thinking – the language of the heart – feeling – and the language of the hands – doing" (O'Connell, 2020).

Nature and art as human needs

Forty years before Francis' conversion, the art historian Ernst Gombrich (1981) perceived the way in which a breach in the "chain of culture" imperiled the order by which humans form expectations, plan, and develop science and art. For his 1981 Leverhulme Memorial lecture titled "Nature and Art as Needs of the Mind," he adopted the theme "With Nature, so with Art," on which the Leverhulme galleries in London were founded. He perceived that the culture was in decline and estranged from the "moral earnestness and unquestioning optimism" (p. 8) of its founding. Although he could offer no solution, he hoped that putting forth a diagnosis of the problem would possibly offer half the cure to the urgent problems affecting the welfare of society, both at home and abroad. Noting a particular disconnection from nature, he observed that his fellows could no longer speak the same well-known language that strikes at the heart.

> The mythology and rituals of countless religions testify to the embeddedness of culture in the natural order; without which order humans could not form expectations, could not plan, could not develop science and, maybe, not art either. For the alternations of day and night, birth and death, the round of the seasons in temperate climates, or the rhythms of the tides, are not like the actions of a clockwork; there is constant variety in regularity which must have impressed itself on the mind since the dawn of consciousness. Like a patient language teacher, nature familiarized the mind of man with recurrent processes in ever-changing modifications, establishing a communicable pattern of events which determined survival but always needed fresh attention.
>
> (Gombrich, 1981, p. 10)

Gombrich's sentiments resonate with that of the conservationist Aldo Leopold, who believes that transforming our ethical appreciation of nature will require an "internal change in our intellectual emphasis, loyalties, affections and convictions" (in Hoffman, 2016, p. 117).

The proof that we have failed in our essential role as stewards to engage and respond to the needs of nature is that at its very foundation, the West lacks a coherent set of ethics to live by much less pass on to its youth.

Looking East

Thomas Merton (1915–1968), Trappist monk, writer, theologian, social activist, and scholar of comparative religion was a vocal champion of interfaith dialogue in no small part due to his communications and contacts with the East. In several of his books he advocated for the necessity of the horizons of Europe to no longer be confined to Europe. He urged Western cultures to pursue new perspectives, so much so that he saw their spiritual and even physical survival was at stake (McDonnell, 1974). His teaching of novices reflected the tradition of 14th-century mystics in expressing a "desire not merely to return to the Divine Source of life but to bring others along with oneself through the exercise of loving concern" (Dupré & Wiseman, 2001, p. 448).

Perhaps that is why Merton was drawn to the rituals and practices of Chinese self-cultivation that had served down through the ages as a means of reviving and rectifying social harmony as well as stabilizing society. He was a serious student of Chinese calligraphy and painting, expressing an affinity with Chinese masters who preserved the cultural heritage of landscape forms of mountains and rivers through the arts.

Although it is unlikely that they ever met in person, it could be said that Merton was of the same mind as his contemporary, Chiang Yee (1903–1977), a Chinese expatriate studying economics in London. While there, Yee employed his traditional Chinese self-cultivation practices of the brush – the

Three Perfections of calligraphy, poetry, and painting. He wrote a series of travel books illustrated with his calligraphy and ink paintings, done on location in England's picturesque Lake District. Yee's painting honored traditional Chinese self-cultivation rituals of venerating landscape forms unbound by geographical limits. Immersion in nature and paying homage to its grandeur and beauty has endured over time in so many diverse cultures, that it may well be the best developed and most considered path to joining us all together to save the planet.

China background

In ancient times China's sage rulers not only offered sacrifices to the mountains and rivers, but they also emulated these landscape forms so that over time they became synonymous with symbols of power and virtue.

China's great philosopher-educator Confucius (c. 551–479 BCE), who lived during the Zhou Dynasty (1046–256 BCE), is believed to have worked for the Prince of Lu in various capacities. Confucius also lobbied his proposal for political and social reforms for a period of 13 years to all the Zhou states. When his policies were soundly rejected, Confucius returned to his home state of Lu (Shandong), where his teaching drew 72 disciples (Chan, 1963). Although he did not author books, he is the chief editor of the *Five Classics*. His teachings, recorded by his students, are contained for the most part in the *Analects* and *Great Learning*, two of the Confucian *Four Books*. In the *Analects*, Confucius notes correspondences between wise individuals and the landscape forms of mountains and rivers. Individuals of *zhi* (wisdom) delight in water, individuals of *ren* (benevolence; humanity) delight in mountains; the former is active; the latter tranquil (Confucius, in Ames & Rosemont, 1998, 6:23, p. 109). After climbing Mt. Tai, China's eastern most sacred mountain and observing from its summit that the world of humans was small (Hay, 1985, pp. 56, 58), Confucius derived a comprehensive understanding not only of the continual flux of existence, but also an all embracing "compassion for one's fellow people as sure an axis of society as the rock mountain is of the landscape" (Hay, 1985, p. 58).

Confucius also provides *measures* for the exceptional virtuous sage-leader, gleaned from observing the correspondences between the attributes of the virtuous individual and metaphysical properties of jade. As the story comes down to us in the Chinese classic *Book of Rites*, a question put to Confucius by a student was, why is it that sages value jade and not soapstone? Is it because soapstone is plentiful, the student asked, and that jade is rarer? Confucius answered that in former times the sage set a high value on jade, not because it is rare, but because the sage sees in jade all the excellent qualities or virtues (*de*) of the noble, profound person (*junzi*) marked by benevolence to all. Jun Shan (2020) provides this translation:

> The wise have likened jade to virtue. For them, its polish and brilliancy represent the whole of purity; its perfect compactness and extreme hardness represent the sureness of intelligence; its angles, which do not cut, although they seem sharp, represent justice; the pure and prolonged sound, which it gives forth when one strikes it, represents music. Its color represents loyalty; its interior flaws, always showing themselves through the transparency, call to mind sincerity; its iridescent brightness represents heaven; its admirable substance, born of mountain and of water, represents the earth. Used alone without ornamentation it represents chastity. The price that the entire world attaches to it represents the truth.

We hear echoes of this wisdom in the writings of the organizational theorist Russell Ackoff (1999) who acknowledged that businesses have been good at the function of science – data, information, knowledge, understanding – but have misunderstood leadership because it is primarily an aesthetic function:

> The pursuit of *truth* is the societal function of science. The pursuit of *plenty* is a function of institutions that are concerned with (1) producing and distribution the resources that make possible the pursuit of ends as efficiently as possible and (2) protecting the resources acquired against their appropriation, theft, or destruction. The pursuit of the *good* involves ethical and moral principles. The pursuits of *beauty* and *fun* are inseparable aspects of aesthetics … expressed as art inspires, produces an unwillingness to settle for what we have and a desire for something better.
>
> (p. 21, emphases in original)

Missing from this version is the inclusion of *wisdom* that appears in an essay of the same title "Transformational Leadership" written one year earlier. In it, Ackoff enlarges both the range of consequences: that is, "making a decision coupled with the length of time to *preventing sacrificing the future for the present by taking into account long – as well as short run consequences*" (1998. pp. 25–26, emphases added).

In the jade example above, humans and nature share both natural and *transcendent* correspondences and remain inextricably linked in the new ecological landscape, as they were in the ancient world. Just as raw jade cannot be carved directly but only worked slowly and methodically over time with abrasives, so too the process of *becoming* a *junzi* requires self-cultivation over a lifetime. As the Chinese proverb goes: "gold has a value; jade is invaluable."

Leading with purpose

As noted above, in their chapter in the *Routledge Companion to Leadership* titled "What is Leadership? Person, Result, Position or Process, or All or None of These?" Grint et al., uncover an absence of a consensus on *leadership* and "a dissensus on all four of these areas" (2016, p. 4). They also note the key omission of *purpose* because its immediate results can be meager when applying the transactional yardstick of dollars and cents. Despite ethics being contested as much as leadership, they hold firm to a leadership model that couples *purpose* and *ethics* corresponding to Moore's (1997) *Public Value Initiative* as a primary prerequisite for successful leadership (in Grint et al., 2016). It also is in keeping with the 2015 United Nations Sustainable Development Goals, SDGS, that are a call for action by all countries – poor, rich, and middle-income – to promote prosperity while protecting the planet. Goal 17 is important in it calls for a global partnership for sustainable development. The goal highlights the importance of global macroeconomic stability and the need to mobilize financial resources for developing countries from international sources, as well as through strengthened domestic capacities for revenue collection (*Make the SDGs a reality*, 2022).

The caveat is that there is no definitive rule book of ethics, rather a gray area that calls for discerning transformational outcomes that effect a deep change in a culture requiring time to measure yet are "more in keeping with the symbolic significance of a system" (Grint et al., 2016, p. 9). They conclude it is critical that leaders and their followers grapple in the gray area of ethics. It is the place where leadership is forged by those willing to engage in the world of practice, not just theory, willing to work and collaborate with others along with committing to actionable items (p. 9). As Hawken (2021) elegantly puts it, "it doesn't mean being right in a way that makes others wrong; it means listening intently and respectfully, stitching together the broken strands that separate us from life and one another" (p. 9).

We see below the way in which a small cadre of Chinese literati, serving as advisors to a nomad conqueror after a hostile takeover, provides such a case study of leadership in the service of the public under extreme circumstances.

Becoming *Inner Sage Outer King*

Through observing the firmaments, Zhang Zai (1020–1077) saw an interconnected planetary universe that conferred on him an active role to fulfill in 11th century China. One traditional route was in China's complex governance system that relied on the appointment of thousands of bureaucratic administrators through a meritocratic examination system and curricula of military strategy, civil law, astronomy, hydrology, economics, and the equivalent of immersion in the humanities based on the foundational texts of the *Four Confucian Books* and *The Five Classics*. In addition to being tested on their formal knowledge, examinees were required to compose a poem or painting on a particular theme from the classics to reveal both their moral and spiritual qualities. Zhang Zai's expresses a cosmic vision in *The Western Inscription*:

> Heaven is my father and earth is my mother, and even such a small creature as I finds an intimate place in their midst. Therefore, that which extends throughout the universe I regard as my body and that which directs the universe, I consider my nature.
>
> (Chan, 1963, p. 497)

The recent trend endorsing self-cultivation practices to dovetail with the UN's Sustainable Development Goals, is that of the Inner Development Goals (IDGs (2022) that have far-reaching antecedents in China.

In ancient China, self-cultivation practices were directed toward that of becoming *Inner Sage, Outer King*. Asian scholar emeritus W. T. de Bary (2004) extends this concept of leadership, *nobility*, and public morality, *civility*, in the Chinese tradition as a humanizing contribution to the current globalization process. In his preface to *Nobility and Civility: Asian Ideas of Leadership and the Common Good,* rather than prescribe behaviors, his intent is to show how history may serve the purpose of a general education rather than what he sees as the "modern rush to often oversimplified, ready-made technical solutions, applied to current dilemmas" (p. xi). His approach is to alert readers to people's past experiences, reflect on their evolving theorizing views, then note what went into the implementation of their own ideal values to fit with the external environment; and finally, to instruct on how to cope with similar problems in the present. Where de Bary's approach is examining and reflecting on views based in classic texts, in this chapter, I take for a ground the corresponding foundation of the classics that the literati applied to landscape painting to refine their intuitive wisdom as did the sages of old. The scholar of Chinese philosophy, Henry Rosemont, Jr., notes that the topic of "intuitive wisdom" is a current research interest for both philosophers and psychologists (personal communication).

The Chinese view on nature

The natural world has long been conceived in Chinese thought as a self-generating, complex arrangement of elements that are continuously changing and interacting. From ancient times onward, the correspondence between human beings and nature continued to evolve, as mountains and rivers came to be seen as representing outward configurations of the earth's inner energy forces.

The Han Dynasty (250 BCE–225 CE) unified China creating the *Han*, the world's largest ethnic group that took its name from this dynasty. It also saw the establishment of the Silk Road, a series of trade routes central to cultural interaction between the West and East. From the Han Dynasty onward, mountains and water became the greatest icons of power in the outer earthly world, just as the emperor was the power of the social and political world.

By the 6th century, critics and historians focused their interest on the problem of a "new transformation." Art historian Wen Fong writes in *Images of the Mind* (1984) the side of the debate that argued for "newness" was countered with the case made for "understanding transformation" guided by the wisdom classics (p. 7). The description below takes as its starting point the design principle of color:

> The color blue is prepared from indigo, and the color red comes from madder. Although blue and red seem to be brighter than their sources, they are incapable of further change … If one wishes to refine upon the blue and to purify the red, one must return to the indigo and the madder and begin there; in the same way to correct pretentiousness and cure superficiality, a writer must return to the *Classics* and begin there. Only when a writer is able to strike a balance between *substance* and the *ornament*, and to make the right choice between a graceful and vulgar expression, are they with whom we may discuss the problem of 'understanding transformation.' (p. 7)

After the 10th century, the history of painting in China was to turn decisively toward landscape (Fong, 1984, p. 17). Literati Painting Theory, (wenrenhua 文人畫) with its focus on landscape painting was practiced by a small group of literati in the early Song Dynasty (1127–1279). Yet, Literati Painting Theory (hereafter *wenrenhua*) would come into full flower in the late Song Dynasty, a dynasty that would end with the Mongol conquest in 1260, resulting in the expulsion of Confucian literati from court. In their forced retirement, the literati returned to their hometowns reengaging with the Classics and The Three Perfections practices – calligraphy, poetry, painting – with renewed emphasis on landscape painting, which attended to the regenerative natural forms of mountains and water that had informed the sage rulers of ancient China.

Purpose into action

Over time, a small cadre of literati, referred to as the Eight Talents of Wuxing, came to be seen by the court as key to dealing with the chaotic aftermath of war and the disastrous outcomes brought on by fiscal missteps. For his part, the Khan recognized that transitioning from nomad warrior to emperor of a vast empire and functional government required the experience of seasoned bureaucrats steeped in wisdom traditions that had prevailed in China over millennia. A small group of Confucian literati did accept Khubulai Khan's invitation to serve in an advisory capacity at his court to initiate his rule as the

Yuan Dynasty (1271–1368), while others refused to do so out of loyalty to the fallen Song Dynasty. Although historians for the past several centuries have elevated the loyalists and disparaged the advisors to the Khan as opportunistic, they are coming around to see an alternative view; that the latter took a deeper, more universal view of history as "sages who take the whole world as their family without distinction between near and far" (Ames, 2019, APA: Personal communications).

Here, Hawken would add that through reciprocity "regeneration is not only about bringing the world back to life; it is about bringing each of us back to life. It has meaning and scope; it expresses faith and kindness; it involves imagination and creativity. It is inclusive, engaging, and generous" (p. 9).

In the absence of both the academy and a civil service examination system in the early Yuan, an extraordinary indicator of the individual's character or intent (yi 意) would fill the void – *wenrenhua* paintings would stand in as both the *method* and the *measure*. *Method* is defined by de Bary (1989) as a specific way to convey a work's message to express the idea of the instruction transmitted from the mind-and-heart of early sage kings. Besides connoting a step, or action, to be taken, *measure* can represent method as a *model* (or norm) that is an observable register of the *junzi*'s character that can advance setting the standard of the moral value or judgment intrinsic to the mind-and-heart (de Bary, 1989, p. xvi).[1]

The *junzi*, according to classic texts, was seen as a *noble, profound* person, the model of someone capable of true leadership as one able to make necessary value distinctions not like the individual who follows natural tendencies only – that of the *untamed nature that leans toward greed*. As the cultural anthropologist, Marshall Sahlins (2008) put it:

> For the greater part of humanity, self-interest as we know it is unnatural in the normative sense: it is considered madness, witchcraft or some such grounds for ostracism, execution or at least therapy. Rather than expressing a pre-social human nature, such avarice is generally taken for a loss of humanity. It puts in abeyance the mutual relationships of being that define a human existence. (p. 51)

Landscape paintings became the observable register for literati refinement in communicating to one another their *heart's intent* by way of the brush – the signatures (heart seals) – that gave visual impressions of the mind-and-heart deep within the individual (Bush, 1971). The beauty of these heart seals lies in their potential for mind-to-mind transference from artist to viewer in a symbiotic relationship, whereby "each shines more brilliantly in the other's company" (Ames, personal communication).

As Confucius taught, anyone who cultivates virtue according to the way of the ancient wisdom tradition could become a *junzi,* even a nomad ruler. Therefore, as de Bary (1981) notes, the role of literati at court consisted of clarifying the luminous virtue that lies in the mind-and-heart of the ruler.

For Khubulai's part, he came to heed the advice of Confucian literati advisors by seeing continuing invasions to expand the empire bolstered by unrelenting taxation of Chinese subjects only served to undermine his rule. The source of such advice could have been drawn from a commentary from *Yijing* (*I Ching*) the *Classic Book of Changes* Hexagram #23, *Po* (Splitting Apart):

> The mountain rests on the earth. When it is steep and narrow, lacking a broad base, it must topple over. Its position is strong only when it rises out of the earth broad and great, not proud, and steep. So likewise, those who rule rest on the broad foundation of the people. They too should be generous and benevolent, like the earth that carries all. Then they will make their position as secure as a mountain is in its tranquility.
> (Wilhelm & Baynes, 1984, p. 94)

The literati not only saw themselves as benefactors of the ancient culture and wisdom traditions, but, more importantly, as preservers and transmitters of essential elements of the cultural legacy, not allowing its collapse, but rather transforming it. For the *junzi*, learning never ceases, for it is an ongoing process of continuous effort toward completion and beauty like a work of art.

That a leadership model based on *purpose* and *ethics* became fertile soil for such virtues of sincerity and reverence (*du gong*), modeled by the literati at court found its completion and realization, not only by being admired, but more so prized in the Chinese officials by the Mongol officers, Uighurs, Tibetans, and Arabs of the inner court (Hearn, 2010).

Nature and art as needs of the mind

As noted above, as much as Gombrich (1981) sees nature and art as needs of the mind, he acknowledges that language serves a primary function. However, as American Philosopher Susanne K. Langer (1953) notes, in navigating our daily habituated lives we become selective and adept at merely recognizing objects such as only reading the labels, rather than seeing further into their hidden contents (p. 238). Navigating our daily lives depends on our use of language, and we become good at it. Because of the **nature** of our habituated daily lives, we become adept at recognizing objects – perhaps reading the labels – rather than seeing further into their hidden contents.

For Gombrich (1981), language is not solely reliable for our needs for there is so much more than communication and labels attached to objects and people in our environment. As rich as it is, language can never address the numberless range of potential experiences, for its store of words is finite. At the point where words leave off, we are left with a supply of *universals* along with those that are movable, *metaphors*, which nature and art provide in rich supply. Using metaphors, we construct pairs such as "the sun is smiling," (p. 7) a seeming tendency of the mind, to consciously order the world of experience with natural phenomena. Moreover, says Gombrich, without this ability of linking the external and our sensory experience of it with the internal emotional life, we could not communicate our feelings to others, much less ourselves, which brings him to conclude that only through this process of creative articulation is the way in which the *mind* becomes *mind*. An updated interpretation of Gombrich's use *becomes mind* likely comes closer to the Chinese concept of mind-and-heart, a *feeling mind*.

As Langer (1953) notes above, we realize in our daily habituated lives that we read from our mental catalog more than we see the actual world before us. Yet we want to *see*, because on some level we know that we *look*, but do not *see*. Creating better practices for a more sustainable world requires what Langer refers to as an "education of the *inward eye* of the creative imagination that guides perception" (p. 404 emphasis in the original).

That is why art is so important to human beings – we want to see what the artist sees – the unrecorded reality, momentarily recognized, yet all too often remains below the surface (Langer, 1954). However, without the participatory role of the viewer who can decipher the artist's intention, the work of art remains incomplete. This important participatory role of the viewer is discussed below.

How nature informed Chinese language

As the language of the world's oldest existing culture, China's language began as pictographic. The earliest pictograph for mountain (shan 山) was rendered as a host mountain flanked by two smaller mountains. Later it evolved to a more calligraphic version in the current rendering of the character. Similarly, the character for water (shui 水), originally drawn to resemble a stream evolved to its current version. When paired *shanshui* (山水) it is translated as mountain-water or landscape. As the Chinese vocabulary increased, the characters had more abstract meanings requiring paired combinations based on sound to express more complex ideas.

The forms of mountains and rivers are images imprinted in the minds of all human beings since the beginning of time. For the Chinese, mountains were especially seen as the containers of vital energy (qi 氣) occupying a potently charged space in ancient geography seen as the spiritual zone of transition between the world of humans and Heaven (Lewis, 2005. p. 290). What sustained this universal model was the free flow between Heaven and Earth of *qi* perceived in the unfolding and workings of the seasons. Individuals who excelled in learning and moral character were seen as transmitters of Heaven's rejuvenating powers, capable of restoring wholeness through their *pure qi*. When doing so they painted from their inner mountains and rivers, presenting to their viewers images of their mind-hearts. Thus, from this heart center of *sincerity* springs creative spontaneity and such individuals are charged with continuing Heaven's creative activity by bringing about new harmonies that would not otherwise materialize without human intervention (Frisnia, 2002).

Art as a need of the mind

In their book *Quantum Leadership*, authors Tsao and Laszlo (2019) identify "consciousness (as) a powerful root cause of who we are, how we behave toward others and nature, and why we act the way we do. Transforming our consciousness is the most effective tool we have for unlocking local and global change" (p. 113). Yet our daily lives leave little room for cultivating *eyes* that shape the world, even knowing that this is not the level that provides meaning to our lives. Langer (1954) notes that as much as common sense is looked on as a desirable knowledge because it is prompt and categorical, it is also inexact (Langer, 1954. p. 216).

Contemporary poet and essayist Mark Strand, who studied painting as a young man told the creativity expert, Mihaly Cziksentmihaly (1996), in an interview that he saw his role as an artist to not only be a witness of recorded experience but also as part of the broader responsibility for keeping the universe ordered through consciousness by paying attention: "I mean, we are – as far as we know – the only part of the universe that's self-conscious. We could even be the universe's *form* of consciousness. We might have come along so that the universe could look at itself" (p. 231, emphasis in original).

Strand's observation resonates with that of the Qing Dynasty (1644–1912) dramatist Li Yu, made three centuries earlier in China: "Landscape is the intellectual and emotional expression of the universe, while intellectual and emotional expression is the landscape of the human mind" (Chen, 2006, p. 2). The Chinese mind that observed correspondences between humans and the properties of jade, also observed in nature patterns that revealed the ways in which the universe operated; that rock was the microcosm of mountain, and mountain a microcosm of the universe (Hay, 1985, p. 56). Moreover, says Hay, although surpassed by mountains, both in mass and scale, human beings, too, are a uniquely situated type of microcosm. As in the West, the Chinese also discerned in nature paradigms of an order that revealed the way in which the universe operated, yet one that differed from the West's concept of the *laws of nature* by eschewing mathematical proof. Interestingly, the Chinese world view comes closer to the epistemology of modern science in its understanding of "great depth, resilience and unifying power" (p. 56). The Chinese sensibility, in contrast to the conceptual logic of the West that found its expression of spatial relations in geometry, established its principles of vision in making order out of sensory chaos that is not linearly defined but amorphous (p. 56). Its logic was more in line with artistic vision for its "biological feeling and its emotional efflorescence, or life on the human level that functions in an essentially deep way in the building up of human consciousness different from discursive thought" (Langer, 1953, p. 62). Whereas language is that of constructing words and propositions, artistic vision develops forms to express basic vital rhythms some of which are so basic they are almost universal. The global omnipresence of such universal rhythmic forms is perhaps nowhere more evident than in landscape painting.

The three tenets of *wenrenhua*

Wenrenhua consisted of three tenets: first, the painter must be a person of the Way; second, the painter must go beyond the correct method; and third, the painter must be capable of bringing about the *awakening* of the viewer, also a person of the Way.

The essence of the Way, according to the philosopher Tu Weiming, has always been conveyed in Confucian thought as never static, but as a process consisting of a

> strong moving power generated by moral and spiritual self-cultivation that opens one up to a dynamic unfolding, through aligning one's vital energy (qi 氣) with the earth's vital energy (氣 – *qi*) that results in personal, social, and cosmic transformation.
>
> (Tu, 1985, p. 9)

Nature created the individual through its physical laws; individuals such as painters, in turn adapt natural materials for their tools – brushes, pigments, paper – for enhancing an embodied self-understanding (Crowther, 2016, p. 14). The Chinese referred to them as the *Four Treasures* of brush, paper, ink, and ink stone. The ink, made from pine soot, was compressed in stick form to be ground in circular motions with water on the surface of the ink stone. Mountains like macro-cosmic pumps exhale *qi* in the form of mist that drops into the water at their base, from which riverbed stones draw in their *qi*. Rubbing the ink stick on the surface of the stone diluted the soot making ink to be uploaded along with the mountain's *qi* from the stone, to combine with the *qi* of the painters when charging their brush with ink and thus mark their *magic* on the paper.

Nature's *qi* found its resonance in the *qi* cultivated by exemplary individuals forming a symbiotic cosmic relationship manifested with the brush in depositing ink and colors on a blank sheet of paper, as visual evidence of the leftover elements of their virtue (*de*) (Fu, 1981). These scholar-amateur painters may have deflected praise for their paintings as simply the *play of the brush*, yet their perceptive viewers knew better – they recognized that the paintings surpassed merely recording an accurate copy of the object by recognizing their genius in not only rendering the forms of objects but more so in transforming them.

Counsel for the *Wenrenhua* viewer

As we have seen above mountains and rivers are visual symbols that can be read on a cursory level that sees them literally, or with the "discerning eye to its highest reaches of symbolic significance of *vitally felt* forms "(Langer, 1953, p. 32, emphases in original).

A person of the Way was well-versed in the *Five Classics* and *Four Confucian Books* with an understanding of the symbols and their deeper meanings. A contemporary student of art history studying the works of the masters would be steeped in the lineage of schools of painting and individual artist styles looking to the art works for the artist's emotional response to their subject.

Shen Kua (1031–1095), the Chinese scientist and statesman provides this instruction for the viewer from one of China's most esteemed painter-poets, Wang Wei (701–761), of the High Tang Dynasty (699–759):

> The wonderful parts (or mystery) of calligraphy and painting must be realized in the soul; hardly discovered in mere forms. Those who look at pictures are always able to point out faults of form, likeness, of design and coloring, but I have seldom found people who have penetrated the mysterious reason and depth of creative activity … the artists had conceived the thing in their mind; their hands responded, and it was done as conceived. This is because their creative activity and their reason resided in the *spiritual* part of their natures and because they grasped to a high degree the 'idea' – the inspiration of Heaven. But this is difficult to explain to common people.
>
> (Li, 1965, pp. 37–38)

The term *spiritual*, according to the religion phenomenologist Louis Dupré (1997) is not exclusively religious, but is also inferred in the arts and literature and can be described "as an *alertness*, a more intense inner awareness of what surpasses ordinary life" (p. 2).

Such an awareness intensified an anticipatory sense of well-being and active motivator of human action, resulted in what the neuroscientist, Antonio Damasio, defines as a sociocultural homeostasis, a new layer of life management in addition to biological homeostasis (2010, p. 293). Storytelling and, in our example landscape painting, became the means of diffusing this wisdom into the ultimate creation of a sociocultural narratives:

> Individuals and groups whose brains made them capable of inventing or using such narratives to improve themselves and the societies they lived in became successful enough for the architectural traits of those brains to be selected, individually and groupwise, and for their frequency to increase over generations. (p. 293)

The next section on 19th-century American landscape painters will highlight similar approaches by Western painters who also turned to nature for inspiration.

This type of aesthetic quality is specifically, not objective fact, but possessing an inner radiating beauty that illuminates the objective message and warms the heart.

Early American landscape painting

The lens on *wenrenhua* painters' symbiotic relationship with nature could also uncover correspondences with the natural landscape by painters in 19th-century USA. The reevaluation of landscape painting from 13th-century China can mirror a shared sensibility of the *sacredness of place* by both global powers despite spanning history and continents. In both instances, it was the painter's brush that indelibly endowed the national consciousness kinship with the natural landscape. Thomas Cole (1801–1848), an economic migrant, artist, and early environmentalist, was the founder of The Hudson River School of Art, the first major art movement in the USA.

With the new nation's expansion, New York City and eventually the entire state – the Empire State – would become both the center from which this westward expansion radiated and the starting point for the painters of the new frontier – hence the name the Hudson River School of Art that embraced an ideal of the natural world imbuing it with an almost religious quality. Under the influence of the movement, Thomas Cole's school of painters favored the natural landscape as noble and sacred where nature and humanity co-existed in peaceful beauty.

The birth of the world's first national park system

Although early USA citizens assumed the birthright of a fledgling new nation, it also adopted from *First Peoples' Nations*, consciously or unconsciously, the concept of stewardship of the land for future generations.

For example, it was in 19th century that USA Congress viewed photographs and sketches of the picturesque landscapes of the West. Yet it would be the awe-inspiring painting of the *Grand Canyon of the Yellowstone* by Hudson River School painter, Thomas Moran (1837–1926), that would move Congress to set aside designated public lands (see Figure 2.1). In 1872, Congress created the first national park in the National Park System of national treasures for future generations, the first of its kind in the world.

Appreciating the American landscape

In his *Lecture on American Landscape* (1841), Thomas Cole wrote that those who felt that the American landscape had nothing to offer, compared to European scenery, were few, and if they did it was out of their ignorance or prejudice, writing:

Figure 2.1 Thomas Moran Painting *Grand Canyon of the Yellowstone* completed and displayed to Congress in 1872. Thomas Moran Oil on canvas mounted on aluminum. H 213, W 266.3 cm Department of the Interior Museum.

> But from whom do these opinions come? From those who have read of European scenery, of Grecian mountains, and Italian skies, and never troubled themselves to look at their own; and from those traveled ones whose eyes were never opened to the beauties of nature until they beheld foreign lands, and when those lands faded from the sight were again closed and forever? (p. 2)

1 Water

Although England's Lake District continued to attract many artists and writers, including Cole and others from the Hudson circle, they specifically considered the lakes of the USA superior for capturing the beautiful and the sublime. Cole had much to say about the rich symbolism of water, that also showed an affinity with the Chinese concept of *qi,* "spirit resonance," cultivated by Chinese *wenrenhua* painters. For example, he described the effect of the "clear" and pristine qualities of both the *purity* and the *transparency* of water:

> In this great element of scenery, what land is so rich? I would not speak of the great Lakes, which are in fact inland seas possessing some of the attributes of the ocean, though destitute of its sublimity; but of those smaller lakes, such as Lake George, Champlain, Winnipisiogee, Otsego, Seneca, and a hundred others, that stud like gems the bosom of this country. There is one delightful quality in nearly all these lakes - the

> purity and transparency of the water. In speaking of scenery it might seem unnecessary to mention this; but independent of the pleasure that we all have in beholding pure water, it is a circumstance which contributes greatly to the beauty of landscape; for the reflections of surrounding objects, trees, mountains, sky, are most perfect in the clearest water; and the most perfect is the most beautiful. (1841, p. 4)

The Neo-Confucian, Shao Yong (1011–1077) compares water with a mirror to show the importance of viewing something "not just with one's physical eyes but with one's mind."

> A mirror reflects because it does not obscure the physical form of things. But water (with its purity) does even better because it reveals the universal character of the physical form of things as they really are. And the sage does still better because he reflects the universal character of the feelings of all things.
>
> (Chan, 1963, pp. 487–488)

In his book titled *Walden*, naturalist Henry David Thoreau (1854) writes in the chapter "The Ponds" that "a lake is the landscape's most beautiful and expressive feature, as if looking into the Earth's eye, the beholder is able to measure the depth of their own nature."

Both the American and Chinese literati painters share in their mutual appreciation of the placidness of a lake as *reflecting* the painters' inner peace and serenity. Thoreau's "Earth's eye" is the same *universal character* of Shao Yong's clear *qi* of water (not turbid *qi*) that corresponds to the cultivated *pure qi* of the individual painter in extending empathy and compassion outward, not just to nature, but to all humanity.

2 Mountains

Cole had this to say, too, about majestic mountains, not near in scale to the towering peaks of other locales such as China, they could still evoke awe and wonder for their own unique grandeur:

> But in the mountains of New Hampshire there is a union of the picturesque, the sublime, and the magnificent; there the bare peaks of granite, broken and desolate, cradle the clouds; while the valleys and broad bases of the mountains rest under the shadow of noble and varied forests; and the traveler who passes the Sandwich range on their way to the White Mountains, of which it is a spur, cannot but acknowledge, that although in some regions of the globe nature has wrought on a more stupendous scale, yet she has nowhere so completely married together grandeur and loveliness – there he sees the sublime melting into the beautiful, the savage tempered by the magnificent (1841, p. 4).

Cole cannot help but acknowledge the sacredness of place that the human mind reciprocates in kind. He continues in his *Essay on American Scenery*

> There is in the human mind an almost inseparable connection between the beautiful and the good … He who looks on nature with a 'loving eye' … in gazing on the pure creations of the Almighty … feels a calm religious tone steal through their minds, and when one has turned to mingle with their fellow men, the chords which have been struck in that sweet communion cease not to vibrate. (1841, p. 2)

Cole's sentiment resonates with that of Ralph Waldo Emerson, who led the transcendentalist movement of the mid-19th century. In his 1849 essay *From Nature,* Emerson famously compared his receptive imagination as exerting the *transparent eyeball* so that in the presence of creation all mean egotism banished writing

> Standing on the bare ground, my head bathed by the blithe air, and uplifted into infinite space, all mean egotism vanishes. I become a transparent eye-ball; I am nothing; I see all; the currents of the Universal Being circulate through me; I am part or particle of God … In the tranquil landscape, and especially in the distant line of the horizon, man beholds somewhat as beautiful as his own nature.
>
> (Kurtz, J., ed. 2020, p. 114)

In addition to his gifts in both painting and writing, Cole was also a forceful voice against the inequity of classes of the immensely poor, compared with the very wealthy, and he may well have been the USA's earliest advocate for urban planning by condemning the destruction of Dutch colonial buildings in New York City to make way for what he sarcastically called "improvements" of modernization and technology.

Conclusion

As we have seen, the rise of *wenrenhua* set the stage for a renewed communication with nature, not just visually, but also through a keener disposition of appreciating the undertones of rhythms in nature, "to perceive unseen norms, structures and forms that unfold harmonically like the goals and aims of nature itself' (Schneider in Godwin, 1989, p. 61). The late Malcolm MacIntosh leaves us with this prescient question: "How do we see the world now, now that we know what we know?" (2015, p. 18).

Are there lessons that can instruct on what Kahneman (2017) identified as a global problem that is endemic – the failure of the imagination, that we now see as short-sightedness. This lack of insight has led us to unrealistic assessments of our abilities and a concomitant inflated self-confidence. We have seen the way in which *wenrenhua* painters resisted formulaic approaches to change by striving continually to revive their intuitions through The Three Perfection practices *to bring new eyes* to ever-increasing complexity that required fresh vision – even if it meant advising a nomad ruler without enmity for the sake of preserving the culture.

In the aesthetic realm, Crowther writes in *How Pictures Complete Us* of the shift in ordinary perception whereby "engaging with meanings that somehow exceed the scope of our perceptual or imaginative capacities moves us beyond the beautiful to the sublime" (2016, p. 6).

For Crowther, pictorial art shows in the highest degree, the way in which painters master their tools through years of practice. More importantly, it is through the intervention of their self-consciousness of the physical universe that is not only made meaningful but also brought to a higher and more complete state of being (p. 151). The Chinese would attribute it to one's *qi,* described earlier in terms of clarity, or *purity* like water that resonates in the writings of Hudson River Painters and Transcendentalists above.

Often art, whether it be a painting or musical composition, is attributed to an artist's or composer's emotion toward their subject. Langer (1954) notes, however, it is not a single feeling but rather an outcome of a complex, permanent attitude not recognizable in any other form but by this formalized *gesture*. For millennia, such forms have been the life-symbols and the basis of human existence – forces of generation, achievement, death – complemented by rituals that have recorded humanity's *response* and feelings. We viewers respond to the given sacred symbols because they make up the emotional pattern that governs our lives. We seek ongoing cultural security through a rite that has been regularly performed over millennia and repeats its sentiments for the present generation toward "first and last things; far from being a free expression of emotions; it is instead a disciplined rehearsal of right *attitudes*" (Langer, p. 131).

Traditionally, Confucian literati in their leisure sometimes packed up their musical instruments and painting tools to go on walks in nature to paint particularly beautiful vistas. We consider an early 13th-century painting by the Song Dynasty (960–1279) painter, Ma Yuan titled "Viewing Plum Blossoms by Moonlight," an example of Chinese *wenrenhua* painting (Figure 2.2).

The format is not the traditional monumental hanging scroll, but that of an album leaf more suitable for sharing works from one's private collection with close friends in an intimate setting. One would have to look carefully at the former for signs of human life for precedence given to the awe and majesty of Nature over humans, whereas in this example, the scholar's form eclipses the distant mountain (Figure 2.2).

We note that the musical instruments and painting materials in the painting remain unpacked, and the Confucian scholar (wearing a white robe) trades a painter's role for that of an observer, lying back to take in the view. Is it a changed attitude toward nature? Is it a rare outing or loss of

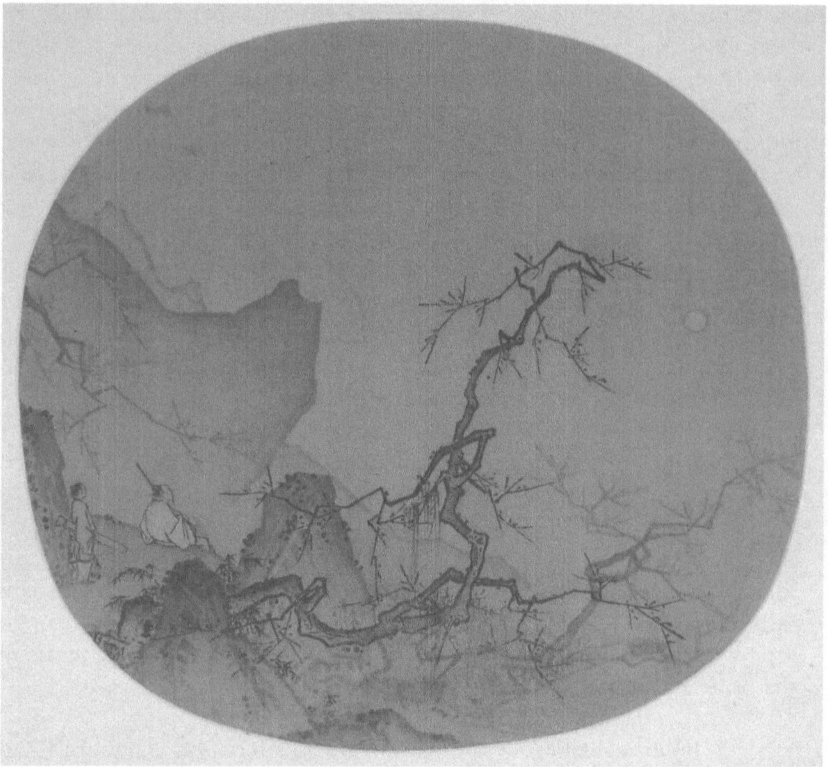

Figure 2.2 **Ma Yuan** Viewing a *Wenrenhua* Painting. Early 13th century. Met Museum, https://www.metmuseum.org/art/collection/search/44638.

a government position? Here appearances can be deceiving for the gentle, calm atmosphere could bely the state of the outer world that is in chaos. The first clue comes from its title: the plum blossom that bears harsh winter weather conditions symbolically corresponds to the "preserving of one's inner beauty and humble display under adverse conditions" (China Online Museum).

What the *wenrenhua* viewer *sees* is a hopeful optimism represented in the figure's *mind landscape* and the message prevails in present time – to viewers such as us – as well as those yet to come in the distant future. The painter has retold a theme from the early 3rd century about a Chinese scholar-official venerated for an ability to reside in a peaceable landscape, an imagined inner mindscape, superimposed on the chaos of the outer world.[2]

The above is an indicator, says Crowther (2016), to yet another space that comes into existence in pictorial art – a virtual space across the horizon of time beyond an occupying space that allows for an aspect *of being* of something that once existed, such as landscape, to have continuing effects in the present of its current reception yet still maintaining a supreme idealization of many possibilities. It's power of a shared experience can be extended to – past, present, future – in dwelling alongside and with the other in *aesthetic empathy*, which facilitates psychological completion in personal as well as social terms through the artists' ability to evoke a sense of the divine by positioning humanity in a more cosmic scheme of things. Moreover, self-conscious beings, despite what they might believe or intend, have a broader ontological role vis-à-vis with the universe that is a mode of being that tends to complete being and this is what painting uniquely accomplishes at the level of space-occupancy (pp. 149–150).

No matter how close we are to another human being, we can never directly know or see the world as another sees it because we cannot get into their experience and know it from their viewpoint. Crowther's (2016) explication of this key role of empathy is that,

> experiencing the other through art is the nearest we can come to such merging. For the artwork at least does more than describe the other's perspective on things, it shows the artist's vision sensuously and imaginatively in a way that allows us to identify with it, yet without being psychologically pressured to do so. Aesthetic empathy of this kind involves our dwelling alongside and with the other … through our wonder at the distinctiveness of human consciousness in terms of its place in nature. (pp. 157–158)

Perhaps it is no exaggeration to say that the literati advisors to Khubulai Khan were particularly influential in what de Bary (1981) notes as a process that not only reasserted the institutionalization that reaffirmed Chinese doctrine, but also restabilizing the imperial bureaucracy in a more mature form:

> …it is important to recognize that the new teaching, while representing the quintessence of Neo-Confucian thought, had transcended its cultural limits and achieved a certain universality by emphasizing the lowest common denominator in its philosophy of human nature; that is, it taught a belief in the inherent moral nature of all individuals irrespective of cultural differences, their *(sic)* perfectibility through self-cultivation, and achievement of an ordered human community through universal self-improvement (p. 71).

What enables one to *see* the alternative to the status quo much less dare to act on it? The lesson from *wenrenhua* painting is how both painter and viewer were able to see what is not there – the *invisible*. We have learned that perfect rendering of an object or scene in a painting while admirable does not make for an extraordinary work of art. It takes *vision* – *seeing what is not there* – all the measures of what the viewer recognized in the *wenrenhua* painter, that is the ability to bring forth with an embodied *sincerity*, the quintessential trait of a true individual of the Way, the one who hits the mark without effort. For it is sincerity that enables humans to live in social harmony with the world.

This key role of the viewer is also in keeping with the concept of the *axiom of cultural innovation* essential to leadership success defined by the late curator, Kirk Varnedoe, of the Museum of Modern Art (MOMA). In his book *A Fine Disregard* (1990), Varnedoe writes on the way in which innovation, like art, is a social phenomenon whereby one individual (or painter) sees an alternative to the status quo and dares to act on it. Yet, equally important is the observer (a viewer) who recognizes it as such, and clears the path to make it happen:

> The axiom of cultural innovation is that it takes two: it requires someone understanding how the rules might be changed and acting on and transforming those rules; but then it also takes someone standing on the sidelines to value this innovation rather than demeaning or suppressing it. (p. 217)

Ultimately, the individual who can see and value the bold action of the disrupter is like the viewer of a painting with a creative mind who recognizes the triumph of the new markers of continuity and change over cultural stagnation, says de Bary (1981). It is through both *vision* and *response* that individuals of potential are empowered to move beyond the untamed nature that leans toward greed. Theologian Evelyn Underhill (1922) writes that such a response fully made on the one hand calls forth

> the most heroic, most beautiful, most tender qualities in human nature; all that we call holiness, the transfiguration of mere ethics … on the other hand, this response of the self is repaid by a new sensitiveness and receptivity, a new influx of power.
>
> (Underhill, 1922, in Dupré & Wiseman, 2001, pp. 434–435)

Yet such a stretch of human realization comes at a price as 13th-century Confucian advisors to Khubulai Khan experienced being rejected by some of their peers and overlooked in recorded history until recently.

Perhaps what Crowther (2016) points out about painting could be applied to business strategy: that although nature encompasses and suggests material forms, it leaves the *unseen* in painting to the artist. When approached with formulaic management fads, strategy like painting becomes restricted to one type of inquiry in that it informs and executes solely on the visible, losing sight that it is also dependent on its *essence* that the artist discerns. In this way, it overlooks the 80% of a company's worth that is *intangible* encompassing such *unmeasurable* entities as brands, good will, and human capital (Tideman, 2005).

This chapter has touched on arts such as music, poetry, calligraphy, and dance while giving precedence to landscape painting. We have seen that it is the latter that eludes linearity given its open spatial unity, that enables the painter to layer strokes, not by a prescribed formula, but that are contingent on one after another, allowing for the artist to pick and choose how it progresses and ultimately decides when it is finished. As Crowther (2016) says:

> If the world is not to one's liking, we would do well to model the artist who through the beauty of art, transforms base matter and makes visible emergent ideas, that rise above the ordinary and create a reality heretofore unimagined. (p. 13)

Just as East and West were connected for centuries by the ancient Silk Road, both share uniquely in their respective national identities being informed by the brush.

Art, particularly Chinese landscape painting over millennia provided the open space for what Damasio (2010) describes as imaginative alternatives to universals once set in stone, either through the extraordinary reaches of art or through the sheer magic of a chance human encounter both sparking lively variations on a theme that evoke awe and wonder (p. 279).

Both East and West have a tradition of landscape painting that can point the way to the actual *seeing* of the innumerable possibilities that hitherto lay dormant but now can be activated by viewers who recognize an energy that is indispensable to the modern world. Nor is it limited to just the two cultures, its valuable renewable source of *qi energy*, *life force*, *spiritual resonance*, resides in the open spatial web of visionary leadership and regenerative business systems, that can enrich, cultivate, transform, and preserve the all-inclusive borderless landscape in which all life flourishes with a continuity for innumerable generations to come.

Notes

1 In Chinese the same word (*xin* 心) – originally a picture of the aorta – is usually translated either as *mind* or *heart*. It is more accurately translated as *mind-and-heart* because it signifies both the seat of thought and the seat of feeling.
2 Zhao Mengfu, 1254–1322. Handscroll; ink and color on silk. Y1984-13. https://artmuseum.princeton.edu/collections/objects/32688

References

Ackoff, R. L. (1998). A systematic view of transformative leadership. *Systemic Practice and Action Research, 11*(1), 23–36.

Ackoff, R. L. (1999). Transformative leadership. *Strategy and Leadership, 27*(1), 20–25.

Ames, R. T., & Rosemont, H. (1998). *The Analects of Confucius: A philosophical translation*. New York, NY: Random House.

AP Press: NBC News. (2017, 4 March). China Premier pledges: We will make our skies blue again. https://www.nbcnews.com/news/world/china-premier-pledges-we-will-make-our-skies-blue-again-n729216

Bush, S. (1971). *The Chinese literati on painting: Su Shih (1037–1101) to Tung Ch'i-ch'ang (1555–1636).* Harvard University Press.

Chan, W-T. (1963). *A source book in Chinese philosophy.* Princeton University Press.

Chen, L. C. (2006). *'Double aperture: Reframing and returning.' Reframing: Writings on the art of Michael Cherney.* Beijing, CN: People's Fine Arts publishing House.

China Online Museum. https://www.comuseum.com/painting/flower-painting/plum-blossom/

Cole, T. (1836). Essay on American scenery. *American Monthly Magazine, 1*, 1–12.

Cort, C., Franceschini, L., & Wang, J. (2015). *Rising leaders on environmental sustainability and climate change.* Yale Center for Business and the Environment.

Crowther, P. (2016). *How pictures complete us: The beautiful, the sublime and the divine.* Stanford University Press.

Csikszenmihályi, M. (1996). *Creativity: Flow and the psychology of discovery and invention.* Harper Collins.

Csikszenmihályi, M. (1997). *Creativity: Flow and the psychology of discovery and invention.* HarperPerennial.

Damasio, A. (2010). *Self comes to mind: Constructing the conscious brain.* Pantheon Books.

de Bary, W. T. (1981). *Neo-Confucian orthodoxy and the learning of the mind-and-heart.* Columbia University Press.

de Bary, W. T. (1989). *The message of the mind in Neo-Confucianism.* Columbia University Press.

de Bary, W. T. (2004). *Nobility and civility: Asian ideals of leadership and the common good.* Harvard University Press.

Dupré, L. (1997, 23 July). Seeking Christian interiority: An interview with Louis Dupré. *Religion Online.* Retrieved 3 August 2018 from https://www.religion-online.org/article/seeking-christian-interiority-an-interview-with-louis-dupr/

Dupré, L. & Wiseman, J., (Eds.). (2001). *Light from light: An anthology of Christian mysticism.* (3rd ed.). Paulist Press.

Fong, W. C. (1984) *Images of the mind.* Princeton University Press.

Friedman, T. L. (2009, 21 November). Advice from grandma. *New York Times.* Retrieved 5 January 2022 from https://www.nytimes.com/2009/11/22/opinion/22friedman.html

Frisnia, W. (2002) *The unity of knowledge and action: Toward a nonrepresentational theory of knowledge.* State University of New York Press.

Fu, M. W. (1981). The impact of reunification: Northern elements in the life and art of Hsien-yu Shu (1257–1302) and their relation to early Yuan literati culture. In J. Langlois, Jr. (Ed.), *China under Mongol rule* (pp. 371–434). Princeton University Press.

Gluckman, R. (2001). World music, according to Yo-Yo Ma. *Ron Gluckman in cyberspace.* Retrieved 5 January 2022 from https://www.gluckman.com/YoYoMa.html

Godwin, J. (Ed.) (1989). *Cosmic music: Musical keys to the interpretation of reality. Essays by Marius Schneider, Rudolf Haase, Hans Erhard Lauer.* Inner Traditions.

Gombrich, E. H. (1981). *Nature and art as needs of the mind (Leverhulme Memorial Lectures).* Liverpool University Press.

Grint, K., Smolovik Jones, O., & Holt, C. (2016). What is leadership: Person, result, position, or process, or all or none of these? In J. Storey, J. Hartley, J.-L. Denis, P. 't Hart, & D. Ulrich (Eds.), *The Routledge companion to leadership* (pp. 3–20). Abingdon: Routledge.

Hawken, P. (2021). *Regeneration: Ending the climate crisis in one generation.* Penguin.

Hay, J. (1985) *Kernels of energy, bones of earth: The rock in Chinese art.* New York: China Institute in America.

Hearn, M. K. (2010). 'Painting and calligraphy under the Mongols' in *The World of Khubilai Khan. Exhibition catalogue of the Metropolitan Museum of Art.* University Press.

Hoffman, A. J. (2016). *Finding purpose: Environmental stewardship as a personal calling.* Greenleaf.

Hoffman, J. (2019). The invention of gunpowder and its introduction into discovery. Retrieved February 28, 2022 from https://www.encyclopedia.com/science/encyclopedias-almanacs-transcripts-and-maps/invention-gunpowder-and-its-introduction-europe

Hug, J. E. (2000). Educating for justice: Any university's major mission is to work for global transformation. *America: The Jesuit Review, 182*(18), 16–22.

IDGs. (2022, April 29). *Inner Development Goals Summit 2022.* https://idg-2022.confetti.events/

Ingegnoli, V. (2001). Landscape ecology. In D. Baltimore, R. Dulbecco, & J. F. LeviMontalcini (Eds.), *Frontiers of life* (pp. 489–508). Academic Press.

Kahneman, D. (2017, 6 May). Why we contradict ourselves and confound each other. *On Being with Krista Tippett.* Retrieved 5 January 2021 from https://onbeing.org/programs/daniel-kahneman-why-we-contradict-ourselves-and-confound-each-other/

Kurtz, J. (Ed.) (2020). *American literature I: An anthology of texts from early America through the civil war.* Viva Publisher. https://open.umn.edu/opentextbooks/textbooks/979

Langer, S. K. (1953). *Feeling and form: A theory of art developed from philosophy in a new key.* Charles Scribner.

Langer, S. K. (1954). *Philosophy in a new key.* Mentor Books.

Lederer, E. (2021). The AP Interview: UN chief warns China, US to avoid Cold War. (September 20) https://apnews.com/article/united-nations-general-assembly-china-climate-united-states-health-f1186707bee7f8376b0be5 523496ddca

Leopold, A. (1949). *A Sand County almanac & sketches here & there.* Oxford University Press.

Lewis, M. E. (2005). *The construction of space in early China.* SUNY Press.

Li, C-T. (1965). *Autumn colors on the Ch'aio and Hua mountains.* (Siven, Trans.) Artibus Asiae.

McDonnell, T. P. (Ed.). (1974). *Christian culture needs Oriental wisdom. Thomas Merton Reader.* Image Books.

McIntosh, M. (2015). *Thinking the twenty-first century. Ideas for the new political economy.* Greenleaf.

Moore, M. (1997). *Creating public value: Strategic management in government.* Harvard University Press.

Needham, J. (1969). Science and China's influence on the world. *The great tradition: Science and society in east and west.* George Allen & Unwin.

O'Connell, G. (2020, 3 September). Pope Francis on the 'ecological conversion' that led him to 'Laudato Si'. *America: The Jesuit Review.* Retrieved 5 January 2022 from https://www.americamagazine.org/politics-society/2020/09/03/pope-francis-ecological-conversion-laudato-si-climate-change

Orr, D. W. (1992). *Ecological literacy: Education and the transition to a postmodern world.* SUNY Press.

Pope Francis. (2015, 24 May). Encyclical letter *Laudato Si* of the Holy Father Francis on care for our common home. *Holy See.* Retrieved 5 January 2022 from https://www.vatican.va/content/francesco/en/encyclicals/documents/papa-francesco_20150524_enciclica-laudato-si.html

Sahlins, M. (2008). *The western illusion of human nature: With reflections on the long history of hierarchy, equality and the sublimation of anarchy in the west, and comparative notes on other conceptions of the human condition.* Prickly Pear Paradigm Press.

Schneider, M. (1989). Acoustic symbolism in foreign cultures. In J. Godwin, (Ed.), *Cosmic music: Musical keys to the interpretation of reality. Essays by Marius Schneider, Rudolf Haase, Hans Erhard Lauer.* Inner Traditions.

Sengupta, S., Einhorn, C., & Andreoni, M. (2021, 14 October). There's a global plan to conserve nature. *Indigenous people could lead the way.* https://www.nytimes.com/2021/03/11/climate/nature-conservation-30-percent.html

Shan, Jun. (2020, 16 September). Importance of jade in Chinese culture. Retrieved from https://www.thoughtco.com/about-jade-culture-629197

Thoreau, H. D. (1854/2015). Walden. Digireads.

Tideman, S. G. (2005). Mind over matter: Towards a new paradigm for business and economics. *The second international conference on gross national happiness rethinking development: Local pathways to global wellbeing.* Antigonish, Nova Scotia, Canada: St. Francis Xavier University. June 20–24.

Tippett, T. (2017). On being. Daniel Kahneman interview with Krista Tippett. American Public Media. Originally aired October 5, 2017. Re-aired January 31, 2021.

Tsao, F. C. & Laszlo, C. (2019). *Quantum leadership: New consciousness in business.* Stanford University Press.

Tu, W-M. (1985). *Confucian thought: Selfhood as creative transformation.* SUNY Press.

Underhill, E. (1922). In L. Dupré, & J. A. Wiseman (Eds.), *Light from light: An anthology of Christian mysticism* (pp. 433–444). Paulist Press.

Varnedoe, K. (1990). *A fine disregard: What makes modern art modern.* Harry N. Abrams.

Wilhelm, R. and Baynes, C. F., trans. (1984). *The I Ching or Book of Changes.* Princeton University Press.

Yee, C. (1942). *A Chinese artist in Lakeland.* Lowe and Brydone Printers.

3 Silent motion to prosperity, leadership from a Chinese perspective

Feng 峰 *Yue* 岳

Introduction

In the past 30 years, China's rapid growth has led it to become the world's second-biggest economy. According to the World Bank,

> Since China began to open up and reform its economy in 1978, GDP growth has averaged almost 10 percent a year, and more than 800 million people have been lifted out of poverty. There have also been significant improvements in access to health, education, and other services over the same period. (2021)

China, as a 5000-year-old continuing civilization, has developed separately from Western influence for most of its existence, and has different perceptions of prosperity and leadership from the West. Throughout its history, China did not have democracy, yet it has consistently acquired prosperity, contributed to humanity, and repeatedly returned to the world stage as an economic, political, and military superpower. Instead of blindly criticizing China based on Western value systems, I recognize that the resilience and longevity of the Chinese civilization provides a learning opportunity for Western civilizations, whose wealth gap has widened in the past 30 years. This chapter provides a Chinese perspective to reveal alternative insights, structures of thinking, and ways of relating and functioning in the world, approaches to leadership and prosperity that are unavailable through a Western lens.

The chapter first explains how to enter a culture from its own perspective. Before I explain how leadership and prosperity can be understood through a Chinese lens, to better demonstrate the contrast between Chinese and Western thinking, the chapter also provides a general summary of how leadership and prosperity are conceived through Western conceptions of reality and thinking structures. Finally, the chapter concludes by providing an interpretation of China's recent economic success from its own perspective.

DOI: 10.4324/9781003213604-3

Cultural perspective and language

Language categorizes the world; it functions as a carrier of thought (Jullien, 2015). The sensory world is not inherently separated, and every way of dividing, conceiving, and investigating one's reality is decided by a mind, which contains unique assumptions, relationships, preferences, and purpose for engaging the sensory world. The biases inherent in a language is shared by the language users, lived as the cultural norms, and acted upon as the basis of everyday operation. French philosopher François Jullien (b. 1951) has spent his career studying Chinese and Western languages, conceptions of reality and thought. He recognizes that a Chinese perspective contains unique categorizations of the world, conceptions of reality, value systems, priorities, and ways of functioning and interacting, and cannot be understood by simply studying it based on Western ontological and epistemological paradigms (Jullien, 2015; Jullien, 2020). A Chinese lens is not obtainable only by interviewing Chinese people, reading Chinese literature, or interpreting them through a Western lens. Studying a non-Western culture based on Western methods can only produce a Western stereotype of the culture, and does not enter its unique perspective. Jullien suggests that entering a Chinese world requires a Western thinker to first depart from their own perspective.

In efforts to explain the separation between languages, Jullien (2002) calls Western languages the languages of "being." By naming the identifiable and stable forms in the world, Western languages create an impression that reality is the sum of separated and independent beings. On the other hand, the Chinese language names silent tendencies that are understood as ever-present, coproducing the propensity of the world through their constant and spontaneous interactions with each other. Conceiving reality on the basis of being, Western scholarship investigates phenomena and situations ontologically, as identifiable and independent beings. However, by conceiving reality through the interplay among motions, nothing is independent, separable, or definable to the ancient Chinese.

Western languages are phonetically based and alphabetic; the Chinese language is ideographic. David Abram (1997) suggests that these two types of languages have separate influences on human cognition. Abram is a philosopher whose work is commonly associated with new materialism and recently founded terms such as ecopsychology, ecophenomenology, and ecological linguistics. Abram says that ideographical symbols contain animals, birds, plants, landscapes, and natural phenomena such as sunrise and rainfall. By using the language, one conceives the self and reality in relation to the sensory world. The Chinese language produces an interactive relationship between the language user and the world, where learning occurs in the living process, in interaction on a moment-to-moment basis, it is a process of maturation, a matter of lived competency, and not intelligibility.

On the other hand, in a phonetic language, the alphabets themselves do not represent the world but the name given to a part of the world by the language user. A name, or a word in an alphabetic language does not represent an aspect of the sensory world, but the meaning the language user gives to the combination of the sounds. In writing, the language user engages with their own thoughts; they operate in a dialogical relationship of meanings created by and among themselves, and not directly with the sensory world. Alphabetical languages produce a sense of an autonomous self, independent from the sensory world, that is unavailable in the cognition of an ideographical language user. Abram (1997) suggests that the Western alphabetical language user's relationship with words created the possibility for the emergence of philosophy, where the philosopher is in constant interactions with their previous statements/meanings and could lead to a dialogical conclusion by themselves through reasoning alone, without needing to interact even with another human.

This separation between the two types of cognitions is also reflected in the characteristics of the two conceptual processes. Jullien recognizes that (Western) philosophy prioritizes reasoning, and uses human meaning and logic to define reality; alternatively, Chinese thought focuses on the sensory world and the principles of change occurring in it. It is practice-based, cares not about "truth" but competency, acquires prosperity in the moment-to-moment interactions with the sensory world's propensities.

Based on the separations between the cultures mentioned above, Chinese and Western ways of thinking emerge from separate roots and cannot be equated under a universal classification. Comparing cultural constructs, stereotypes one through the perspective of the other. Aligned with Jullien, this chapter describes Chinese thought based not on Western ontology-epistemology paradigmatic structures nor theory-and-practice partnerships. Instead, this conception of Chinese thought is constructed through the categorization and conception of reality embodied by the way Chinese language, and value systems prioritizes, sets agendas, and preferences inherent in the characteristics of the language. For readers to appreciate the uniqueness of Chinese thought, this chapter first provides a summary of how leadership and prosperity are conceptualized from a Western perspective.

Leadership through a Western lens

Based on Jullien's work, ancient Greeks conceived prosperity in relation to *order* and *chaos* (Jullien, 2002). In this binary relationship, nature is considered as either chaotic or ordered and can be created directly by human influences. Grounded in a subject-object causal relationship, change, or in this case, prosperity, is an outcome of humans imposing definable, describable, and often measurable intelligible ideals onto the flux and spontaneity of nature. In this process, humans are conceived of as the direct causers of change; prosperity, therefore, is understood to be the outcome of human intentionality, determination, and decisive actions. The centralization of the human is present in existing leadership studies through a humanistic tendency that dominates the field.

Humanism, or privileging the human, is a common theme in leadership thinking. Leader-centric scholars conceive the individual leader as the cause of change; in collective forms, leadership is understood to be directly produced by a group of people (Quick, 2017; Ospina, 2020). In attempts to depart from a leader-centric thinking, meaning, as a collective product of human interactions, has been the basis for new innovations in scholarship. Conceiving human meaning-making as the cause of change, leadership has been understood as a discursive process (Fairhurst, 2007), relationships (Drath, 2008; Uhl-Bien, 2012), everyday working activities (Raelin, 2016), and sociomaterial space (Crevani, 2018). Drath (2008) proposes that leadership is inherently relational because meaning is socially constructed and not generated individually in separation from one's environment. Based on an understanding that meaning is produced during the day-to-day processes of working practices, Raelin (2011) proposes that leadership emerges in practice. In another emerging effort to make leadership more fluid, Crevani (2018) employs the work of social geologist Doreen Massey, and adds sociomaterial space into leadership studies to expand the understanding of the process, from human interactions to the interplay among multiple trajectories occurring in the sociomaterial space beyond human intentionality. However, the inclusion of spatial dimension in her work merely functions to explain how collective meaning is produced; meaning as the cause of leadership remains unquestioned.

Humanism projects a reality where feelings, experiences, meanings, and actions are the direct and dominant causes of change. Leadership has been defined as individual and collective human characteristics and/or activities such as behavior, traits, attributes, power dynamics, and meaning-making. Arguments among scholars tend to focus on the "who" in a subject-object relationship that causes leadership, and not the subject-object causality as the structure for approaching change. Both humanism and the subject-object causal relationship are understood in this chapter as manifestations of the biases inherent in the Western cultural approaches to reality. As these biases are normalized as the carriers of thought, they are often taken for granted. However, these biases influence how leadership can be considered; by investigating leadership through humanism, scholars tend to associate organizational outcomes, both positive and negative, as directly caused by an individual or group. By conceiving change as caused by humans, other possibilities and potential causal relationships are eliminated. Cultural thoughts that do not obtain these specific biases simply cannot produce existing leadership knowledge.

The world is not separated inherently; but each cultural lens is a unique way of dividing the undividable, which both enables and disables certain ways of knowing and relating to the world, making available and unavailable certain insights, to serve the cultural agenda and purpose for participating in the world based on a given value system. Culture decides the validity of knowledge based on its biases; the validity of knowledge determines what information is and is not valuable, will and will not be recorded or passed on by that cultural group.

However, knowledge, insights, and experiences are neither valuable nor objective representations of the sensory world; instead, they are consequences of approaching the sensory world through a cultural lens, filtered through the value system, agenda for studying the world, priorities, and preferences. From this perspective, the available leadership knowledge is a product of perceiving leadership and interpreting the sensory world through a Western lens. The remainder of this chapter introduces how leadership and prosperity can be understood and approached through a Chinese lens. This Chinese conception of reality provides a frame of reference to Western ways of thinking, brings insights about leadership phenomena that are unavailable through a Western lens, and gains an understanding of the Chinese cultural practices, choices, decisions from its own perspective.

The propensity of things: A Chinese conception of reality

Jullien proposes that Chinese thought prioritizes the acquisition of prosperity in the propensity of the everyday living process (Jullien, 2004). Human prosperity, in this case, is no different from the abundances available in the sensory world, like the blooming of a flower, the birthing of lives, and the ripening of a fruit. Prosperity is thus understood as common, is available in the natural and spontaneous propensity of things, and is not determined by human intelligibility, intentionality, meaning, design, or ideal.

According to Jullien (1995), the sensory world is understood by the ancient Chinese through a whole/part relationship. He suggests that Chinese thought did not require metaphysics to understand the sensory world. Instead of referring to a deity, "heaven" is more like meteorology, including reoccurring regulatory motions such as cycles of the sun and rain, day and night, moon and months, and season changes. The ancient Chinese conceived the entire ecosystem as a whole and understood it as the product of constant interplay between the motions of heaven and earth. As part of the earth, every aspect of the world is also constantly changing, not because of their inherent being, but because they are participating in a wider propensity of things. The parts are partners that coproduce the propensity of the world that is the whole. They are not separated from each other; instead, they are influencing and being influenced by each other constantly, at wider and more local levels.

Conceiving the process of living through motion and propensity, the ancient Chinese understood change as permanent (Jullien, 1995). From this perspective, the world is not being-based, but is coproduced in a whole/part relationship through the complex interplays among silent motions that influence each other's propensities constantly. An identifiable form is not a basic unit that makes up reality, but a temporary appearance of the ever-present silent changes in the world. This understanding of reality is evident in the Chinese language, which has no Western equivalent of a noun. A Chinese character represents a silent tendency such as darkening, brightening, contracting, and expanding. A phrase or *ci* is the combination of multiple characters, and represents the Chinese understanding of the whole/part relationship where the propensity of the sensory world is co-produced by the partnership of multiple tendencies. For example, the Chinese phrase for "size" is 大小 *dà xiǎo*, it is the interplay between the character big 大 *dà*, and small 小 *xiǎo*; the phrase "weight" 轻重 *qīng zhòng* combines the characters for "light" 轻 *qīng* and "heavy" 重 *zhòng*. "Length" 长短 *cháng duǎn* is understood through the interplay between "long" 长 *cháng* and "short" 短 *duǎn*. Unlike a Western word, a tendency is not definable, and a Western ontology-epistemology paradigm simply cannot apply to Chinese thought. As Laozi (1989) mentioned, the brightest light and the pure darkness are equally blinding. At an extreme brightness, every form embodies brightness; alternatively, one's entire world can also embody darkness. Anything visible is the spontaneous and temporary interplays between brightness and darkness. Visibility and identifiability do not define the world; they are constantly changing in relation to the interplay between opposing tendencies. Similarly, an identifiable form can only temporarily appear to be long or short in relation to a frame of reference, and neither one way nor the other. Long becomes short when a longer frame of reference appears and vice versa. Human impressions about the world are products of the interplay among silent tendencies. Nothing is big or small, light or heavy, or long or short. Size, weight, and length have no inherent identity to be defined because they are human impressions about the world but do not exist in nature. The identifiable aspects of the world are temporary appearances of the silent motions that drive their emergences, developments, and declines. Conceiving reality on the basis of silent tendencies and not being, Western thinking structures and ways of approaching situations and validating knowledge do not function in a Chinese conception of reality.

Chinese thought also suggests that an identifiable aspect of life such as a form, action, or event is a manifestation of the silent tendency behind it; it also has no basic nature (Jullien, 2011). From this perspective, there is no inherent act of love or care; any activity can be performed to bring freedom, oppression, prosperity, and harm, and be performed by positive and ill intentions. What makes an act loving or caring is the tendency that drove the act, and not the act itself. An opposing tendency can also be the driving force of the same activity under a different circumstance; in that case, the activity embodies the opposing tendency. An identifiable aspect of the world appears to be a certain way not because of its nature, but because of the silent tendency that inspired its temporary and situational emergence.

Following this logic, through a Chinese lens, leadership is not a being, cannot be studied ontologically through ontology-epistemology paradigm; instead, leadership refers to the silent tendency that drives human activities. The prosperity of a human community such as organization and civilization lie not in its institution, structure, the amount of money it possess, resources, or members, but the driving force behind the community's continuing existence as a collective. As a silent tendency, a leadership tendency can be a dominant desire, need, passion, a social or political commitment of the collective that inspires the spontaneous emergences of behaviors, interactions, and ways of working together. As the tendency changes constantly and spontaneously, so are the identifiable aspects of the community. The human activities themselves are thus consequences of leadership and are not inherently leadership related. Art, teaching-learning, governing, and poetry can all reinforce oppression, strengthen domination, promote discrimination, function as weapons to fight for freedom, and act as mediums for equality, nurture, love, care, understanding, and acceptance.

Identifiable human activities are ever-changing in relation to the silent tendency that influences them (Jullien, 2011). Multiple types of activities can be required at different stages of one's progress and under separate circumstances to fulfil a desire or commitment. The power and effect of leadership thus lies not in "what people do" *per se*, but "what drives them" to form the collective, create the structure, have power dynamics, form ways to communicate, obtain relationship dynamics, and work with each other in particular ways and configurations.

Based on the above analysis of Jullien's understanding of a Chinese conception of reality, studying leadership through a Chinese lens prioritizes the change in the driving force of a collective. Changes in human activities are clues to detect the development of the silent driving force behind them; the activities are not in-and-of- themselves leadership-related. While the identifiable aspects of the world are understood as manifestations of the silent tendencies, these are understood to be emergent from a source or 道 *dào*. The Chinese perspective of 道 *dào*, is what makes the inexhaustible renewal and transformations in the world possible.

道 *dào*

道 *dào* is the source of manifestation. According to Jullien (2012), 道*dào* describes neither a truth, prototype, nor meaning; instead, it indicates "where nothing is obstructed by specification, where the determining character of form has not yet come into play, and where haziness, between *there-is* and *there-is-not*, is the very rationality of existence" (p. 47). From a Chinese perspective, what makes an apple is not its essence, but the source from which it manifests. The variations in the types of apples are not inferior versions of a superior form, but spontaneous manifestations of the same source in different environments. 道*dào* is like a seed; it represents infinite potential for manifestation.

道*dào*, as "potential," has no form; it is void, space, and emptiness that creates the possibility for actuality to emerge, and is unmanifested. Potential is the empty space in a room that makes the room useful; as the space becomes occupied, its remaining potential decreases. The first chapter of Laozi (1989) states that 道*dào* is the temporary name given to the source. This is because a name is a manifestation; it represents certain aspects of the sensory world while discriminating against others. When a tendency is manifested from the source, it is committed to a particular direction of growth and development, which also discriminates against other directions. The more actuality takes place, the less potential there is for continuing manifestation. Any identifiable aspect of the world is itself a manifestation; as such, it is limited in its own capacity to manifest, and is not the source. As the inexhaustible potential for manifestation, 道*dào* is unmanifested; to obtain infinite potential, it is hazy, unidentifiable, indistinct, and undefinable. From an unmanifested space, all manifestations become possible; from a place of undifferentiated, no separation, no judgment, all possibilities become possible.

Following this logic, a Chinese lens perceives all leadership tendencies as emergent from 道*dào*. The source of manifestation produces a silent tendency, and the source behind every lifeform's activity is its unique lifeforce. By lifeforce, I mean a tendency that drives a lifeform to continue its existence and development on this earth. I propose that because the Chinese conceive reality through tendencies and not identifiable forms, survival and prosperity are the different stages of the same lifeforce's developing motion. Whether it is a flower, an animal, or a human, any tendency, as it emerges, is vulnerable and at the mercy of its environment. At this stage, to continue its existence, the lifeform's priority is survival. As the same tendency develops, such as when a tree becomes large, and an infant becomes an adult, the lifeform starts to have more autonomy, power, and influence within its environment rather than being at its mercy. At this stage, the lifeform continues its tendency to develop by shifting its priority from survival to expansion and prosperity. Circumstances are ever-changing; driven by the lifeforces, a lifeform's priority constantly modifies between survival and prosperity throughout the propensity of its lifecycle.

Based on this understanding, 道*dào* of leadership in a human community can be conceived as the lifeforce of the collective. 道*dào* spontaneously produces silent driving forces behind the community's activities. However, 道*dào* of a collective differs from that of an individual. Every individual has their own need for survival and prosperity, but they might not associate their needs with the existence of the group. As a consequence, the lifeforce of a collective is the members' overall attachment of their personal survival and prosperity with that of the collective. The 道*dào* of leadership in an organization also differs from that of a region, country, continent, and the human race. Just like the differences between day and night, month cycle, and the cycle of the seasons, while 道*dào* of an organization includes the interplay among its members' lifeforces, 道*dào* of a country includes the interplay among the lifeforces of all organizations, communities, regions, and other interest groups within the country; their propensities occur on different levels and are influenced by separate factors.

Like the potency of a seed that influences the lifeform's growth and development, the potency of 道*dào* also influences the potential strength in the growth and development of leadership tendencies. The potency of leadership's source is related to the community members' association with the collective. The more unified a group is for being a collective, the more powerful motion the collective can generate with consistency and regularity. On the other hand, a lack of interest in the members to be a part of a collective can result in divisions among the group, which is likely to produce weak leadership tendencies. The more potent the source of leadership, the stronger is the collective's lifeforce, and the more likely a leadership tendency emerging from within the collective can survive, grow, withstand challenges, obstacles and develop to produce a powerful effect. Alternatively, a weaker motion produces less effect and is more vulnerable to potential negative influences that its environment presents. This would also suggest that collectives at different levels, like a family, organization, and civilization, have different 道*dào*. They produce different tendencies and have separate cycles. An organization interacts with other organizations, and a country interacts with other countries. A country's prosperity is influenced more by other countries more than by other organizations; an organization's propensity is influenced more by other organizations and the country it is in, than subgroups within the organization. The propensity of each collective is influenced more by peers at the same level and wider levels than lower levels.

道*dào* produces a leadership tendency through its interplay with the environment or situation in which the human community is situated. Just like a seed that only produces a tendency through its interaction with the soil (environment), Chinese thought understands that nothing is knowable in separation from its environment (Jullien, 1995). Every aspect of the sensory world is connected, influencing and being influenced by each other. Like a tree that grows differently in separate terrains, atmosphere, and soil, the lifeforce of a collective can manifest into infinite human tendencies under different circumstances, ranging from loving to hating, protecting to destroying, and contracting to expanding. Even more identifiable human activities can manifest to embody each of these tendencies at different stages of its development.

A leadership tendency emerges for the purpose of continuing its existence as a collective; it is the human community's reaction toward the spontaneous challenges and opportunities temporarily presented by its environment. Meanings, value systems, relationships, structures of organizing are consequences of the interplay between 道*dào* and the environment, and have no inherent value outside of the group's circumstance, nor are they the direct causes of leadership's motion. As the circumstance changes, the leadership tendency modifies, the collective meanings, value systems, relationships, structures of organizing also alter. Prosperity is understood as available in the propensity of the silent tendency; in other words, in the driving force behind the human activities in a collective, and not in an identifiable individual, group, behavior, communication, relationship, or organization's structure *per se*.

Propensity

The ancient Chinese understood propensity as a cyclical regulatory process of emergence, development, decline, diminishment, and renewal (Jullien, 1995). Prosperity is associated with the growth and actualization of a tendency, which is embodied by the blooming of a flower, ripening of a fruit, birthing, and all abundances that occur in nature. Chinese thought suggests that a tendency, as it emerges, is inclined to grow; as the tendency continues to develop and exceeds its capacity to grow, its motion peaks and starts to decline. For example, a human desire or need such as hunger produces a tendency for food that can continue to grow over time; when it is fulfilled, the tendency for food declines and might diminish. When the tendency diminishes, it returns to 道*dào*; from the interaction between 道*dào* and the new environment or circumstance, another tendency emerges. As one is no longer hungry, one's circumstance is changed, and other tendencies such as thirst, need for shelter, human interaction start to emerge and develop. The propensity of a tendency is thus understood to be cyclical.

Cycles occur moment-to-moment, daily, monthly, annually, and all other shorter and longer timeframes. The visible changes in the world, such as the turning of a leaf's color, human aging, the lifespan of an organization, and the rise and fall of a kingdom, are all manifestations of the silent tendency at different stages of its propensity. In other words, it is a silent tendency that drives the change in different stages of the tendency's propensity. Leadership, through a Chinese lens, is the silent tendency that drives a community's activities and not the activities themselves.

A leadership tendency is the dominant response of the entire community toward its situation and is not produced by any individual or subgroup within the collective. The emergence of a leadership tendency includes spontaneous interactions among all members, factions, and/or interest groups. It also involves complex interplays between agreement and disagreement, domination and resistance, and consent and dissent. As a consequence, leadership cannot be understood on the basis of independent parties such as the leader, leadership group, and followers. This is also a reason why there is no concept of democratic or autocratic leadership from a Chinese perspective. Both democratic and autocratic types of leadership divide a unit between leader and follower or authority and non-authority.

Like the sprout of a weed as the interplay between the seed and the weed's environment, the spontaneous leadership tendency is the interplay between 道*dào* and the environment or situation of the community. Free from human limitations, capacities, and ignorance in theorizing, design, reasoning, or judgement, a weed's existence in an environment is the evidence of its compatibility with the environment. Similarly, the leadership tendency that spontaneously emerges within an organization is also a circumstantially compatible tendency in the situation. Just as farming prioritizes on nurturing the crop's inherent tendency to grow and not modifying the form; a Chinese perspective would rely on the spontaneously emerged leadership tendency to acquire prosperity, and not focus on modifying the appearances of a leadership tendency such as the identifiable human activities or form of organizing.

Influence of the environment

By privileging a holistic perspective, Chinese thought is attentive to the influence of the environment on the lives within it. There is no subject-object causality as nothing is static, definable, nor can be understood in separation from any other aspect of its environment (Jullien, 1995 #4012). As an agricultural civilization, it is apparent for ancient Chinese that the growth of a crop is not decided by its inherent nature, but in the interplay of the crop's own tendency to grow and environmental factors, such as the weather, temperature, soil, animals, insects, birds, humidity, and other identifiable and nonidentifiable factors. A tendency's development is influenced by the entire ecosystem in which it is situated. The factors influencing the ecosystem are ever-changing, in turn, constantly affecting the development of the tendency. From this perspective, a leadership tendency's development is not determined by its inherent nature, but by the interplay between the tendency and the entire ecosystem in which the human community is situated.

From a Chinese perspective, a country is an environment for its people, and the condition of the country influences the prosperity of every organization, community, and family within it. Similarly, an organization provides the environment for individual members to succeed and acquire prosperity. This is to say that the foundation for the prosperity of people is not necessarily directly addressing their problems, but for the country to become a prosperous environment. In Chinese thought, problems do not inherently exist; they are appearances of the interplay among factors in a situation. Understandably, a family, organization, or country with limited resources cannot address many needs of its members. If the family remains poor, its children will continue to starve. On the other hand, when a country becomes prosperous, its people's environment changes, circumstances alter, many problems in organizations and families within the country disappear. As a consequence, leadership tendencies within these communities, including their value systems, meanings, priorities, and preferences also change.

The ancient Chinese recognized that the effect of the environment is grand, powerful, but subtle, and also difficult to detect. This is because while an environment influences the available choices and options within it, it does not prescribe the choice. For example, a person who lives on top of a mountain does not have the same resources, terrain, or weather as someone living near an ocean. As a result, the choices that are available for an oceanic lifestyle are unavailable to a mountain person. Similarly, winter erases many options that are available in the summer, and what is possible during the day is impossible at night. An environment does not make choices for you but enables, limits, and even eliminates the potential meanings, choices, and actions available. Placing an individual or a community in a specific situation categorizes the potential decisions and choices for them. Chinese thought recognizes that one's circumstance is not determined by the quality or skill of an individual but by their situation. Based on this understanding, Chinese military strategists can make a patient commander act in a rush and pressure a wise general to make unwise decisions by influencing their physical, political, social, and/or organizational environment. A situation combines multiple factors that are constantly changing. The interplay among the factors creates different circumstances at different times. From this perspective, meaning is not the cause of leadership, but a consequence of an individual, community, organization, society, or a country's situation.

Chinese thought does not recognize free will, but conceives the human awareness, choices, and actions as constantly in a process of influencing and being influenced by the environment (Jullien, 1995; Jullien, 2014). Free will is merely an experience created by providing choices, without a holistic view on the influence of the environment that pre-selects the potential options available. From this perspective, one's value system, agendas, priorities, and knowledge are influenced by the environment. Leadership as a silent tendency is thus produced by the interplay among all factors influencing the situation of a community, and not directly caused by human meaning or activities. To understand prosperity embedded in leadership's propensity, it is more important for the Chinese to study how other motions in its environment influence its propensity than identify the human activities that occur within leadership's motion.

Influenced by wider environments, a leadership tendency emerging within a human community, such as an organization, does not belong just to the organization, nor is it controllable by the organization. Every member of an organization is influenced by multiple aspects of the world, including natural resources, industrial, social, political, religious, cultural, and environmental issues. The outcomes of the interplay among these factors are unique to each individual and is lived and embodied in their decisions, choices, value systems, and activities on a moment-to-moment basis. The organization is a context in which the individual's own tendencies are expressed in a particular configuration. Leadership, as a silent tendency that drives a collective's activities, is an outcome of the complex interactions of the tendencies within the collective. It embodies the interplay among all factors that can affect life, including personal, professional, relational, familial, communal, religious, cultural, social, political, environmental, and other unidentified levels. In other words, a leadership tendency within a collective, such as that of an organization, encompasses the influences of all factors that influence every organizational member's lives beyond the organizational level. This is to say that leadership's motion, even though emergent from within an organization, is not directly produced by the organization. It reflects moving tendencies at multiple levels both narrower and wider than the organization. Motions at all levels are influencing and being influenced by each other; a leadership tendency within a collective is not controllable by the collective.

As a silent driving force of human communities, a leadership tendency is ever-present and changing. Leadership reflects the dominant need or desire of a collective; it is not created by human design, nor is it controllable. Prosperity is available in the development and actualization of a leadership tendency's motion. To take advantage of the propensity of leadership, the ancient Chinese studies the complex process and spontaneous modifications of motion through 陰*yīn* and 陽*yáng*.

陰*yīn* and 陽*yáng*

The ancient Chinese understand that no matter how many factors coproduce a tendency, or how complex are their interplays, a motion is either 陰*yīn* or 陽*yáng*. These two elements do not indicate a precise direction of a motion, but a nature of the tendency's trend. 陰*yīn* indicates a contractive tendency and 陽*yáng* tends toward expansion. 陰*yīn* can embody darkness, the process of change from autumn to winter, afternoon to night, and subtle influence; 陽*yáng* can represent brightness, the process of change from spring to summer, morning to noon, and direct confrontation. In a human community, a leadership tendency emerges either as 陰*yīn*, a contractive tendency that prioritizes on survival or 陽*yáng*, an expansive tendency that focuses on self-expression and prosperity. Each tendency emerges within the situation, and as circumstances change, a new tendency emerges that interacts with the existing tendency and forms a new tendency. If two tendencies are in alignment with each other, they strengthen each other; their partnership produces a more powerful tendency. If the two tendencies are opposite of each other, dependent on the strength of the new tendency, the existing tendency's growth might be slowed down, neutralized, or even reversed by the new tendency. As circumstances change, each new tendency interacts with the existing leadership tendency, influencing the course and speed of its development. Aristotle's law of noncontradiction does not apply in Chinese thought because this law only applies to cultures that conceive reality on the basis of identifiable physical objects and not motion. While two identifiable objects cannot occupy the same physical space at the same time, motions such as rivers or wind, no matter how many motions interact with each other, merge to coproduce a new motion.

At any point of its development, a tendency is either 陰*yīn* or 陽*yáng*; however, the further it develops toward one side, the less likely for its trend to reverse. Further, there are circumstances of contraction even in a process of expansion; the transition from spring to summer is also not a linear process of becoming warmer every single day. 陰*yīn* and 陽*yáng* are both present at every moment. The development of a leadership tendency is thus not a linear process, nor is it determined by one or two circumstances; instead, it is the accumulation of tendencies over time. Prosperity, as an effect produced by motion, is influenced by the accumulated momentum of a tendency. Momentum is studied in Chinese thought through 勢 *shì*.

勢*shì*

Based on Jullien's (2004 #428) work, the ancient Chinese understood that an effect is produced by motion and not form. The effect of a flying arrow is produced by the speed of its motion and not the arrow itself as an object; similarly, prosperity is a manifestation of the silent driving forces behind a human community's activities, and not the activities themselves. On the other hand, copying and pasting the same human activities with the hope of reproducing a leadership effect is like putting the body parts together with the expectation of producing a live human. Conceiving motion, not form, as the basis of reality; 勢 *shì* indicates the strength, speed, range of a motion's development, and is what the ancient Chinese relied on to take advantage of effects produced by a motion.

By conceiving leadership through tendency and not form, power lies not in one or two identifiable outcomes, but the duration of prosperity it brings to a collective. A powerful momentum of the driving force can produce highly profitable results for a long period of time, while a lack of momentum in the driving force is less likely to result in sustainable profitability. 勢 *shì* does not determine an outcome but is suggestive of its likelihood. Jullien (2004) notes that the momentum of 勢 *shì* can become so suggestive that certain types of outcomes become almost inevitable. Water is the most used metaphor in ancient China to understand the effect of 勢 *shì*. The course of a stream can be influenced by many obstacles in its path, such as rocks and the landscape around it; however, as its 勢 *shì* continues to accumulate, it becomes more powerful, more influential to its environment, and less influenced by the environment. The stronger the 勢 *shì*, the more powerful its effect becomes. When the continuing accumulation of water becomes a flood, its overwhelming 勢 *shì* makes the inundation unstoppable. Powerful 勢 *shì* allows it to spread across a wide landscape, making all obstacles in its path seem insignificant. It has a long-lasting impact on the ecosystem as it shapes and modifies the landscape rather than being shaped by it (Jullien, 1995; Jullien, 2004). Similarly, a powerful driving force in a human community can also produce long-lasting effects beyond the collective; a powerful leadership tendency in an organization can produce effects across industries, societies, nations, and the ecosystem of the world.

According to Jullien (1995), 勢 *shì* produces potential. Propensity refers to the potential of a tendency to continue its development. It is like a weed emerging out of the earth in the spring that is inclined to grow. Jullien suggests that potential does not guarantee an outcome because it represents an unmanifested effect that is not yet come about nor is it measurable. However, the more potential a tendency accumulates, the more resilient it is, and the more impactful and long-lasting its effect is likely to be as the potential actualizes itself. Farming crops is an activity of accumulating potential; by nurturing the environment around the crops and not directly modifying it, the farmer maximizes the potential for the crops to grow. As the 勢 *shì* of the crops' tendency continue to pick up momentum over time, the crops' potential for abundance increases.

Conceiving leadership through silent motion, the longevity of prosperity is determined by the remaining potential inherent in the 勢 *shì*. When there is no more potential to be manifested, the momentum peaks and actualizes itself, 勢 *shì* declines (Jullien, 2004). In a human community, as a dominant collective need is fulfilled or is no longer shared by the collective, the driving force starts to decline. While the same behavior, structure, and ways of working together can remain in an organization, these activities are no longer leadership-related and can no longer produce the same leadership effect. As the tendency eventually disappears, an alternative emerges from 道 *dào* in the new circumstance.

To summarize, so far, I have explained that because Chinese thought in Jullien's (1995, 2004, 2011) work conceives reality on the basis of silent tendencies and not form, leadership approached from this perspective is the silent tendency that drives human activities in a community. The community's prosperity is associated with the dominant driving force behind human activities, and not the activities themselves. The effect of leadership is a consequence of accumulated momentum over time, it is not defined by an outcome, but the range, intensity, longevity, and sustainability of its effect on the community and beyond. 勢 *shì* is used to understand, foresee, and leverage the effect of leadership's motion. The following sections explain how prosperity produced by leadership can be leveraged.

Acquiring prosperity through leadership's motion

In the previous sections, I have demonstrated how leadership can be investigated through a Chinese lens described in Jullien's work. I now explain how prosperity can be acquired through leadership from this Chinese perspective.

Prosperity from a Chinese perspective

In Chinese thought, prosperity, as an effect of leadership, is a manifestation of motion. In his studies, Jullien (2004; 2011) uses the term *prosperity* and not *profit* to express preferences because prosperity is not directly associated with immediate gain. In existing studies, the effect of leadership is often associated with the organizational outcome; this is especially so through a functionalist lens (Bass, 1985; Felkins, 2001). Prosperity is often linked to the organization's profit in mainstream leadership scholarship; indeed, a collective's productivity and outcome are often the primary measurements of leadership's effectiveness. On the other hand, prioritizing motion and its momentum allowed the ancient Chinese to predict effects, both positive and negative, including their intensity, scope of influence, and longevity before they come about and become identifiable. The awareness of 勢 *shì* allows the Chinese to recognize and address negative effects before potential harm manifests, and also maximizes profit by leveraging the influence of the positive effects throughout the duration of its entire development and manifestation. From a Chinese perspective, prosperity in human community includes both the potential-for-prosperity and the identifiable profit.

Potentiality is not associated with a predetermined ideal, but the absolute potentiality for a tendency to continue manifesting itself (Jullien, 1995). Potential provides the space for more effects to manifest; when there is no more potential to be leveraged, and profit ceases to come about, and the situation starts to reverse. Identifiable profit represents already-manifested potential and the actualization of past potential. An identifiable profit alone does not inform the effect that is coming about. From this perspective, the potential-for-prosperity has more influence on prosperity than the immediate profit.

Through a Chinese lens, an immediate profit is a manifestation, it has no inherent nature, and its value is circumstantial (Jullien, 2004). Depending on the circumstance, privileging the immediate profit can also harm a community's long-term prosperity. An example to illustrate is the difference between hunting and farming. Hunting privileges the immediate profit but could deplete its potential for future prosperity. On the other hand, crop-farming prioritizes potential over profit; profit in farming can be leveraged once or twice per year. Farming crops requires continuous nurturing of potentiality without profit for a long period of time, but when its potential is leveraged in harvesting, it produces long-lasting and sustainable profits on a regular basis. Farming accumulates potential to be leveraged while hunting does not. As a consequence, farming is more likely to produce long-term prosperity compared to the activities that seek short-term profit such as hunting. If prosperity is measured by immediate profits, an annual harvest would be seen as a loss in profit for three quarters of the year. In modern economic terms, if a country's gross domestic product (GDP) declines more than two quarters in a row it is considered an economic depression. But when both the profit and potential are considered together, what is seemingly unprofitable from a short-term perspective can produce long-term abundance and sustainable prosperity. Prosperity is the interplay between potential-for-prosperity and the immediate profit it manifests. Profit can often contribute to bringing more potential, but it is potential, and not the immediate profit that brings prosperity. Based on this understanding, a prosperous community is not necessarily one that makes the most immediate profit but has inexhaustible potential to leverage. Potential-for-prosperity is embedded in 勢 *shì*. One of the most important parts of acquiring prosperity is how to take advantage of 勢 *shì* and leverage the potential inherent in it.

Prosperity through propensity

Chinese thought acquires prosperity, not by directly tackling perceived problems, but by following the propensity of things. Jullien suggests that the Western tradition tends to tackle issues directly while the Chinese prefer to deal with them indirectly (Jullien, 2000). With a standard format of beginning every study by identifying a problem, the privilege of "problem" is common in leadership scholarship. In fact, many scholars make finding problems and offering criticism the primary tasks of their careers. The ancient Chinese did not associate prosperity in this way because a problem is understood as a matter of perception. An aspect of the world can only be viewed as problematic in relation to a bias and dualism, that opposes itself with certain aspects of the natural propensity of things. A holistic Chinese perspective does not recognize any aspect of the world as a one-sided good or bad, or, right or wrong. One can always find evidence of life as negative and positive; one's opinion might affect one's experience but is separated from the propensity of things and prosperity inherent in it.

Through a Chinese lens, resolving problems does not result in prosperity because the vibrance, diversity, and abundance in the world are not inspired by judgment, discrimination, or fear, but tendencies for growth, development, and prosperity. Nothing is perfect, but flaws and lack of perfection do not stop flowers from blooming, trees from bearing fruit, or people from changing the world. Prosperity is not directly associated with identifiable problems, certainly not by making the problems more significant than the positive aspects of life. Privileging the "problem" centralizes discrimination and division. Prosperity is inherent in the sensory world and available in the propensity of things.

Nothing is inherently wrong in the propensity of things and a problem is only perceived relative to the unproblematic; it is a matter of an individual or a group's ability to identify and recognize, and does not reflect the true nature of life. An aspect of life appears to be problematic not due to its inherent nature but because of its contrast to what is temporarily recognized as not problematic. The propensity of things, like the subtle but constant changes in the weather, temperature, and seasons, and mundane everyday activities of working in an organization, are often undetectable. A problem is perceived because it disrupts the ordinary, but this "extraordinarity" does not make it more impactful than the undetectable and subtle changes.

The ancient Chinese prioritized environmental factors and their influences on the propensity of the situation. 勢 *shì* alters as the interplay among the situational factors change. When 勢 *shì* becomes favorable for a human community, the problem might disappear. From a Chinese perspective, all problems will disappear, and more will come. Prosperity is not directly associated with problems, but the propensity of things. Additionally, every aspect of leadership that can be temporarily perceived as problematic and can also be a resource for acquiring prosperity in other circumstances. From this perspective, regardless of how many problems a leadership scholar can identify in a community such as an organization or a country, it does not stop the community from becoming prosperous. An important skill of acquiring prosperity is of taking advantage of 勢 *shì*.

Follow leadership to acquire prosperity

Leadership is to be followed and not designed. Chinese thought does not create leadership, nor does it propose an ideal; rather, it recognizes that a leadership tendency is always present, and prosperity is inherent in its propensity. Acquiring prosperity requires one to detect and follow the leadership tendency and leverage the effect of its 勢 *shì*.

勢 *shì* that influences prosperity can be separated into 勢 *shì* from within the human community and 勢 *shì* that is beyond. Like the relationship between day and night and season changes, a human community, whether a family, organization, country, or human race itself, is in a whole/part relationship with wider environments, and is influenced by a wider propensity of things. 勢 *shì* within the community is not necessarily separated from 勢 *shì* beyond the community; this is because a community is always being influenced by forces at wider levels. Sustainable prosperity requires the community to form an alignment with both internal and external 勢 *shì*. Alignment with the internal 勢 *shì* produces unity within the community and makes it a powerful force of influence in the wider environment. Alignment with 勢 *shì* at wider levels brings the community long-term prosperity.

From within the community, a leadership tendency spontaneously emerges through the alignment among the members' own tendencies. The leadership tendency can encompass the dominant concerns, motivations, aspirations, needs, and desires of the collective, and is often the complex interplay among all of these factors and other unidentified factors in the current circumstance. As the circumstances of the community and the situation of its members change, so is the development of the leadership tendency. 勢 *shì* is far more than the mere agreement among the members; it includes the intensity of the collective's driving force. Strong momentum is produced by high intensity in the collective's driving force and is accumulated over time. 勢 *shì* indicates potential for producing consistent and high-level effects; it can influence the increase or decrease in the quality of work, morale, and productivity over time. On the other hand, a lack of intensity in the collective's driving force does not obtain potential to generate high productivity nor produce a powerful impact.

Powerful 勢 *shì* encompasses a unified and intensive commitment to a cause shared by the collective. Driven by a powerful 勢 *shì*, members are more likely to do quality work, continue to develop themselves, and tolerate the aspects of the work they do not enjoy because they serve the members' causes and commitments. When this happens, individual members associate their successes with that of the collective. As long as the shared cause remains and its momentum continues, organizational life will be meaningful to the collective; the same force drives the outcomes they produce. Like a rock rolling down a hill, the more momentum it has, the more unstoppable it becomes. With a powerful 勢 *shì*, the collective as a unit can be a powerful force among its peers in the world.

The most powerful 勢 *shì* is a taken-for-granted norm. 勢 *shì* provides an environment, and its norm influences new members and other parties that interact with the collective. Chinese thought recognizes that all norms are biases, either 陰 *yīn* or 陽 *yáng*; and as its 勢 *shì* continues to develop, biases eventually become normalized. Normalized biases, like cultural value systems and preferences function as the foundation for mundane everyday function and are lived as taken-for-granted norms. This is because a taken-for-granted norm is, without being questioned, adopted and embodied by a collective in mundane everyday life. The collective is unified in the tendency as a result. For example, early tendencies for gender, racial, and sexual equality encountered many resistances on different social, political, and religious platforms. As the 勢 *shì* of these tendencies strengthened, these equalities became normalized. The most powerful 勢 *shì* is taken for granted as a norm and the default narrative of the collective. As the 勢 *shì* continues to develop, gender, racial, and sexual equality will become the basis for the everyday function and is unidentifiable; in this situation, speaking of these equalities is repeating the most basic mundane norm in everyday life, and provides no value to the society. Questioning these equalities can become strange to the generation of children who grew up in an environment where these types of equalities are their norms. This is to say that the most powerful 勢 *shì* generated by a collective is one that the entire collective shares and is assumed as the basis of their daily function.

If the leadership tendency within the community can also form an alignment with 勢 *shì* at a wider level, the collective can potentially acquire prosperity beyond the boundary of the community. A community is a part of wider tendencies such as those produced by a society, nation, environment, available resources, and technology; and is likely to be more prosperous by following the value systems of the society and policy of the government, rather than against them. For example, a global tendency toward cleaning the environment of pollution can negatively affect the mining and petroleum industries, while it positively affects renewable energy and electric vehicle companies. Similarly, a social tendency for organic living impacts the food industry, which benefits certain types of companies and disadvantages others. A collective is ever participating in the propensities of the wider environments; if it can follow 勢 *shì* at a wider level, it is possible for the collective to acquire prosperity far beyond the limit of the organizational outcome. Following a social or political 勢 *shì* allows an organization to gain the support of the public, organizations, and/or government, which can lead to an increase in markets, customer base, resources, suppliers, funding, and more. Following 勢 *shì* at wider levels provides the potential for the collective to make an enduring impact on a society, nation, the human race, or the earth, which can provide sustainable prosperity for the community on multiple levels and for multiple generations. Obtaining sustainable prosperity is thus about following the leadership tendencies both from within and beyond the level of the community. The most important component in this process is detecting the existing 勢 *shì*.

Detecting propensity relies on receptivity

From a Chinese perspective, a key component for acquiring prosperity is the skill of detecting 勢 *shì*. Acquiring prosperity through the propensity of leadership requires the human community to align its own motion with both the 勢 *shì* from within the community and 勢 *shì* in wider environments. The 勢 *shì* indicates the stage of a motion's development in its propensity, which influences the actions and prosperity available. The earlier one detects 勢 *shì*, the more potential prosperity there is to be leveraged. However, a tendency is weak at an early stage, and its manifestations are subtle, undifferentiated, and difficult to identify. The more powerful the 勢 *shì*, the more distinct are its manifestations. Events and moments of rupture, which traditional Western thinking conceive as the basis of change, are manifestations of overwhelming 勢 *shì*. These manifestations disrupt the normal and mundane, they are easy to detect, but the potential prosperity left in the 勢 *shì* is less than at an earlier stage of its development. As 勢 *shì* is in a process of declining, less and less prosperity is left to be harnessed. Alternatively, if the community functions against 勢*shì*, detecting it also influences the survival of the community. Depending on the strength of the 勢 *shì* behind the community, a weak unfavorable 勢*shì* at a wider level can be naturalized or survived by the community, but a powerful hostile 勢 *shì* might damage the community if not destroying it. There is no inherent right or wrong, or good or bad in the alternation of 勢*shì*, only positive or negative human experiences based on their own partial and biased perspectives. Either way, 勢 *shì* is understood as a key component that influences the survival and prosperity of a human community.

The ancient Chinese relied on receptivity and not meaning-making to detect 勢 *shì*. Jullien (2020) explains that the propensity of things in the sensory world changes spontaneously, meaning in the form of interpretation, or an idea, creating an obstacle for detecting the propensity of things. This is because any idea, or interpretation of a situation, is attached to a particular discourse or outcome, while the sensory world evolves. As one commits to one's ideas or beliefs in an interpretation, one discriminates against all other possibilities. Instead of following the propensity of the sensory world, a theory imposes that the sensory world follows the idea of a theorist. Chinese thought suggests that the idea then functions as a filter, and creates a reality that is separated from the propensity of things. Privileging meaning centralizes human opinions over the spontaneous motions in the world; it clouds one's ability to detect the continuing course of a motion as it develops.

Receptivity prioritizes *receiving* from the sensory world and not *creating* meaning. Developing receptivity is a process of training. Because early and weak 勢 *shì* are difficult to detect, the propensity of things evolves spontaneously; opportunities can pass by at any moment. The purpose of developing receptivity is to develop one's sensitivity and awareness toward the subtlest motions. This skill is developed as a process of maturation over time. In ancient Chinese culture, learning was embodied, through meditation, *Qigong*, martial art practices, and other forms of practices. Jullien calls Chinese thought wisdom and not philosophy because wisdom is lived, a matter of competency, and is not intellectual. Language is a tool; it only plays the role of assisting humans before they become more competent in knowing each other; it is not the basis for a scholarship or creating a society. A society is understood not as a reflection of what people say, but what is embodied, in everyday reactionary processes of living. A reaction is habitual and formed in constant repetition. Words create meaning, which is separated from the propensity of things; classical books in ancient China were used to reflect and teach the principles to learn from the sensory world in everyday life; the basis for discussions and debates was embodied competency, not intellectual ability, or inability to understand a statement.

Receptivity is a matter of competency; it requires the emptying of ideas, meanings, and interpretations to minimize the attachment to an outcome or discourse and maximize the capability to react to the propensity of things in every moment. The detection of the propensity in the sensory world is a product of receptivity at the moment as motion occurs, and not theorizing in separation from it. One's idea about existing 勢 *shì* is not the basis for certainty, but to make further enquiries about the propensity of the situation. Because a tendency is silent, it can only be identified through its manifestation; in times of uncertainty, it is common to take action, not to execute a theory, but to trigger a more identifiable manifestation of the existing 勢 *shì*. Therefore, propensity dualistic; it simultaneously supports and resists certain outcomes. By taking an action with the intention of triggering an identifiable reaction, 勢 *shì* can sometimes be detected, and one's suspicion about the existing 勢 *shì* can be clarified.

The differences between Western and Chinese understandings of prosperity have resulted in separate understandings of governing and ruling. It is common to this day, that in Western societies, the authority is called the "head"; this can include the Presidents and Prime Ministers of nations or governors of companies. This understanding is also inherited in every corner of the Western society in terms such as the "head" of school, "head" of program, even among students, there is a "head" of the class. Grounded in the cultural norms of subject-object divide, mind-and-body separation, and theory-and-practice format, and the traditional privilege of the subject, mind, and theory, the typical role of the "head" is to dominate, direct, and command the body, design and create ideals for the body to follow. However, grounded in an understanding of change, not created by human intentionality, but is ever occurring in the propensity of things, the authority in China plays the role of the "heart." The heart as the crown of the person is present in every basic training in ancient medical studies (Yu, 2009). This is because the "heart" regulates the flow of blood, which creates an environment for the entire body. Laws and policies have no inherent nature, they can both serve and enslave people. Based on this understanding, the rulers in China are followers of 勢 *shì*. Internally, the rulers' decisions and actions follow the dominant driving force within the country, and externally, function in relation to the propensity of the world. 勢 *shì* within the country is the dominant tendency of the people. By following it, the rulers can gain support by making decisions and taking decisively in alignment with 勢 *shì* from within the country.

An interpretation of China's rise through a Chinese lens

By explaining the relationship between prosperity and leadership from a Chinese perspective, I have demonstrated the unique way a Chinese perspective guides decisions, choices, and daily function in a human community. I would like to provide a brief interpretation on China's recent success from the perspectives I describe in this chapter.

Through a Chinese lens, prosperity is the continuing accumulation and manifestations of potential. This understanding of prosperity produced two important value systems. One is the importance of sovereignty, and another, is long-term thinking. In the Chinese language, one's home country is called 祖国 *zǔ guó*, or ancestral land. The characters reflect an understanding that the civilization, including its land and resources, are left by the ancestors; in other words, ownership is historical and cultural. At the end of each Chinese dynasty, it was common for China to split into tens and even hundreds of separate factions. The division among the factions lasted, at times, for hundreds of years. However, throughout its 5000 years of history, the Chinese civilization restored its sovereignty. Losing sovereignty to foreign invaders is even more unthinkable in terms of filial piety. Sovereignty has been a non-negotiable issue for the Chinese throughout its history to this day, and it is evident in China's diplomatic policies.

When it comes to long-term thinking, the Chinese tend to make 20-, 30-, 50-, and 100-year plans. Because the country's prosperity is understood to be historical and cultural, the civilization continues to accumulate potential for prosperity for future generations. People's immediate experiences in the short term are not the basis for bringing prosperity to future generations and is not the central focus that allowed the Chinese people to enjoy the prosperity they have today.

Through 5000 years of accumulation, China obtained a vast landscape rich in resources, lifeforms, history, and culture. During the Mao era, and following an extreme communist ideal, capitalism was considered evil. However, from a traditional Chinese perspective, capitalist activities are not capitalism, and are not inherently good or evil. Western countries have used capitalist activities to colonize, dominate, and oppress the world; this suggests that the same activities can also be used to decolonize, obtain autonomy and freedom. Deng Xiaoping's opening of the country in 1978 followed the external 勢 *shì* of capitalism. By following the external 勢 *shì*, internally, China mobilized its population to become the forces for producing goods and generating wealth; externally, the big Chinese population also made China one of the largest consumer markets in the world. The United States of America did not want to miss out on the opportunities for capitalist gains and abolished their economic sanctions against China in 1971, and established full diplomatic relations with China in 1979. These outcomes are manifestations of following the capitalist 勢 *shì*. Chapter Twenty in Laozi (1989) states that the highest virtue is like water, because it excels in benefiting the myriad creatures without contending with them, and settles where none would like to be; it comes close to 道*dào*. By becoming Western countries' factories, taking their pollution, manufacturing work and wastes, China silently accumulated 勢 *shì* in the power dynamics of the world. When the Western powers realized that the world has become reliant on China both to be a major consumer and the primary supplier, the propensity of power had already shifted in China's favor.

The country is the environment that provides potential for its people to acquire their own prosperity. Following internal 勢 *shì* is to help the Chinese people acquire prosperity, and it is done by making the country a more prosperous environment that maximizes the potential for the people to acquire their own prosperities. The Chinese government also maintains a prosperous internal environment by regulating the flow of money and resources. In opening new markets, government agencies and organizations take the most risks to create opportunities for companies. In times of global financial crises, the Chinese government often prioritizes minimizing the negative impacts and preserving the internal potential-for-prosperity by using the government agencies, institutions, and organizations to absorb volatile changes in the global market. Additionally, China stayed firm on sovereignty issues in its interactions with Western powers, which is strongly backed by the internal 勢 *shì*.

With an understanding that prosperity is decided by 勢 *shì*, the Chinese government also does not hesitate to act decisively in issues that are controversial under a Western value system. From a Chinese perspective, prosperity is lived, and China's progress is self-evident; it is not caused by lack of problems, but is influenced by 勢 *shì*, and is inherent in the propensity of things. By following both the internal 勢 *shì* for prosperity and external 勢 *shì* of capitalism, China acquired rapid growth and sustainable prosperity, and has eradicated over 800 million people from extreme poverty, which, according to the world bank, was 70% of the entire world's poor. The ideas I explained in this chapter based on Jullien's work, such as a Chinese character representing a tendency and not form, how prosperity is understood, and how to acquire prosperity through propensity, are also lived as taken-for-granted norms in people's everyday lives.

Today's world is dominated by a Western narrative. Under Western influences, Chinese people today are more Westernized. Most cultural value systems remain and are still lived in mundane everyday activities, but Westernization, especially in young people's value systems and ways of being, are visible in today's China. Cultures are ever-evolving. While the non-Western world is becoming more Western, Eastern influences such as yoga, Taiichi, Eastern martial arts, Buddhism, Daoism, and Eastern meditations are being adopted by more and more people in Western societies. As Jullien (2020) says, culture has no inherent identity and is ever-changing in its interactions with each other and the world. As a consequence, to understand a culture, scholars must study it, from beyond Western methods, value systems, interpretations or categorizations of culture, and from its own perspective. Language, as the carrier of thought and the way a culture categorizes the world, can create a solid foundation to start building knowledge about that culture.

Summary

This chapter explores the relationship between prosperity and leadership through a Chinese lens. Based on Jullien's work, I first explained that ancient Chinese conceived reality as the interplay among silent motions that influences the identifiable changes in the world, and that prosperity is an outcome of change that is available, common in nature, inherent in the propensity of things. Leadership, conceived through a Chinese lens, is the silent tendency that drives human activities in a community; prosperity is inherent in the propensity of this driving force. Grounded in Jullien's studies, I used the 道 *dào*, 陰 *yīn*, 陽 *yáng*, and 勢 *shì* to explain a Chinese understanding of how silent motions function to provide insights for acquiring prosperity. Later, I explained how prosperity is understood from a Chinese perspective, which prioritizes potential-for-prosperity over identifiable profit. I also introduced a Chinese value system for acquiring prosperity, that prioritizes not by eliminating the negative (problems), but by acquiring the positive (prosperity). I then explained how prosperity could be acquired by function in alignment with 勢 *shì*. Lastly, I provided a brief interpretation of China's recent development from their perspective introduced in this chapter to demonstrate how a Chinese lens can be applied in investigating phenomena in the world.

Conclusion and recommendations for future research

Cultural thought is still dominated by Western stereotypes. Like many cultural constructs, Chinese thought is often compared with a philosophy of a Western thinker, such as Hegel, Heidegger, and Derrida. In this chapter, I have explained that the two cultures have separate conceptions of reality and obtain different relationships with the world. Comparison puts culture under the same classification, which in this case, imposes Western conceptions of reality and value systems such as being-based constructs, ontology-epistemology paradigms, and theory-and-practice partnerships onto Chinese thought; it is a consequence of stereotyping the culture from a Western perspective. By approaching Chinese thought through the value system inherent in the Chinese language, Jullien's work makes available a Chinese conception of reality, reveals the unique relationship of the language user with nature and the human world, and brings insights that are unavailable from a Western perspective. Investigating situations from a Chinese perspective can resolve issues outside of the strengths of Western scholarship. For example, the non-exclusion of Chinese thought allows Western knowledge to be utilized to benefit the acquisition of prosperity; researchers can conduct extensive further research on the aspects of leadership identified here, like 道 *dào* and 勢 *shì*. Through a Chinese lens, the identifiable aspects of leadership inform the silent driving force behind it. The identifiable is a sign or clue about 勢 *shì* and its momentum. For example, heroic leaders tend to appear in times of uncertainty, when people look to follow strong people; on the other hand, when people are competent in their abilities, leadership is more likely to be collective and distributed. The different types of leadership can be indicators of the type of leadership tendency that is spontaneously emerging in an organization. Similarly, the temporary organizational discourse, including its intensity, can also indicate the current dominant leadership tendency and 勢 *shì* behind the group's activities. Leadership knowledge such as the identifiable behavior, organizational structure, form of leadership, and the relationally and sociomaterially produced meaning in the moment-to-moment process of work can all indicate the motion of 勢 *shì*, and the stage of the propensity toward a leadership tendency. Additionally, monitoring the changes in the identifiable aspects of leadership over time can also detect the changes in a leadership tendency's development and its propensity. Through partnership between cultural thinking like the Chinese and Western traditions, leadership can be understood with more complexity and depth and approached from multiple angles to produce effects that serve various purposes and address pressing concerns.

References

Abram, D. (1997). *The spell of the sensuous: Perception and language in a more-than-human world*. Vintage Books.

Bass, B. M. (1985). *Leadership and performance beyond expectations*. Free Press.

Crevani, L. (2018). Is there leadership in a fluid world? Exploring the ongoing production of direction in organising. *Leadership*, *14*(1), 83–109. 10.1177/1742715015616667

Drath, W. H., McCauley, C. D., Palus, C. J., Van Velsor, E., O'Connor, P. M. G., & McGuire, J. B. (2008). Direction, alignment, commitment: Toward a more integrative ontology of leadership. *The Leadership Quarterly*, *19*, 635–653. 10.1016/j.leaqua.2008.09.003

Fairhurst, G. T. (2007). *Discursive leadership: In conversation with leadership psychology*. SAGE.

Felkins, P. K., Chakiris, B. J., & Chakiris, K. N. (2001). *Change management: A model for effective organisational performance* (1st pbk. ed ed.). Productivity Press.

Jullien, F. (1995). *The propensity of things: Toward a history of efficacy in China* (J. Lloyd, Trans.). Zone Books.

Jullien, F. (2000). *Detour and access: Strategies of meanings in China and Greece* (S. Hawkes, Trans.). Zone Books.

Jullien, F. (2002). Did philosophers have to become fixated on Truth? (J. Lloyd, Trans.). In F. Jullien (Ed.), *Un sage est sans idée: Ou l'autre de la philosophie*(pp. 803–824). Seuil. 10.1086/341235

Jullien, F. (2004). *A treatise on efficacy: Between Western and Chinese thinking* (J. Lloyd, Trans.). University of Hawai'i Press.

Jullien, F. (2011). *The silent transformations* (K. Fijalkowski & M. Richardson, Trans.). Seagull Books.

Jullien, F. (2012). *The great image has no form, or on the nonobject through painting* (J. M. Todd, Trans.). University of Chicago Press.

Jullien, F. (2014). *On the universal: The uniform, the common and dialogue between cultures* (M. Richardson & K. Fijalkowski, Trans.). Polity.

Jullien, F. (2015). *The book of beginnings* (J. Gladding, Trans.). Yale University Press.

Jullien, F. (2020). *From being to living: A Euro-Chinese lexicon of thought* (K. Fijalkowski & M. Richardson, Trans.). Sage Publications Inc.

Laozi. (1989). *Daodejing* (D. C. Lau, Trans.; Rev ed.). Chinese University Press.

Ospina, S. M., Foldy, E. G., Fairhurst, G. T., & Jackson, B. (2020). Collective dimensions of leadership: Connecting theory and method. *Human Relations*, *73*(4), 441–463. 10.1177/0018726719899714

Quick, K. S. (2017). Locating and building collective leadership and impact. *Leadership*, *13*(4), 445–471. 10.1177/1742715015605348

Raelin, J. A. (2011). From leadership-as-practice to leaderful practice. *Leadership*, 7(2), 195–211. 10.1177/1742715010394808

Raelin, J. A. (2016). *Leadership-as-practice: Theory and application*. Routledge.

Uhl-Bien, M., & Ospina, S. (2012). *Advancing relational leadership research: A dialogue among perspectives*. Information Age Pub.

The World Bank In China. (2021). The World Bank. https://www.worldbank.org/en/country/china/overview#1

Yu, N. (2009). *The Chinese heart in a cognitive perspective: Culture, body, and language*, Vol. 12. Mouton de Gruyter.

4 Investigating tensions in sustainability in Chinese and New Zealand business partnerships: An empirical analysis

Michelle Sitong Chen

Introduction

The growing global interest in sustainability has focused attention on the business sector. Calls for organizations to operate beyond the narrow computations of financial benefit to embrace environmental and social measures are being amplified (Chen, 2021). This chapter examines tensions in addressing divergent sustainability issues between Chinese and New Zealand firms in business partnerships. Our selection of New Zealand-Chinese partnerships is motivated by the 2008 trade agreement between the two countries, the first such agreement that China made with a Western country in contemporary times. This agreement has endured and was upgraded in 2021. Therefore, lessons learned from companies operating under its aegis will be valuable for those in other jurisdictions.

Sustainability requires companies to integrate environmental integrity, economic prosperity, and social equity in the present and future in a dynamic equilibrium (Elkington, 1994; Elkington, 1997; Elkington, 2004; Bansal, 2002; Bartunek, 1983; Hahn, 2011). However, the problem of achieving multiple sustainability objectives results in tensions, because progressing on one issue might have detrimental effects on others (Chen, 2019; Hahn, 2015; Van der Byl, 2016).

As Chinese and New Zealand firms continue to develop partnerships, major challenges are anticipated. With the rise of organizations operating in global markets that address social and environmental problems (Margolis, 2003; Smith, 2013), contradictory sustainability practices become evident (Smith, 2011; Besharov, 2014; Li, 2016). However, exploring tensions in sustainability is a new area with few empirical studies in business contexts (Van der Byl, 2016; Hahn, 2016; Hahn, 2018). As suggested by Smith (2016), it is imperative for future research to "develop more compelling insights by discovering tensions inductively and by seeking, as far as is possible, to view the world from the perspective of their informants, rather than assuming a set of tensions at the outset" (p. 461). Further, they also argued that prior research focuses on one element, whereas organizations

DOI: 10.4324/9781003213604-4

may experience multiple tensions interwoven with one another in their daily business activities. In a similar vein, Joseph et al. (2018) asserted that empirical research on sustainability tensions is limited and thus requires future empirical research in different industries and various contexts. Moreover, the majority of the prior literature has examined tensions in sustainability within firms, while the context of collaborative business partnerships between firms has received very little attention (Li, 2016; Hahn, 2018).

This chapter is structured as follows: the theoretical background conceptualizing holistic sustainability is explored through literature that investigates tensions in sustainability within business. We then describe the research design and explore the results of the study. The discussion section interprets our novel insights, and the chapter concludes with limitations and suggests opportunities for future scholarly exploration of tensions in addressing sustainability issues in the business contexts.

Literature review

Conceptualizing holistic sustainability

Sustainability is also called "sustainable development" which has proven to be a difficult concept to define, yielding little consensus on its constitutive elements (Gladwin, 1995). However, there are two main research streams. One trajectory holds the view that sustainability is an integrated concept which requires three elements of environmental integrity, economic prosperity, and social equity to be satisfied for both the present and future (World Commission on Environment and Development, 1987; Bansal, 2002; Barbier, 1987; Elkington, 1994; Elkington, 1994). The second broad stream has reached a consensus that sustainability should be regarded as a dynamic concept. Here, the relationships among environmental, social, and economic performance are maintained by managing one dimension well, which then transforms the others (Epstein, 2003; Schmidheiny, 1992; Gladwin, 1995; World Commission on Environment and Development, 1987; Bansal, 2002; Rondinelli, 2000; Bartunek, 1983; Hahn, 2011; Gladwin, 1995; Hahn, 2015; Ozanne, 2016). By integrating these two streams, sustainability is conceptualized as a holistic concept that requires an integration of environmental integrity, economic prosperity, and social equity to be satisfied simultaneously in both the present and future in a dynamic equilibrium (World Commission on Environment and Development, 1987; Elkington, 1994; Elkington, 1997; Elkington, 2004; Bansal, 2002; Bartunek, 1983; Hahn, 2011). However, it is difficult for organizations to achieve holistic sustainability, because progressing one issue has detrimental effects for others (Hahn, 2018; Hahn, 2015; Slawinski, 2015; Epstein, 2015).

Tensions in sustainability in business contexts

In recent years, there has been an increasing amount of literature on tensions in sustainability in business contexts, which can be illustrated from the following sustainability areas: strategic, intertemporal, instrumental and moral, and spatial tensions (see Figure 4.1).

First, Smith (2014) defined strategic tensions "as contradictory, yet interrelated, demands embedded in an organization's goals" (p. 1592). According to Hahn (2015), most firms have experienced strategic tensions, because decision-makers often have contradictory strategies in addressing environmental, social, and economic performance. Hahn (2018) further asserts that these kinds of tensions touch the very heart of sustainability, because it concerns a diverse set of potentially competing issues, such as climate change, biodiversity conservation, poverty alleviation, public health, and education. For example, Li (2016) proposed that tensions may exist in addressing environmental, economic, and social objectives between firms. As he explained, while some companies may focus more on their financial over social values, others take a more rigorous approach in privileging financial returns with little or no concern for social performance.

Second, as required by the World Commission on Environment and Development, firms should address short-term business targets and

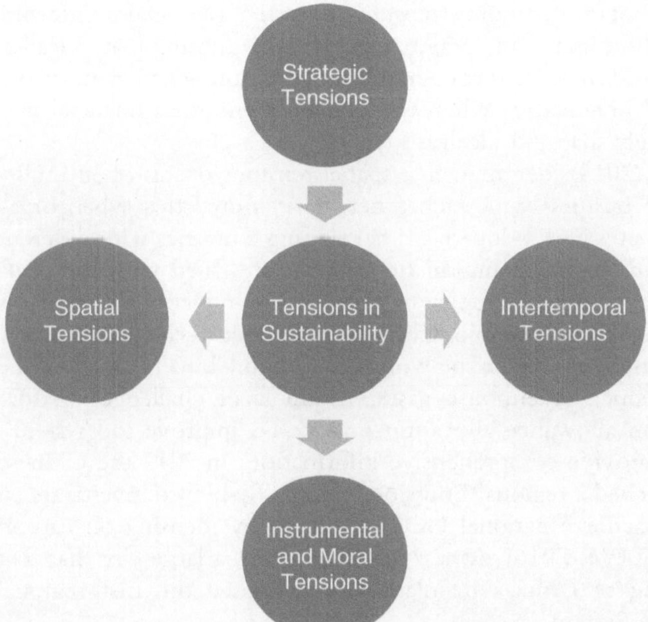

Figure 4.1 Tensions in sustainability in business contexts: Source based on Smith (2011), Hahn (2015), Slawinski (2015) and Hahn (2016).

long-term societal goals at the same time. This indicates that the long-term nature of the benefits that a business provides may conflict with short-term business benefits (Carollo, 2017; Slawinski, 2012; Slawinski, 2015). The short-term vs. long-term tensions were named by Slawinski (2015) as "intertemporal tensions" (p. 531); when "the demands of today differ from the needs for tomorrow" (Smith, 2011, p. 389). For example, Slawinski and Bansal (2015) explored the short-term and long-term tensions in the case of the Alberta oil sands in Canada, where they compared 5 firms, finding that some companies have chosen to focus on immediate profits and to delay investments in greenhouse gas emissions reductions, while others have chosen to forgo some short-term profits to mitigate climate change in anticipation of future regulations and shifts in market demand.

Third, citing Margolis and Walsh (2003), Hahn (2016) propose that firms are faced with tensions in addressing instrumental and moral initiatives. They argue that firms focused on instrumental capabilities are driven by organizational benefits, so social issues are only considered if they can bring some economic benefits (McWilliams, 2011). In contrast, firms which are driven by moral imperatives ensure that their activities are based on "doing the right thing." Firms thus "rest upon fundamentally different and contradicting foundations – i.e. the business case and the moral case, respectively – which gives rise to considerable tensions" (Hahn, 2016, p. 214). Similarly, Ashforth (2014) investigated the ideal and pragmatic tensions in a natural food corporation, finding tensions between two major informal groups, labelled "idealists" and "pragmatists" (p. 479), noting that "idealists endorsed social idealism such as cooperative and environmental values more strongly than did pragmatists, whereas pragmatists endorsed financial viability more strongly than did idealists" (p. 479).

Fourth, Hahn (2015) identified that spatial tensions occur when multinational firms do business with each other. They noted that when organizations operate sites in developed and developing countries with different sustainability standards, these multinational firms are faced with the challenge of either obeying host country or their own home country standards (Okereke, 2006). As one example, China is the largest developing country and the largest carbon emitter in the world. Although China has made some regulations to reduce greenhouse gases, it still faces challenges in formulating a carbon allowance allocation policy. To improve the system's complexity and provide comprehensive information, in 2012 the Chinese government launched a regional Emission Trading System to investigate an efficient way to achieve national CO2 reduction by focusing on carbon emission intensity (Ye, 2016). As a result, Shenzhen, a large city that that links Hong Kong to China's mainland, implemented the first regional Emission Trading System.

Compared to China, New Zealand already has an advanced national Emission Trading System which covers the sectors of industrial processing, transport fuel, agriculture, and electricity production for reducing greenhouse gas volume (New Zealand Ministry for the Environment, 2015). China still needs to establish its own Emission Trading System for CO2 reduction by exploring and testing the results of the regional efforts, while New Zealand's Emission Trading System is developing at an advanced stage. Chinese CO2 policies focus on how to reduce the intensity while New Zealand's emphasis is on reducing the total volume of CO2. From this case, China and New Zealand have different regulations reducing greenhouse gas emissions. Measures of intensity and volume result in tensions which arise when firms do business in deciding either to follow low host country or higher home country standards in regulating greenhouse gas emissions. However, these studies have focused on conceptual interpretations (Van der Byl, 2016; Hahn, 2016; Hahn, 2018), while empirical work is still lagging behind, particularly lacking investigation in the specific context between companies (Li, 2016; Hahn, 2018).

Methodology

Research philosophy and methods

We are interpretivists who used abductive reasoning when we examined how Chinese and New Zealand firms manage their divergent sustainability issues in their partnerships. We wanted to explore and interpret subjective perceptions of reality (Bryman, 2003; Creswell, 2013), to help us understand how sustainability tensions arise and are managed. Further, based on the recent literature in sustainability research, most of the empirical studies have adopted the qualitative approach. For example, Xiao (2019) argued this in their study of managers' sensemaking and their responses to sustainability tensions in buying companies.

Using an abductive approach to reasoning afforded the ability to go back and forth between theory and empirical data, a process that develops continuous dialogue between observation and the interpreters' pre-existing understanding (Hatch & Yanow 2008), and thus is more likely to create a dynamic relationship between the existing theory of tensions and empirical data, providing enriched perceptions of tensions in the sustainability research field.

Drawing from the traditions of qualitative research, we utilized interviewing as the preferred data collection method. Before the main investigations, we carried out pilot interviews out to test the scope of the study (Baker, 1994; Mann, 1985). Semi-structured interviews offer freedom and flexibility to explore issues (Yin, 2010), and these were enriched by an informal group discussion of key stakeholders. Thus, participants in the informal group discussed tensions related to sustainability in their business partnerships by expressing diverse opinions and views, providing an in-depth exploration of the issues (Wibeck, 2007).

To gather data we used purposeful sampling and snowballing to identify companies and potential participants (Miles, 1994; Mason, 2002). Based on the information provided by the New Zealand China Council (2015) and Statistics NZ Ministry of Business Innovation and Employment (2016), we found that the majority of Chinese and New Zealand firms in business partnerships were large corporations. The next step was to ensure that selected companies had mature sustainability strategies and evidence of implementation so that participants would be knowledgeable. In doing so, we read relevant documents and archival records to discover if the firms had annual sustainability reports, and whether they provided information on sustainability activities on their websites and through social media. Firms were approached by personal contacts through emails, LinkedIn and WeChat. The empirical material was based on interviews with 34 respondents from 11 Chinese and New Zealand firms (see Table 4.1).

Data analysis

This study followed the thematic analysis process in the four steps suggested by Miles (1994) and Braun (2006), in particular, we used the Grounded Theory coding technique advised by Corbin (1990) to generate all the themes and sub-themes. As suggested by Waldman (2019), qualitative research coding processes such as grounded theory and organizational discourse analysis are helpful for researchers to "identify tensions, situating them in a cultural/organizational context, examine how they develop into categories or sequential moves over time, and examine strategies that actors use to manage them" (p. 4). The main reason why their coding technique was followed is because the level of development and specificity is distinguished from other coding techniques, and it has a well-defined process that begins with basic description and moves to conceptual ordering and then on to theorizing.

For coding, we followed the three stages suggested by Corbin (1998), open, axial, and selective coding. In the open coding, we went through the data, examining it, comparing one part with another and began to make categorizations. As described by Corbin (1990), open codes are a group of incidents with conceptual labels, which are assigned to each phrase, sentence or paragraph. At this stage we kept asking what was happening in the data and focused on the events, actions, and interactions. These actions "sustained the researcher's theoretical sensitivity, transcended descriptive details, and encouraged a focus on patterns among incidents that yielded codes" (Holton, 2007, p. 275). In this way, "conceptually similar events/actions/interactions" can be grouped together to form a conceptual category (p. 12). For example, to identify the tensions, we looked for indicator terms described by informants such as "problems," "difficulty," "challenging," "tensions," and "opposed/opposing" suggested by related empirical studies (Smith, 2014; Ferns, 2017; Slawinski, 2015). As a director from company G1 said, their

Table 4.1 Companies and Participant Profiles

No. of business partnerships	*Labelled selected companies*	*Type of business partnerships*	*Time of partnership*	*Industry*	*No. of interviewed participants*	*Type of interviewing*	*Labelled interviewed participants*	*Titles of interviewed participants*	*Years of working experience of participants*
Partnership 1	A: New Zealand	Joint venture business partnership	2 years	Farming	3	telephone	A1	Director	over 15 years
						telephone	A2	Senior Manager	less than a year
						telephone	A3	Director	6 months
	B: Chinese				2	telephone	B1	Non-Executive Director	one and a half years
						face-to-face	B2	Director	10 months
Partnership 2	C: New Zealand	Acquisition business partnership	6 years	Appliance manufacturing	2	telephone	C1	Chief Executive Officer	29 years
						telephone	C2	Director	3.5 years
	D: Chinese				2	telephone	D1	Director	19 years
						telephone	D2	Manager	11 years
Partnership 3	E: New Zealand	Strategic business partnership	5 years	Telecommunications	8	face-to-face	E1	Manager	12 years
						face-to-face	E2	Manager	12 years
						telephone	E3	Senior Manager	About 12 years
						face-to-face	E4	Senior Manager	5.5 years
						face-to-face	E5	General Manager	Nearly 23 years
						face-to-face	E6	Senior Manager	15 years
						face-to-face	E7	Manager	7.5 years
						telephone	E8	Manager	9 years
	F: Chinese				3	face-to-face	F1	Director	7 7 years
						face-to-face	F2	Director	11 years
						face-to-face	F3	Manager	5 years

(*Continued*)

Table 4.1 (Continued)

No. of business partnerships	*Labelled selected companies*	*Type of business partnerships*	*Time of partnership*	*Industry*	*No. of interviewed participants*	*Type of interviewing*	*Labelled interviewed participants*	*Titles of interviewed participants*	*Years of working experience of participants*
Partnership 4	G: New Zealand	Joint venture business partnerships	15 years	Health and safety	2	telephone	G1	Director	Over 10 years
						telephone	G2	Independent Director	1.5 years
	H: Chinese				0				
Partnership 5	I: New Zealand	Joint venture business partnership	2 years	Aviation	5	face-to-face	I1	Manager	3 years
						face-to-face	I2	Senior Manager	4 years
						telephone	I3	Senior Manager	5 years
						face-to-face	I4	Manager	10 years
						telephone	I5	Manager	2.5 years
	J: Chinese				0				
Partnership 6	K: New Zealand	Joint venture business partnership	4 years	Dairy	5	face-to-face	K1	Director	9 years
						face-to-face	K2	Manager	6.5 years
						face-to-face	K3	Senior Manager	7 years
						telephone	K4	Senior Manager	6 years
						face-to-face	K5	Director	15 years
	L: Chinese				0				
Partnership 7	M: New Zealand	Acquisition business partnership	4 years	Disposal	1	telephone	M1	Chief Executive Officer	10 years
	N: Chinese				0				
Partnership 8	O: New Zealand	Acquisition business partnership	1 year	Health and safety	1	face-to-face	O1	Senior Manager	Over 20 years
	P: Chinese				0				

Chinese partner preferred expensive packaging to please customers, whereas the New Zealand firm wanted to reduce packaging, offering "a simpler presentation" to reduce their carbon footprint.

In that interview, the words "tensions" and "opposed," we notated as "Chinese firm: Increasing margin to gain purely financial profits vs. New Zealand partner firm: Ensuring their business profits were made based on doing less damage to the environment" to form an open code.

To further identify tensions in the Chinese and New Zealand firms in business partnerships, we also searched for contradictory statements mentioned by participants. For example, as asserted by one informant:

> I think our Chinese partner company has a very strong business mindset driven by financial performance such as looking at growth and market share. However, I think our company is trying to balance performance between financial and social development.
>
> (Senior Manager E6)

This statement highlighted contrasting sustainability practices between these two companies; we therefore coded this paragraph as "Chinese firm: Balancing performance between financial and social development vs. New Zealand partner firm: Not taking social initiative into consideration" as an open code. As a result, sets of open codes were labelled as such, and over time, they were compared and grouped to formulate conceptual categories.

Once the conceptual codes began to accumulate, we categorized them by grouping them under more abstract explanatory terms, as Corbin and Strauss (1998) advise. In further analysis of the first-order codes, axial coding identified more theoretically informed second-order themes Corbin, 1990). In this axial coding phase we used data to "determine the conditions that gave rise to the work, the context in which it was carried out, the action/interactions through which it occurred, and its consequences" (p. 13). Accordingly, we identified a set of codes that were developed more fully as we moved through each additional interview and company. During axial coding, a set of conceptual categories was generated.

The third coding step is selective coding which is the final part where the main themes are drawn; it is "the process by which all categories are unified around a core category" (Corbin, 1990, p. 14}. In this process, coding was delimited to sub-core categories related to the core category. The core category represents the central phenomenon of the study, and the sub-core categories need to stand in relationship to the core category as conditions, action/interactional strategies, and/or consequences, where open, axial, and selective coding overlap (Corbin, 1998). As a result of selective coding, categories and their sub-core categories became more integrated and elaborate to build up the core category for this research.

Findings

In this section, we discuss the main tensions and how managers made sense of them. The findings identified multiple tensions in three sustainability areas – triple bottom line, temporal, commercial, and moral, as illustrated below. The details of frequency of them are shown in Table 4.2.

Identification of multiple tensions

Financial dominance of triple bottom line tensions

With comments from 15 participants, the findings of identified triple bottom line tensions: issues that require firms to contribute to environmental, economic, and social performance (Elkington, 1997). The tensions between Chinese and New Zealand firms in business partnerships thus can be understood as these firms having contradictory strategies in addressing environmental protection, economic prosperity, and social justice in their daily business activities. This finding reflects the strategic tensions which were identified in recent conceptual studies from a within-firm perspective (Hahn, 2018; Hahn, 2015). However, the empirical analysis demonstrated the differences between Chinese and New Zealand firms in addressing triple bottom line issues. With comments from 11 participants at 7 firms, the findings showed that Chinese firms tended to pursue financial growth, while their New Zealand partners tended to achieve financial returns and environmental or social objectives. For example, one director reported:

> Our Chinese partner firm has a big focus on the financial performance. I think their main driver is to return a dividend for their shareholders whereas we are focusing on returning a dividend for our shareholders and also maintaining sustainable farming such as setting goals around animal treatment and wastewater management.
>
> (Director A1)

Similarly, one non-executive director asserted:

> Honestly, we do not worry about sustainability issues. To us it is just about looking at whether business activities can meet financial goals or not. Our Chinese directors do not understand the business, they only can look at budgets and if the New Zealand partner firm does not meet the monthly budget, then there is something wrong. We believe that our New Zealand partner will look after the environment such as protecting waterways and animal welfare.
>
> (Non-Executive Director B1)

These leaders' comments suggested that company A tended to make sure

Table 4.2 Identification of Tensions

Open Coding	*Axial Coding*	*Selective Coding*	
Conceptual Codes	*Conceptual Categories*	*Sub-core Categories*	*Core Category*
Chinese firms: Economic performance vs. NZ partner firms: Economic and environmental/social performance NZ firms: Economic performance vs. Chinese partner firms: Economic and environmental/social performance Financial tensions dominant, addressing sustainability issues becomes secondary	**Financial Dominance of Triple Bottom Line Tensions**	**Identification of Multiple Tensions (IMT)**	**Mastery of Tensions in Sustainability (MTS)**
Chinese firms: Today's business success vs. NZ partner firms: Tomorrow's business development and public welfare NZ firms: Today's business success vs. Chinese partner firms: Tomorrow's business development and public welfare	**Temporal Tensions**		
Commercial imperatives vs. Moral Imperatives Hardly any commercial and moral tensions as both parties behave ethically according to the law	**Insignificant Commercial and Moral Tensions**		
Adopting Chinese law in regulating social and environmental issues vs. Utilising NZ's law in regulating social and environmental issues No statement of spatial tensions as both parties just need to make sure their business activities obey the local regulations	**Minor Spatial Tensions**		

that its financial growth is built on protecting the natural environment, while its Chinese partner company B tended to only look at how to get financial returns driven by shareholders' interests. More evidence was also found in other business partnerships firms. A good example was highlighted in the partnership between companies G and H regarding tensions over product packaging. As director G1 mentioned:

> So sometimes there are some tensions with the representatives of our partner company in addressing how to package products. From our Chinese partner's perspective, products should ideally come in a very expensive outer box with some very decorative designs on it, because this is what Chinese customers want. However, this is opposed to our desire to reduce packaging, have less environmental impact and a simpler presentation, because our company embeds reducing carbon footprint into our business plan.
>
> (Director G1)

These leaders indicated that while the New Zealand firm G tended to ensure that its business profits were based on doing less damage to the environment, thus aiming to address economic and environmental objectives at the same time, its Chinese partner firm H was driven by financial profits without taking sustainability into consideration in its business activities.

Similar tensions were also revealed in the partnership between companies I and J, where the New Zealand leader I1 reported that their company tried to design air flights with lower carbon emissions and safer routes to gain financial growth, but their Chinese partner firm considered flying to more destinations with more passengers a higher priority, thus ensuring economic growth. She reported:

> There are always some tensions that happen in our meeting room. Our Chinese partner firm does not like looking after the environment, for example, our partner company has a great growth aspiration by flying to more destinations to increase financial growth. What they are always looking at is where to fly to and how to fly more. However, our company is thinking of flying with less carbon emissions and also making sure it is profitable.
>
> (Manager I1)

The tensions between economic and environmental performance in this business partnership are reflected in a recent empirical study of Ferns (2017) who identified tensions between economic growth and environmental protection among the European supermajor oil companies such as BP, Shell, and Total.

In addition, three participants at company E mentioned the economic and social tensions (Sharma, 2017; Howard, 2013) with their partner company F. While their firm tended to balance performance between financial and social development, their Chinese partner firm does not take the social aspect into consideration:

> I think our Chinese partner company has a very strong business mind-set driven by financial performance such as looking at growth and market share. However, I think our company is trying to balance performance between financial and social development.
>
> (Senior Manager E6)

Another two informants from company E shared a similar view that their Chinese partner company F's business mind-set neglected the community:

> There was a local arts festival that was looking for sponsorship and I thought that would have been a great fit for our business partner. Although they were interested, they could not get involved, because it was out of their annual budget.
>
> (Manager E1)

> Honestly, the social perspective is not engaged in our partner company. We told them about several great events, but they do not want to sponsor them. I have to say that our partner company has not contributed to the local community; from brand recognition, they are not socially responsible.
>
> (Manager E2)

The above participants' comments endorsed the view that while one firm addresses both financial and social goals, the partner firm has an exclusive focus on financial profit, while ignoring the social aspect (Li, 2016).

In contrast to the findings above, only 4 participants noted that the Chinese firm tended to gain business by producing eco-friendly products for the customers, while its New Zealand partner firm tended to focus more on financial returns. According to one director at company D:

> Of course, there are sometimes contradictions between environmental performance and economic performance in our business partnership. For example, how to conserve energy for the home appliances and reduce carbon emission for more environment-friendly products has become a very top priority for our company's values.
>
> (Director D1)

Tensions also exist within companies when incorporating sustainability practices. One New Zealand leader made a case for sustainability because of its potential to reap financial rewards. "We practice sustainability because being socially and environmentally responsible is a fundamental consideration of gaining financial profits," noted its CEO.

Interestingly, the findings also indicated that, although some participants reflected that Chinese and New Zealand firms in business partnerships had tensions in addressing these environmental, financial, and social issues, the majority of tensions in their business partnerships are around commercial activities while how to deal with sustainability issues had not yet come up, or had been relegated to an unimportant position. As evidence, one director at firm A stated:

> I think it is quite early days for us and our Chinese partner to have some tensions in addressing environmental or social issues. As this partnership has lasted only about 2 years, the only tension we have come across was about economic goals.
>
> (Director A3)

They described the rationale for this: that the main reason why this partnership was established was because it is a win-win joint venture partnership for both firms. As he continued:

> We could see the benefits of this joint venture partnership. The reality was our company was carrying a lot of debt. At this time, forming this partnership helped us out of financial difficulty and also realized our ambition to grow exports into the Chinese market. While on the other side, it is also beneficial for our Chinese partner firm, because they can get sustainable food from us.
>
> (Director A3)

Similarly, one director at company A stated:

> At the end of the day, our Chinese partner firm put a very good deal on the table of paying us around 300 million New Zealand dollars. In addition to that, they also offered us access into the world's fastest growing market, which is a huge bonus for us. I suppose that addressing sustainability issues is still in progress until our Chinese partner has a greater understanding of it. Therefore, some of those environmental issues we probably just need to operate in New Zealand. In the meantime, both parties are still trying to balance tensions in financial performance.
>
> (Director A1)

This comment was also affirmed by a non-executive director at firm B, who confirmed that the business partnership with the New Zealand partner company had only been in place for about 2 years, and the only tensions were economic, meaning that how to address environmental and social performance was not discussed:

> It is still a kind of new partnership for both parties; if we decide to work together in the future, we need to sort out these financial tensions first. The only tension I would call an economic one. We have not talked about sustainability or the environment.
>
> (Non-Executive Director B1)

The reciprocal arrangement here is that their firm can get sustainable-branded products for the Chinese market, while their New Zealand partner firm can get financial support from their firm to wipe their debts. As this director commented:

> Our New Zealand partner firm was suffering from serious financial trouble and the banks were very unhappy with them and so they found us to form a joint venture partnership so we can help them out of this difficulty. The reason why we partner with them is because they produce sustainable products in a good quality environment, very high standards of food safety and presentation, which can provide premium products to customers in China.
>
> (Non-Executive Director B1)

Similarly, two informants at firm E reported that the tensions with their Chinese firm F are mainly about financial issues. According to senior manager E3: "Under most circumstances, tensions with our Chinese partner firm are from a commercial point of view. So, addressing sustainability issues becomes secondary to us. It is a consideration, but it is definitely not our overwhelming driving force." This statement was also echoed by another senior manager, as he remarked:

> I think more tensions with our Chinese partner firm are around how to allocate the budgets, so this is where the tension is. I cannot see tensions playing out necessarily in sustainability or environmental issues; it is more of a business tension with our Chinese partner firm than it is necessarily a sustainability tension that we are asking to trade off.
>
> (Senior Manager E6)

> A similar opinion was also held on the partnership between New Zealand firm I and Chinese firm J.

As senior manager I2 said:

> Well, the difficulties in our partnership range from negotiating a commercial outcome that works for both parties. What seems

> acceptable in our Chinese partner firm may not be acceptable in our firm. What is acceptable here behaviorally may not be acceptable in our Chinese partner firm. This is because we are two organizations, thus often with different objectives.
>
> (Senior Manager I2)

To better explain this statement, another participant asserted:

> We are in a joint venture partnership. Both of our companies work together and then split the revenue between us. Addressing sustainability issues is not part of the objectives of partnership with the Chinese firm, we are not signing up to agree with sustainability goals, we are here for business, and we practice sustainability separately. (Senior Manager I3)

This statement was also affirmed by manager I1: "What makes this partnership really attractive to us is because of the large Chinese market, so about 80% of the customers are Chinese, 20% are New Zealanders." These three leaders' comments indicate that the reason why tensions are not identified in this business partnership is because they only entered the partnership for financial gain.

Based on the above discussion, it can be said that tensions exist in addressing triple bottom line issues between Chinese and New Zealand firms in business partnerships. Interestingly, the findings revealed that Chinese firms tended to only concentrate on how to achieve financial returns that are beneficial for shareholders and the company itself, while their New Zealand partner firms tended to see the connections between or among three dimensions of sustainability practice, thus ensuring that their firms' financial profits are gained through protecting the natural environment and implementing social initiatives. Further, it can also be seen that most of the tensions between Chinese and New Zealand are about financial issues and the triple bottom line tensions were somehow neglected or being put into a secondary position.

Temporal tensions

Temporal tensions occur as partner firms confront strategies for addressing today's success and tomorrow's business development and public welfare. Our findings reveal significant differences in that New Zealand firms tended to have a sustainable business plan as well as being socially responsible, while their Chinese partner firms just wanted to achieve short-term business profits without thinking of long-term plans. For example, one senior manager at firm E said:

> There are many short-term and long-term tensions in our business partnership. Our Chinese partner firm is like any company, which is driven by short-term profits and financial positions. They have targets

> and they have things to achieve for the financial year, so that drives them very heavily and it skews their decision-making. They will recommend to us and try to push us towards things that are commercially favorable for them. However, our firm on the other side probably will be more focusing on the long-term development.
>
> (Senior Manager E3)

This argument was also confirmed by another participant at firm E.

> From my perspective, our Chinese partner firm does not play a long game. They play a short to medium-term game, because they do not think about what they are going to do next. However, we are looking at, for example, 25% to 30% less power consumption for the same output in our products. This has a big impact not only on business development but also for environmental protection, which means we can run some devices in cold temperatures with less carbon emissions.
>
> (Senior Manager E2)

These leaders revealed temporal tensions when developing the business and managing public goods that are "nonexcludable and nonrivalrous such as water and air" (Slawinski, 2015, p. 533}. Similar tensions were also apparent in the business partnership between companies G and H. As one director asserted:

> We are sometimes in tension with our Chinese partner firm, because they just want us to maximize sales in China almost at all costs. In doing so, they are asking us to drop the price and lower the cost of the products and the ingredients for bigger sales. However, our desire is in conflict with our Chinese partner company, our company wants to have a sustainable business by pushing the price up through increasing standards of products, which is also beneficial for consumers' health. That is exactly the tension in our business partnership.
>
> (Director G1)

Another informant at firm G reported the same tension in their business partnership:

> I can give you a good example of a tension between our company and our Chinese partner company. Our Chinese partner company always wants to drop prices of products and make something cheap with poor quality ingredients. From our company's point of view, it would be a very short-term and damaging decision to make some quick money. Eventually, it is going to damage our reputation as being a socially responsible company. In the end, we will lose our loyal consumers who trust our brand. In contrast, our company will buy the more expensive ingredient that is

sustainably produced, which enables us to be a premium top brand from long-term strategy.

(Independent Director G2)

These comments suggest that their company planned to develop a premium brand by providing beneficial ingredients to their customers. By contrast, their Chinese partner company focused on to how to maximize sales by dropping the costs and standards of products. This contradictory action thus caused temporal tensions. Furthermore, their Chinese partner company's behavior demonstrated what Marginson (2008) called "short-termism which is defined as a preference for actions in the near term that have detrimental consequences for the long term" (p. 274).

In contrast, only 4 participants at 2 companies reported the temporal tension that the Chinese firm tended to ensure that their activities are beneficial for sustainable business and public welfare. However, this promoted tensions since their New Zealand partner firm is more interested in achieving today's financial targets for their business. For example, all participants at New Zealand firm C and its Chinese firm D expressed this view. According to one director at firm D:

> Our New Zealand partner firm is short-term focused, which means they are more financial results-driven to gain profits for the shareholders. But sometimes for a socially responsible company it is a bit short-term. How to deliver a financial report to the shareholders, that is the key for them. As we can see in the past, our New Zealand partner firm gave very little investment to the long-term development like new products and new technologies to save more energy and produce less carbon emission. In contrast, our firm wants the company to be more far-reaching for the welfare of company and society. So those are some differences.
>
> (Director D1)

Similar tension was also reported by the CEO of New Zealand firm C:

> For a number of years, we had a much shorter-term focus. However, our Chinese partner firm thinks long term. We had this tension before, for example, our firm wanted to buy a business, because it is for sale and good for short-term returns. However, our Chinese partner firm came in and said we do not want to defend this decision, we want to invest it all in higher technology regarding using less energy, less water, supporting our environment and what is important to people. It is very important to think how we can grow our business substantially for the next five years.
>
> (CEO C1)

This CEO's comment suggested that their Chinese partner company invested more resources in developing a premium brand by improving technology such as reducing carbon emissions and saving energy. This action helped them to develop a sustainable business, while at the same time, meeting water and air standards for the public's benefit will also be managed over the long term. Instead, their New Zealand company has been guided by gaining short-term financial profits.

Minor commercial and moral tensions

Firms focused on commercial imperatives are driven by the profit motive benefits for the organization and its shareholders (McWilliams, 2011; Berger, 2007; Yuan, 2011). In contrast, organizations adhering to moral imperatives focus on doing the right thing to benefit various stakeholders' interests to create value for the local community (Rodrigue, 2013; Hahn, 2016). The empirical analysis showed that only 5 participants reported commercial and moral tensions in their business partnerships. Rather, 19 informants at 8 firms announced that there is hardly any such tension in their business partnerships, because participants have different understandings toward being moral and ethical compared to the literature.

For example, three participants at company K remarked that their company and its defunct partner company experienced tensions in managing the health and safety standards of products. A senior manager at that company said that they approached customers' health as a serious ethical issue with implications for consumers:

> What we really care about is long-term developing the best products that we possibly can to provide the maximum benefits to the population. We have very ambitious goals around wanting people around the world to be enjoying our products. In doing so, we are making sure that products come out of the farm, right through to being used in the pharmaceutical industry and nutritional products.
>
> (Senior Manager K3)

This value conflicted with its defunct Chinese partner company, who chose an unethical supplier who contaminated products, threatening consumers' health; this behavior was driven by the aim to gain pure financial profit. As professed by senior manager K3: "It is a classic food safety thing, our defunct Chinese partner not thinking beyond a very short-term view, not thinking it might harm babies. Instead, they just go for a better price. And it is a morally bankrupt thing to do really." This participant then stated that their company will not choose suppliers who cannot assure the quality of products, because these unethical behaviors will have a negative impact on customers' health:

> I am aware of incidents where there have been questions raised over behavior of a customer in relation to our products. We will stop supplying to them if we believe they might damage the quality of our products or could potentially reflect poorly on us. It is the same with our farmers, if they do not meet the exact environmental requirements, then we will stop taking.
>
> (Senior Manager K3)

This statement was also supported by another informant, as one director at company K announced:

> Mistakes happened all the time. I do think our company acts ethically and does what is right. It is our company who blew the whistle on what was happening. However, it was our defunct Chinese company who chose the wrong supplier that contaminated [products]. It was us who reported to the authorities and yes we could have been unethical and we could have hidden that, but that's not where we are.
>
> (Director K1)

These comments indicated that the defunct Chinese partner firm tended to be driven by commercial imperatives by pursuing financial return at any cost regardless of breaking the law and regulations, while their local firm tended to ensure their business actions are based on a moral perspective without doing any harm to people's health or putting their lives at risk. These conflicting behaviors raised tensions within commercial and moral imperatives between Chinese and New Zealand firms.

Other partnership companies also experienced similar tensions. For instance, the CEO of company C reported the tensions with their Chinese partner company D in shutting down one important factory:

> We shut an important factory only late last year. In fact, the decision was made locally and it did have a bad impact as a large number of people lost jobs. Before the final decision was made, there were some debates between our leadership team and our partner company. The Chinese team wanted to keep it open for longer because they did not want to see many people lose jobs, but we wanted to shut it down, as it was no longer financially profitable.
>
> (Chief Executive Officer C1)

From this perspective, tensions arose between the New Zealand company C and its Chinese partner company D. While company C's action tended to be driven by commercial imperatives, company D cared more about moral responsibility by considering employee interests, and its potential impact on the local community. This finding is consistent with Hahn (2016) who proposed that firms are faced with tensions in addressing instrumental and moral initiatives, thus highlighting firms confronting tensions "resting upon [a] different, contradicting foundation, the business case and the moral case, respectively" (p. 215).

However, our research does not fully support Hahn et al.'s (2016) conceptual study because the empirical analysis also showed that most informants reported that there were few such tensions in their business partnerships. This is because these participants interpreted following a moral rationale as just about making sure their business obeys local laws and regulations, rather than going beyond compliance to look at wider responsibility toward people and their related community. According to the CEO at firm C, "There is no conflict there. We have never had to compromise our beliefs and moral judgements for pursuing commercial benefits." This assertion was also supported by one director at company D, who emphasized that there was hardly any contradiction or discord between moral and commercial considerations in their Chinese partner company, and both companies make sure their business practices are in line with the law:

> I do not see very clear evidence that there is such a contradiction between moral and commercial considerations. Our company has been strictly governed by the company and local laws. When the company makes any decision, we have to first consider whether it is in line with these laws and regulations in order to conform to ethical norms. Therefore, I do not think that is really an issue here with our Chinese partner firm.
>
> (Director D1)

Similarly, a senior manager at company E asserted: "I do not think we have come across commercial and moral tensions with our Chinese partner company." Both parties were always making sure their business decisions obey the law and regulations, he continued:

> We think about those sorts of things when we do business with other parties or with other companies, for example, the employment contracts of a third party and what their hiring policies are. If we disagree with the way that they treat their employees, we will not do business with them.
>
> (Senior Manager E3)

A good example was provided by one senior manager at firm I:

> No, there is no such tension in our business partnership. From my perspective, it is moral to shut a factory in a community. For example, I shut one important factory overnight. As a result, 50 workers who had full-time jobs went into an environment that was completely ... they would never get another job in that area. So, is that immoral? Then

> business does that and business is immoral all of the time. I am doing these sorts of things now in my firm.
>
> (Senior Manager I2)

In short, the above illustrations indicated that there are few commercial and moral tensions perceived between Chinese and New Zealand firms in business partnerships, because most participants expressed that as long as their activities conform to the laws and regulations, then they are performing adequately from their moral perspective.

Minor spatial tensions

With comments from 10 participants at 5 firms, the empirical analysis also identified spatial tensions between Chinese and New Zealand companies in business partnerships. Based on participants' sentiments, spatial tension can be defined as "when Chinese and New Zealand firms do business with each other, they are faced with the challenge of either obeying China or New Zealand sustainability standards in addressing social and environmental issues." For example, the senior manager at firm O asserted:

> Every country has different regulations. So New Zealand regulations are our backbone because that's where we make all the products. So, every product in the factory needs to meet the New Zealand regulations. However, China has different standards to regulate healthy products, for example, it is legal in China to put 90% flour outside capsules with only 10% healthy ingredients. Therefore, our Chinese partner firm asked us to provide such products to Chinese customers, which causes tensions in our partnership.
>
> (Senior Manager O1)

This leader's comment revealed spatial tensions in their business partnership, as China and New Zealand have different laws in regulating health products, raising tensions in addressing social responsibility. Similar tension was also identified in the partnership between company E and F. As remarked by a senior manager at firm E:

> I think the other big conflict is basically just the regulatory conflict. Based on New Zealand regulations, we have to put all the products through our national security testing lab, which raised some conflicts with our Chinese partner firm. They suggested that they have got a great tool that they can implement to help with doing this, but it does not pass the security clearance of New Zealand. So that's probably where conflict plays out from a regulatory and a sort of security perspective mostly.
>
> (Senior Manager E6)

This leader's statements indicate that spatial tension occur in their business partnership in addressing national security issues. This is consistent with prior research arguing that different national regulations lead to tensions when firms operate sites in developed and developing countries with different environmental or social standards (Christmann, 2004; Hahn, 2015).

Further, these findings do not support Hahn et al.'s (2015) conceptual argument either, because the empirical analysis also showed that most informants (20 participants at 9 firms) announced that there is no such tension in their business partnerships in relation to Chinese and New Zealand laws and regulations in addressing sustainability issues as long as these companies ensure their business activities obey the local regulations. For example, one director at firm B said that there is hardly any spatial tension with their New Zealand partner firm, because both firms ensured that their business activities conform to national standards such as addressing health and safety issues:

> I do not think there is such tension. For example, in terms of health and safety issues, our New Zealand partner company must comply with the New Zealand regulations. If they export products to China, they need to comply with standards that meet the laws of the People's Republic of China.
>
> (Director B2)

Similarly, other participants also expressed similar opinions about their business partnerships. According to the CEO at firm C:

> There is no argument regarding this issue. The regulatory standards are different in most countries. Both of us have to comply with the standards in the markets that we sell our products. When our firm sells products in New Zealand, all of those products have to meet New Zealand standards in regard to energy savings and health and safety requirements. When our Chinese partner firm sells branded products in China, they have to meet China's standards. There's not much room for us to define how we meet those. They are quite clear and there is certainly little judgement to be made there.
>
> (Chief Executive Officer C1)

This comment was also affirmed by one director at their Chinese partner firm:

> We do not really have such tension in our partnership. We are global companies, and the first ability to be global companies is to conform to local standards. Different regions have different standards. But if we want to sell products in certain markets, we have to conform to the local standards. That is the first thing.
>
> (Director D1)

Similar sentiment was also reflected in the partnership between company G and H. A good example was demonstrated by one independent director:

> For example, all health and wellness food products sold in China must have a blue hat certification which is based on Chinese government regulations. It is very hard for us to get it. In order to get this, our firm works very well with our Chinese partner firm through understanding and making sure we comply with the Chinese regime in terms of products' health and safety standards. We want to be sure that we comply with the local laws and regulations. It is very important to us.
> (Independent Director G2)

The comments confirm the absence of spatial tension in their business partnerships, because it is compulsory for them to obey Chinese and New Zealand regulations and laws in addressing sustainability issues such as health and safety standards.

Discussion

By looking at previous studies in tensions in sustainability, it is apparent that the majority of the research tended to focus on one type of tension such as the intertemporal tensions between short-term business profits and long-term societal goals (Slawinski, 2015), and tensions between economic prosperity and social initiatives (Sharma, 2017; Iivonen, 2018). Nevertheless, this study found four types of sustainability tensions between Chinese and New Zealand firms in business partnerships: triple bottom line, temporal, commercial and moral, and spatial tensions.

First, our study identified the triple bottom line tensions in that these companies have contradictory strategies in addressing environmental protection, economic prosperity explored from a conceptual perspective (Hahn, 2018; Hahn, 2015). However, the findings tend to not support the claim proposed by Li (2016) that while some companies may focus more on financial profits than social values, others may look at financial returns with no or little concern for social performance. For example, the empirical analysis illustrated that some Chinese firms tended to pursue financial growth, while their New Zealand partner firms tended to achieve financial returns and environmental/social objectives at the same time.

Second, prior studies argued that short-term and long-term tensions have received relatively little attention in business sustainability research (Bansal, 2014; Ortiz-de-Mandojana, 2016). Rather, temporal tensions were identified in this study in that the Chinese and New Zealand firms confront strategies in addressing today's success and tomorrow's business development and public welfare. This finding confirms the short-term and long-term sustainability tensions in which "the demands of today differ from the needs for tomorrow" (Smith, 2011, p. 389). However, this finding is different from what Slawinski (2015) called "intertemporal tensions" (p. 531) which illustrates the tensions between short-term business profits and long-term societal development. For example, some participants suggested that New Zealand firms tended to focus more on tomorrow's business development and public welfare, while their Chinese partner firms put more emphasis on achieving today's success without taking long-term plans into consideration. This indicated that the long-term benefits that firms provide to both business and society conflict with a short-term focus that is only beneficial for organizations themselves, thus highlighting the tension between short-term private interests and long-term for both private and public concerns.

Third, the findings of this study identified commercial and moral tensions which affirms Hahn et al.'s (2016) argument that firms are confronting tensions which are "resting upon [a] different, contradicting foundation, the business case and the moral case, respectively" (p. 215). Fourth, the empirical analysis also identified spatial tensions in that when Chinese and New Zealand firms do business with each other, they are faced with the challenge of either obeying China or New Zealand sustainability standards in addressing social and environmental issues. This is in accordance with the spatial tensions that were also identified conceptually by Hahn (2015) who suggested that when multinational firms do business with each other, firms operating sites in developed and developing countries with different sustainability standards are faced with the challenge of either obeying the host country's or their own home country's standards.

Existing tensions in addressing divergent sustainability issues between Chinese and New Zealand firms are not only restricted to one area of sustainability; rather, they are related to multiple areas. This creates more difficulty and challenges for these companies to manage them at the same time.

In terms of these multiple sustainability tensions, the findings of our study demonstrate the differences between Chinese and New Zealand companies in addressing sustainability issues as evident from the triple bottom line and temporal tensions. For example, in terms of the triple bottom line, the empirical findings showed that the majority of participants reported that Chinese firms tended to pursue financial growth, while their New Zealand partner firms tended to achieve financial return and environmental or social objectives. In contrast, some participants also demonstrated that their Chinese firm tended to gain sales by producing eco-friendly products for the customers, while its New Zealand partner firm tended to focus more on gaining financial return. Similarly, as illustrated in the temporal tensions, the empirical analysis demonstrated that most New Zealand firms intended to have a sustainable business as well as being socially responsible, while their Chinese partner firms just wanted to achieve short-term business profits without thinking of long-term plans. In comparison, some informants reported that the Chinese firm tended to ensure that their activities are beneficial for sustainable business and public welfare, while their New

Zealand partner firm was more interested in achieving today's financial interests for their business.

In comparison to New Zealand companies, some of Chinese partner companies have started to be aware of the importance of sustainability improvements. In doing so, these companies have made efforts to achieve financial and non-financial sustainability such as incorporating environmental and social performance at the same time.

Interestingly, although the findings of this research identified multiple sustainability tensions between Chinese and New Zealand companies, most of these have been relegated to unimportant positions or have been neglected. For example, one of the important conceptual categories is "financial dominance of triple bottom line tensions," which demonstrated that, although some participants reflected that their companies had tensions in addressing these environmental, financial and social issues, the majority of tensions are around commercial activities while how to deal with sustainability issues had not yet been raised or had been considered unimportant. Moreover, another conceptual category elaborated is "minor commercial and moral tensions." This revealed that although a few participants reported these tensions, most participants felt that there is hardly any in their business partnerships, because these participants interpret following a moral rationale as just making sure their business obeys the laws and regulations, rather than going beyond this to look at the responsibility for doing the right thing for individuals and their related communities. Further, only a few participants announced the existence of spatial tensions in their business partnerships. In contrast, most informants said that there were no such tensions in their business partnerships in relation to Chinese and New Zealand laws and regulations in addressing sustainability issues if these companies ensured their business activities obeyed the local regulations.

Although the Chinese and New Zealand companies are faced with multiple sustainability tensions to manage at the same time, these companies tended to focus on settling financial issues; hence, how to manage these multiple sustainability tensions has been neglected or considered less important, which denotes that these companies lack acknowledgement and awareness of the importance of these tensions.

Practical and managerial implications

As well as the theoretical contributions, this study has also underscored some practical implications for firms which face similar tensions in addressing sustainability issues in collaborative business partnerships. The findings of this study are based on the perceptions from participants who are in management, senior management, and executive positions and are involved in managing the partnerships between themselves and their partner firms. Here, the main practical implications of this empirical study are illustrated from the following perspectives.

First, this research can help the practitioners to recognize that they face multiple sustainability tensions to manage at the same time which partially overlap across individual, organizational, and societal levels in a knotted and nested relationship. This reminds practitioners that it is difficult and challenging for them to manage the sustainability tensions simultaneously, because moving one competing demand may affect another. Further, based on the empirical analysis of this study, compared to New Zealand companies, Chinese partner companies do not have rigid sustainability policies and regulations which are dominated by financial performance, thus causing tensions in their business partnerships. From this perspective, we argue that, although Chinese companies have started to be aware of the importance of sustainability implementation, they need to learn from New Zealand companies how to achieve financial and non-financial sustainability through improving their organizational sustainability regulations and standards.

Limitations and future research

Despite its contributions and implications, this research has some limitations that call for further investigation in future research. The first limitation is about generalizability, because data collection was restricted to a specific context between Chinese and New Zealand companies in business partnerships, which suggests that the findings of this research may not be applicable to other contexts. Further, the unit of analysis in this research focused on a small sample of participants in Chinese and New Zealand companies. However, following abductive reasoning, the purpose and objective of this qualitative research is to gain a richer understanding of tensions in sustainability based on participants' real experience and subjective interpretations, which helped us as researchers to achieve analytical instead of statistical generalizability. From this perspective, we encourage future studies to extend this work by exploring the tensions in other empirical contexts through conducting quantitative studies.

The second limitation is the use of one-person coding. Due to the subjective nature of qualitative research, the relationships within and among codes and categories are complicated. Some of the codes and categories overlapped and were redundant. In terms of this research, it was difficult for us to get other people to do coding at the same time, which suggests that the same information can be coded in a different way by other researchers, thus generating different codes and categories, consequently, producing different results and propositions for this research.

Conclusions

In conclusion, this empirical study investigated tensions in sustainability between Chinese and New Zealand firms in business partnerships through showing how tensions arise and are managed. In doing so, 33 in-depth individual interviews alongside one informal group discussion were carried out at 16 relatively large Chinese and New Zealand firms in business partnerships, with staff who are in management, senior management, and executive positions, and directly managing their business partnerships. Accordingly, this study manifests that Chinese and New Zealand firms in business partnership are faced with complex and multiple sustainability tensions. However, these companies tended to ignore and neglect them by putting their focus on financial issues. In particular, the findings suggest that not all New Zealand companies address financial and non-financial sustainability performance simultaneously, while some Chinese companies have started to realize the importance of sustainability implementations and made efforts to achieve both at the same time. This study contributes to scholarly understanding of tensions in sustainability between firms in collaborative business partnerships.

References

Ashforth, B. E., & Reingen, P. H. (2014). Functions of dysfunction: Managing the dynamics of an organizational duality in a natural food cooperative. *Administrative Science Quarterly*, *59*(3), 474–516. 10.1177/0001839214537811

Baker, T. (1994). *Doing social research* (2nd ed.). McGraw-Hill.

Bansal, P. (2002). The corporate challenges of sustainable development. *Academy of Management Executive*, *16*(2), 122–131. 10.5465/AME.2002.7173572

Bansal, P., & DesJardine, M. R. (2014). Business sustainability: It is about time. *Strategic Organization*, *12*(1), 70–78. 10.1177/1476127013520265

Barbier, E. B. (1987). The concept of sustainable economic development. *Environmental Conservation*, *14*(2), 101–110. 10.1017/S0376892900011449

Bartunek, J. M., Gordon, J. R., & Weathersby, R. P. (1983). Developing "complicated" understanding in administrators. *Academy of Management Review*, *8*(2), 273–284. 10.5465/AMR.1983.4284737

Berger, I. E., Cunningham, P. H., & Drumwright, M. E. (2007). Mainstreaming corporate social responsibility: Developing markets for virtue. *California Management Review*, *49*(4), 132–157. 10.2307/41166409

Besharov, M. L. (2014). The relational ecology of identification: How organizational identification emerges when individuals hold divergent values. *Academy of Management Journal*, *57*(5), 1485–1512. 10.5465/amj.2011.0761

Braun, V., & Clarke, V. (2006). Using thematic analysis in psychology. *Qualitative Research in Psychology*, *3*(2), 77–101. 10.1191/1478088706qp063oa

Bryman, A., & Bell, E. (2003). *Business research methods* (4th ed.). Oxford University Press.

Carollo, L., & Guerci, M. (2017). 'Activists in a suit': Paradoxes and metaphors in sustainability managers' identity work. *Journal of Business Ethics*, *148*(2), 249–268. 10.1007/s10551-017-3582-7

Chen, M. S., Eweje, G., & Kennedy, J. C. (2019). Managing tensions in sustainability in Chinese and New Zealand business partnerships: A conceptual perspective. In N.

Capaldi, S. O. Idowu, R. Schmidpeter, & M. Brueckner (Eds.), *Responsible business in uncertain times and for a sustainable future* (pp. 145–168). Springer. 10.1007/978-3-030-11217-2_7

Chen, M. S., Eweje, G., & Kennedy, J. C. (2021). Managerial sensemaking of tensions in sustainability: Empirical evidence from Chinese and New Zealand business partnerships. *Journal of Cleaner Production, 319*, 1–15. 10.1016/j.jclepro.2021.128699

Christmann, P. (2004). Multinational companies and the natural environment: Determinants of global environmental policy standardization. *Academy of Management Journal, 47*(5), 747–760. 10.5465/20159616

Corbin, J. M., & Strauss, A. (1990). Grounded theory research: Procedures, canons, and evaluative criteria. *Qualitative Sociology, 13*(1), 3–21. 10.1007/BF00988593

Corbin, J. M., & Strauss, A. (1998). *Basics of qualitative research: Techniques and procedures for developing grounded theory* (2nd ed.). Sage.

Creswell, J. W. (2013). *Qualitative inquiry and research design: Choosing among five approaches* (3rd ed.). Sage.

Eisenhardt, K. M., & Graebner, M. E. (2007). Theory building from cases: Opportunities and challenges. *Academy of Management Journal, 50*(1), 25–32. 10.5465/AMJ.2007.24160888

Elkington, J. (1994). Towards the suitable corporation: Win–win–win business strategies for sustainable development. *California Management Review, 36*(2), 90–100. 10.2307/41165746

Elkington, J. (1997). *Cannibals with forks: The triple bottom line of 21st century business.* New Society.

Elkington, J. (2004). Enter the triple bottom line. In A. Henriques & J. Richardson (Eds.), *The triple bottom line: Does it all add up?* (pp. 1–16). Earthscan. https://doi.org/

Epstein, M. J., Buhovac, A. R., & Yuthas, K. (2015). Managing social, environmental and financial performance simultaneously. *Long Range Planning, 48*(1), 35–45. 10.1016/j.lrp.2012.11.001

Epstein, M. J., & Roy, M.-J. (2003). Making the business case for sustainability: Linking social and environmental actions to financial performance. *The Journal of Corporate Citizenship, 9*, 79–96. http://www.jstor.org/stable/jcorpciti.9.79

Ferns, G., Amaeshi, K., & Lambert, A. (2017). Drilling their own graves: How the European oil and gas supermajors avoid sustainability tensions through mythmaking. *Journal of Business Ethics, 158*(1), 201–231. 10.1007/s10551-017-3733-x

Gladwin, T. N., Kennelly, J. J., & Krause, T.-S. (1995). Shifting paradigms for sustainable development: Implications for management theory and research. *Academy of Management Review, 20*(4), 874–907. 10.5465/amr.1995.9512280024

Hahn, T., & Figge, F. (2011). Beyond the bounded instrumentality in current corporate sustainability research: Toward an inclusive notion of profitability. *Journal of Business Ethics, 104*(3), 325–345. 10.1007/s10551-011-0911-0

Hahn, T., Figge, F., Pinkse, J., & Preuss, L. (2018). A paradox perspective on corporate sustainability: Descriptive, instrumental, and normative aspects. *Journal of Business Ethics, 148*(2), 235–248. 10.1007/s10551-017-3587-2

Hahn, T., Pinkse, J., & Preuss, L. (2015). Tensions in corporate sustainability: Towards an integrative framework. *Journal of Business Ethics, 127*(2), 297–316. 10.1007/s10551-014-2047-5

Hahn, T., Pinkse, J., Preuss, L., & Figge, F. (2016). Ambidexterity for corporate social performance. *Organization Studies, 37*(2), 213–235. 10.1177/0170840615604506

Hatch, M. J., & Yanow, D. (2008). Methodology by Metaphor: Ways of Seeing in Painting and Research. *Organization Studies, 29*(1), 23–44. https://dx.doi.org/10.1177/0170840607086635

Holton, J. A. (2007). The coding process and its challenges. In A. Bryant & K. Charmaz (Eds.), *The sage handbook of grounded theory* (pp. 265–290). Sage.

Howard, P. H., & Jaffee, D. (2013). Tensions between firm size and sustainability goals: Fair trade coffee in the United States. *Sustainability, 5*(1), 72–89. 10.3390/su5010072

Iivonen, K. (2018). Defensive responses to strategic sustainability paradoxes: Have your coke and drink it too! *Journal of Business Ethics, 148*(2), 309–327. 10.1007/s10551-017-3580-9

Joseph, J., Borland, H., Orlitzky, M., & Lindgreen, A. (2018). Seeing Versus Doing: How Businesses Manage Tensions in Pursuit of Sustainability. *Journal of Business Ethics, First online*, 1–22. https://doi.org/10.1007/s10551-018-4065-1

Joseph, J., Borland, H., Orlitzky, M., & Lindgreen, A. (2020). Seeing versus doing: How businesses manage tensions in pursuit of sustainability. *Journal of Business Ethics, 164*(2), 349–370. 10.1007/s10551-018-4065-1

Li, P. P. (2016). Global implications of the indigenous epistemological system from the East: How to apply Yin-Yang balancing to paradox management. *Cross Cultural & Strategic Management, 23*(1), 42–77. 10.1108/CCSM-10-2015-0137

Mann, P. H. (1985). *Methods of social investigation*. Basil Blackwell.

Marginson, D., & McAulay, L. (2008). Exploring the debate on shorttermism: A theoretical and empirical analysis. *Strategic Management Journal, 29*(3), 273–292. 10.1002/smj.657

Margolis, J. D., & Walsh, J. P. (2003). Misery loves company: Rethinking social initiatives by business. *Administrative Science Quarterly, 48*(2), 268–305. 10.2307/3556659

Mason, J. (2002). *Qualitative researching* (2nd ed.). Sage.

McWilliams, A., & Siegel, D. S. (2011). Creating and capturing value: Strategic corporate social responsibility, resource-based theory, and sustainable competitive advantage. *Journal of Management, 37*(5), 1480–1495. 10.1177/0149206310385696

Miles, M. B., & Huberman, A. M. (1994). *Qualitative data analysis: An expanded sourcebook* (2nd ed.). Sage.

Ministry of Business Innovation and Employment. (2016). *New Zealand companies*. https://www.companiesoffice.govt.nz/companies/learn-about/updating-company-details/financial-reporting/new-zealand-companies

New Zealand China Council. (2015). *New Zealand China Council investment report: Fostering growth*. https://www.nzchinacouncil.com/partnership-forum-2015

New Zealand Ministry for the Environment. (2015). *An overview of the New Zealand Emissions Trading Scheme*. Retrieved 24/11/15 from http://www.mfe.govt.nz/climate-change/reducing-greenhouse-gas-emissions

Okereke, C. (2006). Global environmental sustainability: Intragenerational equity and conceptions of justice in multilateral environmental regimes. *Geoforum, 37*(5), 725–738. 10.1016/j.geoforum.2005.10.005

Ortiz-de-Mandojana, N., & Bansal, P. (2016). The long-term benefits of organizational resilience through sustainable business practices. *Strategic Management Journal, 37*(8), 1615–1631. 10.1002/smj.2410

Ozanne, L. K., Phipps, M., Weaver, T., Carrington, M., Luchs, M., Catlin, J., Gupta, S., Santos, N., Scott, K., & Williams, J. (2016). Managing the tensions at the intersection of the triple bottom line: A paradox theory approach to sustainability management. *Journal of Public Policy and Marketing, 35*(2), 249–261. 10.1509/jppm.15.143

Rodrigue, M., Magnan, M., & Cho, C. H. (2013). Is environmental governance substantive or symbolic? An empirical investigation. *Journal of Business Ethics, 114*(1), 107–129. 10.1007/s10551-012-1331-5

Rondinelli, D. A., & Berry, M. A. (2000). Environmental citizenship in multinational corporations: Social responsibility and sustainable development. *European Management Journal of Applied Psychology, 18*(1), 70–84. 10.1016/S0263-2373(99)00070-5

Schmidheiny, S. (1992). *Changing course: A global business perspective on development and the environment.* MIT Press.

Sharma, G., & Bansal, P. (2017). Partners for good: How business and NGOs engage the commercial–social paradox. *Organization Studies, 38*(3/4), 341–364. 10.1177/0170840616683739

Slawinski, N., & Bansal, P. (2012). A matter of time: The temporal perspectives of organizational responses to climate change. *Organization Studies, 33*(11), 1537–1563. 10.1177/0170840612463319

Slawinski, N., & Bansal, P. (2015). Short on time: Intertemporal tensions in business sustainability. *Organization Science, 26*(2), 531–549. 10.1287/orsc.2014.0960

Smith, W. K. (2014). Dynamic decision making: A model of senior leaders managing strategic paradoxes. *Academic Management Review, 57*(6), 1592–1623. 10.5465/amj.2011.0932

Smith, W. K., Gonin, M., & Besharov, M. L. (2013). Managing social-business tensions: A review and research agenda for social enterprise. *Business Ethics Quarterly, 23*(3), 407–442. 10.5840/beq201323327

Smith, W. K., & Lewis, M. W. (2011). Toward a theory of paradox: A dynamic equilibrium model of organizing. *Academy of Management Review, 36*(2), 381–403. 10.5465/amr.2009.0223

Smith, W. K., & Tracey, P. (2016). Institutional complexity and paradox theory: Complementarities of competing demands. *Strategic Organization, 14*(4), 455–466. 10.1177/1476127016638565

Van der Byl, C. A., & Slawinski, N. (2016). Embracing tensions in Corporate Sustainability: A review of research from win-wins and trade-offs to paradoxes and beyond. *Organization & Environment, 28*(1), 54–79. 10.1177/1086026615575047

Waldman, D. A., Putnam, L. L., Miron-Spektor, E., & Siegel, D. (2019). The role of paradox theory in decision making and management research. *Organizational Behavior and Human Decision Processes, 155*, 1–6. 10.1016/j.obhdp.2019.04.006

Wibeck, V., Dahlgren, M. A., & Öberg, G. (2007). Learning in focus groups: An analytical dimension for enhancing focus group research. *Qualitative Research*, 7(2), 249–267. 10.1177/1468794107076023

Xiao, C., Wilhelm, M., van der Vaart, T., & van Donk, D. P. (2019). Inside the buying firm: Exploring responses to paradoxical tensions in sustainable supply chain management. *Journal of Supply Chain Management, 55*(1), 3–20. 10.1111/jscm.12170

Ye, B., Jiang, J., Miao, L., Li, J., & Peng, Y. (2016). Innovative carbon allowance allocation policy for the Shenzhen emission Trading scheme in China. *Sustainability, 8*(1), 1–23. 10.3390/su8010003

Yin, R. K. (2010). *Qualitative research from start to finish.* Guilford Press.

Yuan, W., Bao, Y., & Verbeke, A. (2011). Integrating CSR initiatives in business: An organizing framework. *Journal of Business Ethics, 101*(1), 75–92. 10.1007/s10551-010-0710-z

5 Leading the way guided by the Tao Te Ching

Hunter Meng Qingyu and Selina Yang Xiaona

Introduction

In this chapter, we discuss the relevance of the ancient Chinese text *Tao Te Ching* to leadership as understood today. Lao Tzu, a 6th-century BCE sage, and the text associated with him continues to hold fascination today because it appears to bring together a spiritual orientation without being dogmatic.

Lao Tzu is a mysterious person who is reported to have lived in 6th-century BCE or later in the Warring States period of 4th-century BCE China. Barbalet (2014) notes that the text "is a collection of sayings developed in and applied by a group, community, or college of moral-political thinkers and practitioners" (p. 14). It may be, then, that Laozi which simply means Old Master, may represent a circle of colleagues rather than an individual, and that the ideas expressed in the *Tao Te Ching* developed over time. To be sure, however, the political and practical background of the work makes it interesting for 21st leadership scholars seeking alternative constructs that refresh the field, while keeping to ancient paths.

Ames and Hall (2004) write in the introduction to their translation, expressed in pinyin as *Dao de jing* that there are two crucial words in the title: *de* (德) and *dao* (道). They state that *de* embraces a sense of "the ceaseless and usually cadenced flow of experience" (p. 14), and *dao* "the discernible rhythm and regularly of the world as it folds around and through us" (p. 23), often expressed as the *Way*.

The text is constructed in the belief that the world in which we live is in a state of constant change and that humans can find ways of cooperating with this fluidity by *not* trying to control their environment. It is the *dao* that governs behavior, for, as Ames and Hall (2004) note, the *dao* "is non impositional" (p. 23). The two words, *dao* and *de*, draw on a dominant metaphor of water, indicating that throughout our lives, and as leaders, we need to act in like manner. This is an issue we will return to later in the chapter, but suffice to note here, that despite the title "leader" and its implied mandate to direct and control, the *dao* reveals more flexible alternatives.

In this chapter, we claim that the *Tao Te Ching* is a leadership text. For example, Pheng (1995) states that the fundamental purpose of its creation

DOI: 10.4324/9781003213604-5

was to guide ancient rulers in their governance and is, therefore, instructive for leaders. Indeed, this is the same approach that Heider (1996) takes in his explorations of the *Tao of leadership*. He claims that the original intent of the *Tao Te Ching* can be translated into today's environment as leaders pay close attention to what is happening around them, and by focusing on processes rather than controlling for outcomes.

Engaging with any ancient text is no easy task, the *Tao Te Ching* included. For a start, the original is written in Old Chinese characters and metaphors that made sense at the time but have now lost their primary meaning. Because of these obscurities there is some disagreement among scholars about its interpretation. Some studies show that it emphasizes the realization of collective interests, the balance between leaders and followers, or human responsibility to the world (Amaghlobeli & Celepli, 2012; Zhang & Foo, 2012; Zu, 2019). Others have pointed out that it contains many management theories, such as servant leadership, Theory X, and Theory Y (McManus & Perruci, 2015). These varieties show that a unified view is all but impossible, and this adds to the text's appeal.

In our study we also wondered how a 1000-year-old Chinese book could help leaders in organizations. We began by deciphering and reconstructing the text in the version as close to the original as we could source. The results revealed many unique leadership concepts, but we lacked practical evidence confirming the salience for today.

To address this historical gap, we interviewed 9 Chinese leaders working in New Zealand. Our interests were in understanding how leaders build partnerships with others from outside their cultural milieu. We wanted to test the relevance of the *Tao Te Ching* on these native Chinese people given they would have at least a vague sense of the text. By exploring how they function in a non-Chinese context enabled us to examine their ideas in sharp relief to their tacit beliefs and assumptions developed in their childhoods in China.

While the leaders we interviewed revealed some basic awareness if Taoism, most had never read the *Tao Te Ching*. We found, though, several interesting points from the experiences of Chinese managers on how to build partnerships in New Zealand. This led us to examine interview data against Taoist concepts to observe if and how the past and present may intersect.

Our 9 respondents were a construction manager, franchise hotel manager, butchery manager, a leader in an accounting firm, and owners of various businesses including a barbershop, bicycle shop, massage chair company, beauty salon, and an educational agency. In each case the leader was born and raised in China and is now working in New Zealand under quite different conditions from home. For example, the construction manager's work requires him to access building materials from local suppliers, maintain constant contact with engineers, city council staff, designers, and clients to ensure the follow-up and revision of the project where necessary. He needs to communicate at multiple levels: technical, linguistic, and political, while keeping a positive relationship with clients.

The flexibility and multifaceted skills needed to operate in a new environment were evident in our other participants. For example, the franchise hotel manager deals with business travelers and needs to maintain regular communication with the offshore hotel headquarters to complete the assigned performance tasks. However, most of her daily interactions are with local firms who provide laundry services and other consumables.

The barbershop owner has been in the hairdressing industry for 14 years. During his work with clients, he discusses other issues that help him work in the local environment. For example, he spoke of having to choose a decoration company to outfit his redesigned shop and he selected a company that he had heard about from a regular customer. This approach was similar with the owner of the beauty salon who graduated from a beauty school in New Zealand, becoming more familiar with the local industry. She has run this shop for more than two years, and the target market is local. She also cooperates with local companies who supply products and help with marketing. Her leadership ensures the smooth running of the operation and building rapport with customers about their lives.

The international educational agency requires leadership that attends to multiple requirements. Referral schools, parents in China and host families in New Zealand all require different communication styles and understandings. Here flexibility is paramount when meeting these complex and sometimes competing needs.

During interviews, we asked open-ending questions allowing participants to talk freely about their experiences. Here we generalize the findings into 5 areas: the quality of work, adapting to the environment, communication, learning from water, and choosing partners when preparing for long-term collaboration. In each case we overlay ideas from the *Tao Te Ching* to explore the interviewees' experiences. In what follows, we discuss these 5 elements and when referring to the original text, we use Ames and Hall's (2004) translation.

The quality of work

Taoist philosophy can guide people to improve the quality of their work, products, and services. Leaders may be able to gain a clearer picture of their own purpose and in the process help them identify and avoid distracting factors. Furthermore, they can identify and select partners who have similar values around quality, which establishes long-term mutual trust. In sum, we found that completing work to a high standard improves cooperation between Chinese and New Zealand enterprises.

The *intention* to produce good work is in-and-of-itself insufficient and must be matched with the quality of the finished product. For example, the construction manager said, "I will see how the walls are plastered and whether they meet my standards." Assessing the quality of the plastering is an intuitive measure reflecting the actual work done.

This attention paid to the final outcome flows into products and services. For example, the bicycle shop owner stated that "I place much value on the quality of bicycles, after-sales service, maintenance, distribution, and other issues. What is more, customers' needs will be satisfied as much as possible." This relationship does not, therefore, imply a single transaction, but rather, implies an ongoing attention to product quality and the trusting relationship among parties.

For example, the construction company manager noted that "New Zealand managers pay more attention to concrete performance during the work." He thinks that it takes time for both parties to build trust, during which collaborators can show their strength and competence to achieve quality and build trust by completing the work.

The quality of work is an essential measure among partners. The franchising director of a hotel emphasized this point when talking about the relationship with the headquarters. She said:

> the headquarters will regularly arrange performance tasks for staff on the system and will check the completion status. There will also be training, workshops, and test questions, and the headquarters will give marks to the directors. In addition, a meeting for 2 or 3 days will be organized. There may be a third-party company at the meeting to evaluate the business.

These continuous evaluations ensure that quality is prioritized.

In addition, when selecting partners, managers will also assess their counterparts' quality of work. The barbershop owner spoke of choosing an interior furnishings company for his salon. He said,

> First, I will look at Google review and choose a company with a relatively high score. Then, I will check whether they are serious in the measurement, whether the completion effect is satisfactory to me and whether the construction period is delayed. All these determine whether I will choose this company next time." When the manager chooses a partner, he will evaluate that company, a process that runs through the entire sequence of events and is the decisive factor long-term cooperation. Therefore, this kind of evaluation between partners determines their business partnership.

In short, performance appraisal is widespread, and compared with other less important factors, such as price, it is the basis for establishing cooperative relations. As the barbershop owner said, "the average price is good." The price is not the major concern so that the general price can be accepted. That is to say, leaders will not just pursue the lowest price regardless of other factors, making the quality of work as the priority.

Taoist philosophy tends to guide people to discover their inner goals and motivates them to work toward quality. It helps to change perceptions by exploring the essential properties of things and life experiences. Then it prompts conscious improvement in both personal character and support for practical activities. For example, the *Tao Te Ching* says:

> 天下皆知美之為美，
> 斯惡已；
> 皆知善之為善，
> 斯不善矣。
> As soon as everyone in the world knows that the beautiful is beautiful,
> There is already ugliness.
> As soon as everyone knows the able,
> There is ineptness.
>
> (Ames & Hall, 2004, pp. 79–80)

This text shows that things generally exhibit relative properties, such as beauty and ugliness, or able and ineptness. On the contrary, there is no absolute full and final "thing" because everything is in process. The labels given to things are prescribed by humans, but the *Tao Te Ching* insists that there is no good or bad in the nature of anything. There are only causes, laws of operation, and effects, and while different conditions influence perceptions, this subjective consciousness cannot change their attributes.

Therefore, leaders do not need to overthink the judgments from others or even society as they seek quality. However, this does not imply a quest for perfections. It is that:

> 大成若缺，
> 其用不敝。
> 大盈若盅，
> 其用不窘。
> 大直如詘，
> 大巧如拙，
> 大贏如絀，
> 大辯如訥。
> What is most consummate seems defective,
> Yet using it does not wear it out.
> What is fullest seems empty,
> Yet using it does not use it up.
> What is truest seems crooked;
> What is most skillful seems bungling;
> What is most prosperous seems wanting.
> What is most eloquent seems halting.
>
> (Ames & Hall, 2004, p. 147)

Quality products have their flaws and things that seem flawless are often out of touch with reality. Defects are a common feature of everything. Thus, the unremarkable may be irreplaceable and the glamorous goals that people all yearn for must also have their drawbacks. For instance, there is an expression in the *Tao Te Ching*.

> 金玉盈室，
> 莫之能守也。
> 貴福而驕，
> 自遺咎也。
> When treasure fills the hall,
> No one is able to keep it safe.
> Those who are arrogant because of station and wealth
> Bring calamity upon themselves.
>
> (Ames & Hall, 2004, p. 88)

Glamorous things such as wealth and status bring people a sense of accomplishment, but they also come with many troubles. It takes much energy to enjoy and protect them, making those who become immersed in them to lose their way.

Therefore, Taoist philosophy guides people to discover the essence of things beyond the glossy exterior.

> 故必貴而以賤為本，
> 必高矣而以下為基。
> 夫是以侯王自謂孤、寡、不穀。
> 此其賤之本與非也？
> 故至譽無譽。
> 是故不欲琭琭若玉。
> 硌硌若石。
> Thus for something to be noble it must take the humble as its root;
> For something to be high it must take the low as its foundation.
> It is for this reason that the lords and kings use "friendless," "unworthy," and "inept" as terms to refer to themselves.
> This is a clear case of taking the humble as the root, is it not?
> The highest renown is to be without renown.
> They do not want to be precious like jade,
> But common like stone.
>
> (Ames & Hall, 2004, pp. 137–138)

Herein is a paradox that flips ideals on their head. For example, humility and not striving for profile become the keys to leadership success rather than grasping after fame from the outset. Glamorous things are just some extra gains in the development process, and these ought not be used as an overriding goal. Wise leaders are able to shield themselves from outside distractions; they are alert finding ways to do their best in pursuit of their organization's goals.

In sum, wise leaders know that achieving quality relies on hard work and avoiding distractions. While others may be trying their best to seize every bit of wealth and status, the wise have little interest in acquiring glamorous things, only to find that this pursuit makes them seem stupid. However, wise leaders they are constantly improving their work toward quality.

Adapting to the environment

Taoist philosophy helps people explore the world. It is inevitable to encounter various situations and challenges in work and life. Some content in *Tao Te Ching* can give guidance on how to face and analyze these problems.

> 道,可道也,非恆道也。
> 名,可名也,非恆名也。
> 無名，萬物之始也;
> 有名，萬物之母也。
> Way-making (*dao*) that can be put into words is not really way-making.
> And naming (*ming*) that can assign fixed reference to things is not really naming.
> The nameless (*wuming*) is the fetal beginnings of everything that is happening (*wanwu*),
> While that which is named is their mother.
>
> (Ames & Hall, 2004, p. 77)

Taoist philosophy is based on the exploration of the concept of 道*dao*, and how to understand it is the key to presenting the worldview. The earliest *Tao Te Ching* discovered by archaeology has no punctuation (Yin, 2016). If the commas and periods were removed, *dao* might be seen as containing two essential components, 無*wu* and 有*you*.

無*Wu* is called "the fetal beginnings of everything." It refers to the state prior to the creation of all things, including matter and spirit. It can also be considered the root causes of things. In other words, nothing can arise out of nothingness. There are reasons for their presence.

Another component is 有*you* that is named as the mother of everything. It is arranged after 無*wu*, which might manifest the logical relationship between them. There is a further interpretation of it in the text.

> 是謂天地之根。
> 緜緜呵若存，
> 用之不勤。
> This is called the root of the world.

Wispy and delicate, it only seems to be there,
Yet its productivity is bottomless.
(Ames & Hall, 2004, p. 85)

This paragraph shows that 有 *you* is the basis of things, and its influence accompanies their development over time. Therefore, it should be able to represent the laws and effects on which things operate.

Taoist philosophy attempts to lead people to realize that everything has fundamental causes, laws of operation, and effects. People should spend more energy exploring these factors in each of the issues they face when they are in unfamiliar environments, enabling them to make purposeful and comprehensive analyses of problems. Then it is easier for them to grasp the essence of things and make corresponding measures based on their assessments.

Our study found widespread differences in business between Chinese and New Zealand managers, which brings significant challenges for the Chinese. For example, the butcher shop owner said, "Chinese people often talk about business at the dinner table and pay more attention to each other's feelings." In China, principals among partners often entertain each other, building their relationship and promoting mutual understanding. It also makes their relationship closer and firmer, thus promoting the smooth development of business cooperation. It is an essential part of the Chinese business context. However, the butcher shop manager also said, "It does not matter who is in charge for New Zealand managers." She noted that New Zealanders pay more attention to customer loyalty, such as the size of the order, whether orders are consistent, and whether the monthly payment is or is not in arrears. In this respect Chinese and New Zealand leaders diverge in their approach to social events.

In addition, New Zealand companies have time boundaries, while Chinese companies prefer being able to respond whenever customers need them. The manager from the accounting firm said that they share the office with other New Zealand companies.

> One day, near the end of getting off work, I gave the front desk a document that needed to be sent out on the same day. However, it may be that it was not explained clearly, or it may be time to get off work. The document was not sent out on the same day, which led to the loss of customers.

The misunderstanding here was around work hours. For Chinese working after official hours is common, meaning that daily life and work are mixed. However, the boundaries between their work and life are clearer for New Zealanders. As another manager complained, "I usually do not receive email replies during off-hours, no matter how urgent it is."

Leaders who follow the *dao* can observe differences in habits and temporality, exploring the cultural and conceptual diversity underlying these issues. This ability to be present to the moment helps build empathy with local people by understanding their work life behaviors. This facilitates more targeted planning and action as they integrate8 into the environment.

Adapting to the New Zealand business environment is challenging for Chinese managers. Taoist philosophy gives some inspiration as they seek to understand the environment. As they pay attention to dissecting the nature of various problems, differences in behaviors may be seen to be a manifestation of some social characteristic or habit. A comprehensive and in-depth understanding of causes, operational laws, and effects are critical to planning their actions. In this way, no matter the situation, they have the means to respond and are more likely to have a clearer appreciation of the issues.

Furthermore, Taoist philosophy requires people to integrate into the environment rather than just adapt to it.

> 善行者，無轍迹。
> Able travelers leave no ruts or tracks along the way.
> (Ames & Hall, 2004, pp. 118–119)

People can benefit from the favorable elements of the environment and avoid obstacles so that their steps are so light that they do not leave a trace. This metaphor reflects Taoism's desire for people to integrate with the external environment.

Many respondents in our interviews mentioned the importance of merging into the local environment. To reduce the losses due to cultural differences, and establish and maintain business relationships with New Zealand companies, most people usually integrate themselves into it as soon as possible by learning and imitating each other's manners and habits. For example, one leader observed, "the Chinese usually like to cooperate with close and familiar friends, and they usually acquiesce in oral agreements. However, New Zealand managers believe more in the contract." After negotiation, both parties agree on the details and requirements of the business. Then, cooperation through the contract guarantees both parties. Cooperation can be completed without unnecessary contradictions and conflicts. When discussing cooperation he went on to say, "it has been agreed in black and white, and there will be no problems." He adapted to local values by drafting a written contract together with his partners. In this way, they understood and grasped the details and requirements of co-operation to reduce conflicts.

At the same time, Chinese enterprises' advantages and culture cannot be ignored or underestimated. For example, the franchise hotel manager said, "Chinese companies usually assume multiple responsibilities for one person, but foreign companies usually have specific responsibility." She believes that the Chinese way makes it easier to deal with problems. On the other hand, the butcher's shop gave an example of rough delivery by a New Zealand third-party company. Furthermore, after contacting the New Zealand supplier, the problem was not solved. It may be because the supplier also has to do a lot of intermediate contacts and confirmation. Therefore, Chinese managers should go beyond adapting to the local context by using their merits.

For example, the construction company manager attends to cultural symbols by saying, "I will send moon cakes to my business partners on the Mid-Autumn Festival, and I will also give holiday blessings on other Chinese festivals." The manager of the beauty salon feels the same. She integrated the culture of traditional Chinese medicine into beauty, which also helped her build many long-term clients. They all agree that these cultural expressions can bring new positive things to the relationship with their partners.

These practices of the interviewees also correspond to the requirements of Taoism.

> 知已者知也，
> 自知者明也。
> To know others is wisdom;
> To know oneself is acuity (*ming*).
> (Ames & Hall, 2004, p. 128)

Integration is based on a comprehensive understanding of all internal and external factors by using the guidance of the Taoist worldview to discover and analyze themselves and others, so that they can use their own strengths to contribute to the development of the whole environment.

In sum, wise leaders pay attention to dissecting the local business environment. They value exploring the causes, laws, and effects of various factors so that they can get a more comprehensive and in-depth understanding of themselves and external conditions, which can facilitate their integration process.

Communication

Respondents often mentioned that they kept close contact with their partners, and this effective communication promoted mutual understanding among them, thus enhancing mutual trust. For instance, the construction manager talked about two aspects of communication. First, "I often communicate with sub-constructors to monitor their completion." This kind of communication in daily work guarantees cooperation. Second, timely communication helps understand the needs of partners and the specific situation. Problems can be solved in time to protect the interests of all parties and achieve joint development. Moreover, he also mentioned communication with an inspector. He said,

> At work, I may have seen him dozens of times, and he recognized me very much. If there is a minor problem during the inspection, he will ask me to make it up again and show him a photo, or he would refuse it directly.

Through continual cooperation and communication at work, it is evident that these parties have developed trust through the leader's strengths and responsible working attitude. Therefore, communication provides the cornerstone for cooperation.

In *Tao Te Ching*, cooperation is described as follows.

> 天長地久。
> 天地之所以能長久者，
> 以其不自生也，
> 故能長生。
> The heavens are lasting and the earth enduring.
> The reason the world is able to be lasting and enduring
> Is because it does not live for itself
> Thus it is able to be long-lived.
> (Ames & Hall, 2004, p. 86)

The heavens and earth have the characteristic of not living for themselves, which is the fundamental reason for their enduring existence. They provide an environment in which all things can be born, grow, and die. In turn, the flourishing of things sets off their eternity. Therefore, it requires managers to create an environment that can host the development of all stakeholders. Keeping an understanding of the needs of others, then, is the foundation.

Frequent exchanges can help partners maintain positive business relations. A simple exchange, such as "how is the business?" stabilizes relationships, thus building loyalty and makes communication between managers more straightforward. When facing minor problems, they do not have to worry about losing their business partners. For example, the construction manager said,

> If I find something is wrong with the wall painting, I will negotiate with them, clarify my standards and let them repair until they are up to standard. After that, I will still cooperate with them because I think it has done well.

This lays the foundation for addressing more significant problems because, after frequent and effective contact, their ability and credibility in solving small problems has been proven, thus solidifying trust.

Guidance given by Taoist philosophy encourages leaders to not strive for profile or to gain an advantage through manipulation. Open and honest communication creates an environment where needs of both interlocuters are met.

> 是以聖人退其身而身先，
> 外其身而身存。
> It is on this model that the sages withdraw their persons from contention yet find themselves out in front,
> Put their own persons out of mind yet find themselves taken care of.
> (Ames & Hall, 2004, p. 86)

This passage demonstrates that valuing the interests and needs of others is an essential part of virtuous cooperation that managers maintain the humility to help sustain relationships. With a modest demeanor, they should understand the needs and demands of their partners, which helps maintain effective and continuous communication.

Taoist philosophy also opposes an overemphasis on self-interest.

> 何謂寵辱若驚？
> 寵之為下也，
> 得之若驚，
> 失之若驚，
> 是謂寵辱若驚。
> What does it mean in saying "Favor and disgrace are both cause for alarm?"
> It means that whenever favor is bestowed, both gaining it and losing it should be cause for alarm.
> (Ames & Hall, 2004, p. 93)

Excessive consideration of the gains and losses of self-interest will not only occupy people's energy but also inevitably lose some potential resources. Such an approach may not maximize leaders' interests in the long term. Therefore, Taoist philosophy guides people to respect and fulfill the interests of others while not compromising their own, whether they are communicating or cooperating. It promotes building close relationships and realizing mutual benefits.

Therefore, effective communication is conducive to business development. For example, when the barbershop manager discussed his choice of a renovation company, he said, "He is a client of mine and chats a lot while cutting his hair. I know he is doing renovations. I know what kind of person he is. That is the reason why I choose this company." They promoted mutual understanding through frequent exchanges, discussing their occupations and exploring personality differences. Their open communication created mutual trust and promoted cooperation between them.

In addition, managers should not pretend to be in a dominant position with any partner.

> 是以聖人之能成大也，
> 以其不為大也，
> 故能成大。
> It is thus that the capacity of the sages to become great
> Is simply because they do not try to do great things.
> This is why they are indeed able to be great.
> (Ames & Hall, 2004, p. 130)

Sages can be considered wise because they do not put themselves above others. For managers, even if some partners are demanding or too dependent on them, they should remain humble and low-key. They should not try to interfere with the operations of other organizations, and it should not only be shown in communication but also in cooperation. Long-term trust requires all parties to be on an equal footing. Taoist philosophy requires leaders to create an environment that can carry people's development and not let them disturb the actions of others.

In conclusion, Taoist philosophy requires leaders to create an environment in which all stakeholders can develop together. Communication as the basis for cooperation should be open and continuous. All parties should maintain a humble attitude to respect and realize the interests of others, which is also based on mutual equality.

Learning from water

According to Ames and Hall (2004), "the highest efficacy is like water" (p. 87). In the *Tao Te Ching*, water is an important metaphor. It is considered to embody the essence of Taoist philosophy, and it is an example that managers should follow. Interestingly, some of the experiences mentioned by the interviewees have similarities to some of the characteristics depicted in the text.

There is a manager from an international education agent who introduces students from China to New Zealand. He said, "Many parents' demands often upset my plans, and there are some unexcepted issues almost every day." It shows significant uncertainty in his work, and there is no perfect plan to solve all problems. He also said, "When we encounter various situations, we will try our best to communicate with customers and partners. Then we change plans and seek ways to coordinate their relations and meet their needs." His attitude in dealing with problems is not static, rather, he maintains flexibility. In addition, the manager of the bicycle shop also put forward a similar point of view. "When developing new customers, I may lose them because the price is relatively high. But I will make appropriate adjustments to our long-term customers." Prices are fixed, but to build or maintain a long-term partnership, they also make adjustments based on the conditions, which means that they are capable of adapting to different contexts. Therefore, it also shows that flexibility is necessary for dealing with partnerships.

In the *Tao Te Ching*, water is depicted as the softest thing in the world.

> 天下莫柔弱於水，
> 而攻堅強者莫之能先也，
> 以其無以易之也。
> Nothing in the world is as soft and weak as water
> And yet in attacking what is hard and strong,
> There is nothing that can surpass it.
> This is because there is nothing that can be used in its stead.
> (Ames & Hall, 2004, p. 197)

Although water contains great energy, it appears soft and weak. It has the power to destroy everything, but it does not even have its own shape and many objects are capable of changing the direction of its original flow. No matter its size, whether it is a stream or a river, the water ends in the sea. To reach the sea, water adapts to a variety of environments, including mountains and plains. This flexibility is what people should learn.

Therefore, it is necessary for managers to have a flexible attitude to deal with problems and maintain partnerships.

> 人之生也柔弱，
> 其死也恆仞堅強。
> 萬物草木之生也柔脆，
> 其死也枯槀。
> 故曰堅強者死之徒也，
> 柔弱者生之徒也。
> While living, people are supple and soft,
> But once dead, they become hard and rigid cadavers.
> While living, the things of this world and its grasses and trees are pliant and fragile,
> But once dead, they become withered and dry.
> Thus it is said: Things that are hard and rigid are the companions of death;
> Things that are supple and soft are the companions of life.
> (Ames & Hall, 2004, p. 195)

Softness and flexibility are qualities that people should have. It is necessary for managers to stick to their own goals, but they should try to change their attitudes and plans to suit different circumstances. Similarly, the interviewees also mentioned the need to use flexible ways to coordinate and meet the demands of all parties while establishing and maintaining partnerships.

The interviewees also mentioned that they should tolerate some issues. For example, when the butchery manager talked about the rough delivery of the third-party delivery company in New Zealand damaged the supermarket shelves, she said, "We have contacted the suppliers before, but the problem has not been solved. As long as there is no problem with the meat's quality, I will not find out who is to blame." This example shows that when faced with such small losses instead of core interests, she chooses to take responsibility instead of just considering her own interests. She is tolerant of minor problems to promote their long-term cooperation.

There is a similar discussion in *Tao Te Ching*.

> 水利萬物而又爭居眾人之所惡，
> 故幾於道矣。
> It is because water benefits everything (*wanwu*)
> Yet vies to dwell in places loathed by the crowd
> That it comes nearest to proper way-making.
> (Ames & Hall, 2004, p. 87)

Water nourishes all kinds of life, but it is in a dirty and detested low-lying place. While it is indispensable, it chooses to tolerate others with humility and suffer what they do not like rather than placing itself above them. Hence, managers should also have a tolerant attitude in maintaining partnerships.

> 受邦之詬，
> 是謂社稷之主；
> 受邦之不祥，
> 是謂天下之王。
> Only the person who accepts invective against the state
> Is to be called its legitimate ruler;
> Only the person who accepts the misfortunes of the state
> Is to be called its true king.
> (Ames & Hall, 2004, pp. 197–198)

People who can afford to lose and take risks deserve to be the heads of others. Thus, it is a positive way to give others appropriate tolerance without affecting goals. As the interviewee mentioned, she does not haggle over minor issues with a longtime partner. A tolerant leader might get more help which can contribute to their development.

In sum, wise leaders focus on cooperation. They have a tolerant attitude and use flexible ways to deal with conflicts and problems. "What enables the rivers and seas to be king over all the valleys is that they are good at staying lower than them. It is this that enables them to be the king of all the valleys" (Ames & Hall, 2004, p. 181). They should be able to adapt themselves to different situations like a river and should also learn to be tolerant of others, like an ocean.

Choosing partners when preparing for long-term collaboration

Building long-term partnerships is not an easy task, requiring significant effort from managers. Selecting an experienced partner who matches the actual needs is the foundation of continuous cooperation. The coordination and changes among parties are also conditions to support them in establishing mutual trust.

It can be seen from interviews that it is crucial for professional things to be done by experts. For example, the owner of the beauty salon explained. First, she chose beauty machines and products from a New Zealand company. She said, "I used them when studying at the local beauty school. This company specializes in making beauty products and providing related products to beauty distributors." Therefore, she expressed her confidence in its products since the supplier is experienced in this area. Second, she selected a local company that focused more on the New Zealand market when partnering with a marketing company. "Because my target market is everyone in this region, not just the Chinese, I would cooperate with local companies. Then I looked at several copy writings. After that, I felt that this company was more in line with consumers' preferences and could better embody the features of my beauty shop." It shows that she made a full investigation about potential partners at the beginning of her choice.

In the *Tao Te Ching*, it is also suggested that people should leave professional work to experts.

> 夫代大匠斲者，
> 則希不傷其手矣。
> Of those who would thus stand in for the master carpenter,
> Few get away without injuring their own hands.
> (Ames & Hall, 2004, p. 193)

Those who want to replace the carpenter to carve wood run the risk of hurting their hands. Similarly, it is hard to get positive results when inexperienced people handle professional work. That requires organizational leaders to have a clearer understanding of both parties when seeking collaboration. They should identify their own needs and conduct in-depth research on potential partners. Therefore, managers need to remain vigilant in analyzing internal and external factors, such as specific needs and others' business scope. They should make choices based on their actual needs, laying the foundation for a long-term business relationship.

Additionally, we noticed that most interviewees and their partners encountered some difficulties and resistance in the initial cooperation. The manager of the study abroad agency talked about his experience. In the beginning, when he had just stepped into the New Zealand market, everything was new. He said, "I was only trying to get in touch with the local high schools very carefully in emails to get the initial cooperation with them and help the student clients to get the opportunity to study in New Zealand." Gradually, with the increase of cooperation, the agency dealt sensitively with students' problems about their learning, their relations with host families, and adapting to the local environment. He added, "Our company has been approved. At the same time, the schools took students' problems seriously in cooperation, which made us feel at ease to send students to these schools." The building of their mutual trust was not all plain sailing. Many respondents also mentioned similar views that some misunderstandings would be when the cooperation started. They have all gone through a process of reconciliation and change.

It also corresponds to the operation of *dao* in Taoist philosophy.

> 天之道，猶張弓者也？
> 高者抑之，
> 下者舉之，
> 有餘者損之，
> 不足者補之。
> 故天之道，
> 損有餘而益不足。
> The way of tian (the sky) is like archers drawing their bows.
> To hit something high in the air, they pull the string downward;
> To hit something lower, they pull the string upward.
> When they have drawn the string too far back, they let some go,
> And when they have not drawn it far enough, they pull harder.
> The way of tian is also to let some go where there is excess
> And to augment where there is not enough.
>
> (Ames & Hall, 2004, p. 196)

Anything, including building and maintaining partnerships, requires people to undergo a complex process. As the interviewees shared their experiences, there were initial contradictions and differences between them and their partners. They often needed to confront and respond to questions. Even if they had established some degree of mutual trust, there is still room for improvement in their cooperation. Establishing a long-term partnership is different from a simple transactional relationship. As stated in the text, it requires some changes and adjustments on all sides. Hence, managers need to be prepared mentally and put effort into implementing partnership processes.

In conclusion, the experiences of the interviewees and the content of the *Tao Te Ching* show that managers should understand their own needs and potential partners before making choices. Also, a business partnership is different from a transactional, buying and selling relationship. Organizational leaders should be prepared to deal with conflicts and problems that may arise at any time. Constant coordination and change are inevitable.

Conclusion

In this chapter, we have considered the *Tao Te Ching*, experimenting with it to understand its relevance for leaders today. Our working assumption has been that ancient texts hold a repository of truths that can be accessed in all generations. For, while there are constraints in our reading which are bound by the time and place in which the ideas were generated, there are timeless ideas which can be appropriated in these times.

The *Tao Te Ching* is a Chinese text, written in ancient ideographs from within a community concerned with maintaining balance between humans and the rest of the natural world. Perhaps because it was generated during troubled times, the Warring States Period, that the notion of harmony became important for these early Taoist scholars, for this was a time of political turmoil where different states with their vassal territories vied for dominance over others, as China evolved to a more unified country.

By noting this context, we can confirm that China is the proscenium. We wanted to explore, therefore, how the *Tao Te Ching* informs contemporary Chinese leaders working in a foreign environment. Our further assumption was that these people would have at least an intuitive awareness of Taoist values. We were surprised at our findings. Although the interviewees expressed little formal knowledge of Taoism or the *Tao Te Ching*, they seemed to draw on an innate awareness of Taoism in their work.

This was unanticipated given that China made a deliberate break from Taoism and Confucianism during the Communist takeover of the country in the mid-20th century. A counterargument might point out that both the interviewees and Taoism come from China, and that the participants in our study would understand those connections. However, there is little evidence that contemporary Chinese cultural traditions reflect a Taoist worldview. We might say, therefore, that Taoism is part of the cultural DNA of Chinese people though their knowledge of the texts and philosophical reasonings behind them might be cursory.

Our interviews prompted us to think further about the connections between ancient Taoist beliefs and contemporary leadership practice. This caused us to return to the text itself and mine it for ideas that can be transferred into this context. We concluded that the *Tao Te Ching* can provide guidance for leaders today.

To be sure, the *Tao Te Ching* is not concerned with the origins of the world and humanity. It is more a political than an ontological document, and is focused on causes, laws, and effects of situations. Therefore, those who follow the *dao* are called to turn their attention toward their environment in the present, now. Being attentive to and analyzing the natural world such as the sky, earth, and water provides learning opportunities, and by being integrated into the external environment, leaders can avoid potential risks and embrace positive forces.

Being centered in the present gives leaders a flexible attitude when analyzing situations and dealing with problems. The water metaphor that is so prevalent within the text makes sense when seen from this perspective. However, to adopt this, leaders must take a counterintuitive path where they renounce strength and control, and embrace fluidity as the martial artist and movie star Bruce Lee (2016) declared:

> You must be shapeless, formless, like water. When you pour water in a cup, it becomes the cup. When you pour water in a bottle, it becomes the bottle. When you pour water in a teapot, it becomes the teapot. Water can drip and it can crash. Become like water my friend.

Lee's understanding of Taoism makes this potent connection to leadership. Here he takes the conceptual metaphor of water and incorporates it into his body. Although not original, his statement confirms our assumption that this ancient text is still relevant, especially in the exhortation for leaders to know the world and cultivate their style. Strong posturing and authoritative declamations are as antithetical to leaders who follow the *Way* as they are to and Lee's hybrid form of mixed martial arts. Therefore, by attending to the *dao*, leaders can change their character and adapt to the needs of the moment.

For example, a pugnacious person may learn to help others to achieve their dreams and, in the process, become cooperative. Or, an arrogant individual may discover what it means to be low-key and modest after observing and becoming like water. Therefore, although personality may be considered stable, fixed, and innate, Taoism proposes that inner change can occur, even in small bits, over time.

Therefore, the *Tao Te Ching* offers guidance for thinking. It is not a response to specific issues, but instead gives leaders the posture they should have when facing various problems, including the methods, inspirations, and warnings they need when putting their ideas into action. Hence, the text can give inspiration to leaders whatever their situation. It draws out potential within people and enables them to break out of predetermined constraints, particularly those passed on through leadership theories developed in other places and times. The *dao* gives freedom to leaders to express their abilities beyond the shackles and limitations of current practice. From this point of view, it realizes benign leadership by prompting development and change from the inside out.

Taoist leadership differs from contemporary theories. It does not focus on solving problems, nor does it give measure of behaviors or style; neither does it propose professional skills. It succeeds where contemporary leadership theories are weak, by encouraging people to focus on the here and now, and to analyze what is occurring in the moment.

We remain persuaded about our beginning assumption that the *Tao Te Ching* can provide a worldview to help leaders develop their thinking and character. Furthermore, we think that these ideas can be enhanced beyond innate reactions to situations based on cultural mores, if today's business leaders become more familiar with the text itself, in all its delightful complexity.

References

Amaghlobeli, G., & Celepli, M. (2012). Understanding Taoism leadership from the Western perspective. *Journal of Business, 1*(2), 47–52.

Ames, R. T., & Hall, D. L. (2004). *Dao de Jing: Making this life significant: Translation and philosophical interpretation of the Dao de Jing*. Ballantine Books.

Barbalet, J. (2014). Laozi's *Daodejing* (6th century BC). In J. Helin, T. Hernes, D. Hjorth, & R. Holt (Eds.), *The Oxford handbook of process philosophy and organisation studies* (pp. 17–31). Oxford, UK: Oxford University Press.

Heider, J. (1996). *The Tao of leadership*. Gower.

Lee, B. (2016, March 2). Be like water inspirational video. *YouTube*. Retrieved from https://www.youtube.com/watch?v=v1GpUB3OFuw

McManus, R. M., & Perruci, G. (2015). *Understanding leadership: an arts and humanities perspective*. Routledge, Taylor & Francis Group.

Pheng, L. S. (1995). Lao Tzu's Tao Te Ching and its relevance to project leadership in construction. *International Journal of Project Management, 13*(5), 295–302.

Yin, J. J. H. (2016). Chinese characters. In S. W. Chan (Eds.), *The Routledge encyclopedia of the Chinese language* (pp. 89–101). Routledge Press.

Zhang, Y., & Foo, S. F. (2012). Balanced leadership: Perspectives, principles and practices. *Chinese Management Studies, 6*(2), 245–256. https://doi.org/10.1108/17506141211236686

Zu, L. (2019). Purpose-driven leadership for sustainable business: From the perspective of Taoism. *International Journal of Corporate Social Responsibility, 4*(1), 1–31.

6 When the Dragon and Taniwha meet: Doing business with China

Ralph J. Bathurst

Global interconnectivity

China's Belt and Road Initiative (*Yí Dài Yí Lù*; 一带一路) is perhaps the most significant business development in the 21st century in its potential to impact on international trade across the entire globe. Ambitious in its reach, the Belt and Road Initiative is a signature policy of the Communist Party of China and is tied constitutionally to Xi Jinping's presidency. As businesses located in other nations consider possible partnership arrangements with their Chinese counterparts, it is timely to explore how to work with the inevitable difficulties that arise.

The concept of integrated trade routes beyond State boundaries is not new, with the ancient Old Silk Road network, developed during the Chinese Han Dynasty who ruled from about 206 BCE to 220 CE, being perhaps one of the most enduring. The Old Silk Road was more a system of networks rather than a single road, and was named after the highly prized silk fabric, which stimulated land and sea trading, from China in the East to Europe in the West.

Today's Belt and Road Initiative was first announced in 2013 as "One Belt One Road," and planned to mimic and extend its ancient counterpart, linking by road and sea, all countries on the planet in one vast trading conglomerate, embracing the African Continent, and reaching down to the South Pacific, through its island nations to its southern-most destination, Aotearoa New Zealand. In 2016, the name changed in translation to its now preferred "Belt and Road Initiative" to overcome the potential misunderstandings and misinterpretations of the word *One*, with its totalitarian overtones. Notwithstanding this adaptation, the number 1 (*Yí* 一) remains in the Chinese version.

The Belt and Road Initiative is first and foremost concerned with infrastructure development: roads and rail networks. To that end, the Chinese government with its US$40 billion Silk Road Fund administered through the Asian Infrastructure Investment Bank, by December 2015 reached agreement with 57 countries (HKTDC, 2019), which undertook to co-administer funds for local developments.

DOI: 10.4324/9781003213604-6

Infrastructure developments are but a beginning and it is anticipated that the Initiative will enable businesses across the globe to work together for the benefit of all humanity. However, a grand plan as aspirational as the Belt and Road will take considerable effort and wisdom on the part of national and business leaders, and entrepreneurs, to work with the multiple cultures represented in the countries that have signed up to the plan to date.

Despite the Initiative's ambitions, generalized plans on how businesses can cooperate in a global market, do little to help managers understand the specific values that each party brings to the partnership. In this chapter, I address this problem by narrowing the focus to the relationship between China and New Zealand's indigenous Māori people. By exploring partnership developments in this context, I aim to offer advice to managers and leaders in other jurisdictions as they seek to explore the potentials in multilateral business arrangements. I focus on core cultural issues that have the potential to animate partnerships beyond paying perfunctory attention to cultural values, to a position where they accrue social and economic benefits for all parties.

There are philosophical and practical reasons for the choice of jurisdictions. Philosophically, partnership arrangements call on all parties to protect each other's integrity, especially in valuing the differences that each brings to the arrangement. The current trends in organizations to value diversity and inclusion at local levels (Pless & Maak, 2004), where people of difference (gender, ethnicity, and religious persuasion, for example) are valued, also calls us to consider the benefits of international diversity where peoples of differing political and social persuasions come together. Indeed, the ancient Chinese word for "person" (仁) used by Confucius and recorded in the *Analects* is a compound of *ren* (人 person) and *er* (二 two). Thus, note translators Ames and Rosemont (1998), "This etymological analysis underscores the Confucian assumption that one cannot become a person by oneself – we are, from our inchoate beginnings, irreducibly social" (p. 48). This being the case, businesses are challenged first to be places of vibrant social connection, with financial considerations and profit margins coming second.

Practically, our choice is informed by several complementary issues. First, New Zealand was the first country to establish a free-trade agreement with China in 2008 (MFAT, 2018), and during the subsequent decade, leaders in both jurisdictions have learned much about how each other operates; knowledge that is now available to leaders in other countries as they too develop partnerships with Chinese firms through the Belt and Road Initiative. Second, as a small liberal democracy that values "private" enterprise, New Zealand companies have learned to cooperate with their Chinese counterparts who function in a much larger system that seeks to balance communist and capitalist ideals.

My ideas here are also underpinned by a sense of urgency, given the trade war initiated by the world's largest economy, the United States of America. This disagreement acts as a foil for this discussion in that it places cooperation in sharp relief against its damaging impacts and accompanying isolationism.

Multilateralism or trade war?

Throughout his tenure, US President Donald Trump targeted Chinese imports by imposing tariffs, a step that came with some approbation, especially among US farmers who in August 2019 showed 79% approval of Trump's stand (Breuninger & Schoen, 2019), despite a projected loss of some USD9.2 billion resulting from China's retaliatory measures in cancelling agriculture products.

In further reprisals, China devalued its renminbi to "'weaponise' its currency" (Strauss, 2019). In response, President Trump continued his stand, by imposing further tariffs that came into effect on September 1, 2019. Domestic consumers were impacted as the prices of Chinese-made children's clothes, shoes, TVs, and smart devices increased. Even before the September 1 tariffs, "J.P. Morgan had estimated that [Trump-imposed] import taxes would cost the average household roughly $1,000 a year" (Wiseman & D'innocenzio, 2019), meaning that domestic consumers would bear the brunt of President Trump's intransigence.

Certainly, job losses and a concomitant slowing down of investment, accompany trade tariffs. In a plea for softening his stance, 200 US-based footwear companies wrote an open letter to President Trump claiming: "This uncertainty the China trade war has brought to our industry is stifling U.S. growth and halting capital investment in jobs, infrastructure, technologies, and more competitive pricing for our customers" (Lobosco, 2019). Trump replied with a surprising riposte, placing blame for the economic downturn on the Federal Reserve Bank and the complaining companies themselves, tweeting:

> If the Fed would cut, we would have one of the biggest Stock Market increases in a long time. Badly run and weak companies are smartly blaming these small Tariffs instead of themselves for bad management … and who can really blame them for doing that? Excuses!
>
> (Trump, quoted in Semones, 2019).

Playing this blame game works well for leaders wanting to boost their profile among constituents at home and sympathizers abroad. According to the Trump narrative, weak companies become victims of a volatile stock market and fall prey to forces outside the country seeking control. In the case of China, rhetoric by the President and other members of his inner circle, reinforced their need to withstand malevolent powers pressing in on the nation.

Yet statements for public consumption are crafted as "good versus evil" obviate the need for understanding the rich complexities that multinational partnerships require. For example, former Secretary of State Mike Pompeo declared that the current president, Joe Biden, "'fails to understand' the 'harsh reality' of good versus evil" (Singman, 2021). In a similar yet more strident voice, former Vice President Mike Pence declared China to be an "evil empire" and "the greatest threat on the face of the Earth" (Fink, 2021). In both cases where evil is being resisted and conquered, trade wars and military campaigns become justifiable.

For countries to espouse business freedom on the one hand and then to damage those same businesses by engaging in direct confrontation appears at best to be unwise, and at worst a dereliction of political leadership. Bellicosity does not nurture long-term business partnerships, which calls for tolerance and mutual respect. Furthermore, it inhibits the ability to work through vicissitudes and conflicts as they arise.

If, then, there is to be any resolution to trade wars of this kind we must find other ways of operating that avoid ever-increasing vicious cycles of resistances and reprisals. For, this trade war impacted on nations outside the immediate orbits of these two economic super-powers; nations that had very little opportunity to demand that China and the USA cease and desist from their mutually destructive path.

To address this impasse, I offer an alternative approach by shifting the focus away from China and the USA's arm-wrestle for dominance and turn to the relationship between Chinese and New Zealand companies, particularly firms which are led by indigenous Māori people. Insights from these contexts, I argue, can be generalized to wider jurisdictions, and may help address deadlocks that impair global trade.

Chinese–New Zealand partnerships have been characterized by the Dragon–Taniwha rubric. The *Dragon*, the mythological figure which features in traditional Chinese art, and according to Jullien (1995), represents the life and vitality with which Chinese people identify. The *Taniwha* is also mythological with Polynesian roots and is considered by New Zealand's indigenous people, Māori, to have a guardianship (*kaitiaki*) function. It is said to dwell in deep waters and may become menacing if sacred (*tapu*) places are violated.

Acknowledging these mythological symbols is important because they articulate what is at stake with the Belt and Road's global expansion. The two figures help identify the potential for life-full engagement across cultural and State boundaries, while warning of perils ahead, if the dignity of either party is infracted. The Dragon and Taniwha represent, therefore, the cultural forces at work behind business partnerships, and by exploring localized arrangements, leaders across the globe may be better equipped to realize the potential benefits for all parties when embracing the Chinese Belt and Road Initiative.

By drilling down into specifics, we are better able to get past purely instrumental economic drivers, to then examine the cultural values that enable business synergies to develop. Thus, I turn our attention to a 2017 meeting between a group of New Zealand indigenous entrepreneurs and Chinese corporate leaders. In this chapter, "going small" enables an examination at a micro level by exploring the core cultural values at work, and to then generalize those out to larger contexts. I identify several crucial elements the facilitate partnerships including understanding historical antecedents, a willingness to learn from each other, and finally, developing a poly-dexterity that takes account for paradox and ambiguity in business partnerships.

A brief history of cultural relationships

New Zealand is an island nation yet despite its small population size which occupies a total land area of only some 268,021 km^2 (compared to the USA's 9.834 million km^2 and China's 9.597 million km^2), it has one of the world's largest exporters of dairy products; and given its coast line that pushes out to a 200 mile exclusive economic zone, it has 4,083,744 km^2 fifteen times its land area, under its jurisdiction, making fishing a significant economic driver for the nation.

Because the primary production sector dominates the New Zealand economy, it has become a target for Chinese investors keen to secure access to guaranteed food supplies. These Chinese interests are not motivated just for financial return, but also for reasons of food security, and New Zealand with its high-quality produce, is an apt "breadbasket" to complement Chinese dietary needs.

However, the history of relationships among Chinese and European migrants, and local indigenous Māori in New Zealand is replete with tensions and paradoxes. As with other Pacific Rim nations, including Canada and the USA, evidence of the presence of ethnic Chinese is in concert with European migrations in the first half of the 19th century, prompted in part by the discovery of gold. In New Zealand although these first Chinese migrants suffered discrimination from European colonizers, the relationships between Māori and Chinese were on the whole cordial, as scholars from both communities testify (Ip, 2009; Mutu, 2009).

Asian studies Professor Manying Ip (2009, p. 2) notes that Māori–Chinese relationships were mostly "symbiotic" (compared with relationships with European settlers that were more combative), and Margaret Mutu (2009) Professor of Māori Studies, writes of the warmth in her associations with Chinese New Zealanders, and of her discovery of "Austronesian indigenous communities in Southern Taiwan" (p. vii). Mutu also declared that the affinities between Māori and Chinese people in New Zealand were reinforced by becoming "natural allies … Not only do we have shared cultural values and practices, we have similarities in our histories of contact with the British as a colonial power" (p. vii). However, this was more than just the friend of my enemy is my friend, but also a reflection of their shared cultures.

In New Zealand, these early synergies between Chinese migrants and local Māori were contrasted with ambivalences between these same Chinese and European settlers. What, though, accounts for the equivocal relationship between the growing European population and Chinese? Notwithstanding the sense of solidarity that developed between Māori and Chinese as a defensive measure against the European settlers, there was also deep philosophical divide between the two northern hemisphere groups of newcomers.

The European settlers brought with them worlds views informed by Judeo-Christian ethical systems and Greek philosophical inquiry; while the Chinese came with belief systems grounded in Confucian "secular" ideologies which had little affinity with the religious/theological ideals of the Europeans. Not only did the European settlers fail to understand Chinese values, they also brought with them a sense of superiority that perceived others as inferior to their social and cultural norms. People of difference (Māori and Chinese) were therefore in need of conversion to European ways, before taking their place at the table of commerce as equals. Or, as Eric Nelson puts it:

> The comparative or intercultural pursuit might only yield a mixing of incompatible categories and violate the uniqueness of each perspective it addresses, whereas globalism and cosmopolitanism might demand the exclusion of nonuniversalizable claims diverging from modern Western rationality.
>
> (Nelson, 2009, p. 177)

Therefore, while contemporary trade wars may be carried out in the name of pursuing national sovereignty, they also cover for a deeper, more lasting sense of mistrust of peoples representing divergent political, business, and social systems. This inherent suspicion can be addressed, however, and current attempts by Māori and Chinese business leaders to bridge ideological gaps are exemplary.

A Dragon Taniwha meeting

In February 2017, the inaugural "Dragon Taniwha" conference was held, hosted by the Hawke's Bay iwi (tribe) Ngati Kahungunu, and some 50 representatives of large Chinese companies. The name of the conference represented at its most basic level the coming together of people from two different cultural backgrounds for the benefit of both.

The February 2017 conference was characterized as "a meeting of cultures and a meeting of minds" (NZH, 2017) with attendees from Alibaba (the world's largest retailer), Lei Garden (which operates 24 Michelin-star restaurants around China), and Shanghai Cred (Chinese property investment company which in 2017 bought Australia's largest private landholding for almost $400 million).

The New Zealand-based conference organizer, former All Blacks (New Zealand's most popular sport and Rugby World Cup winning team) captain Taine Randell, said that the conference came on the back of significant time and energy being put into building relationships with potential Chinese partners. Following his career as a professional sportsman, Randell spent some time in London as a commodity trader, and then returned to his New Zealand home in 2008 to take on a role as a "director of the Kahungunu Asset Holding Company, which manages the business interests of Ngati Kahungunu, New Zealand's third largest iwi" (NZH, 2016).

The Kahungunu Asset Holding Company owns shares in the Fiordland Lobster Company and sells lobster directly to restaurants in Shanghai, where diners pay NZ$250 per kg as the "plated price" (NZH, 2016) for a taste of the delicacy. There is an even higher return on lobster over the Chinese New Year period.

During the February 2017 conference, John O'Loghlen, the Alibaba Group director ofbusiness development Australia and New Zealand, said that the Māori story and its links with Chinese culture was something many businesses "would die to have" (O'Sullivan, 2017). The desire for Chinese business representatives to find affinities within Māoridom was also reflected by Shanghai Pengxin president of investment Terry Lee, who said that there was a natural affinity between Māori and Chinese, because of a common ancestry. Lee noted that Te Reo Māori (the Māori language) was more accessible than the English language, "Maybe … because we are relatives" (NZH, 2017). However, assumptions of a common genetic history are probably overstated given that the anthropological evidence suggests that the Chinese connections are through the indigenous people of Taiwan, who number only about 500,000 people (Dudding, 2015).

A more accurate assessment came from Justin Wong, the Executive Director Lei Garden, when he placed cultural values at the heart of their desire for partnerships with Māori; values which draw on similarities of trust, the centrality of the family, and a sustainability focus. "Where ever we do business we look for building a long-term partnership. It is not transactional" (NZH, 2017) Wong said of his desire that the two peoples explore their commonalities.

The ability to look beyond transactional arrangements is not one-way. Māori leaders at the February 2017 Dragon Taniwha summit expressed confidence in Chinese leaders because of their cultural sensitivities. Professor Margaret Mutu, a keen advocate for Māori resurgence and for holding the New Zealand Government to its responsibilities under the Treaty of Waitangi, declared confidence in Shanghai Cred and the sensitive ways it had worked with the people of her region, Ngāti Kahu in particular. She recounted to the summit attendees that a banker from the USA, after purchasing a Northland property, had violated the *tapu* (sacred restrictions) of the area. Mutu said that "our people paid the price," and the Taniwha was aroused, only to be assuaged when Shanghai Cred stepped in and purchased the property in 2013 for NZ$29 million. She further said that Shanghai Cred was "a pleasure to work with" because of their sensitivities to shared culture and values. Mutu's assessment was that "Shanghai Cred took over the resort and in our first meeting they agreed to protect all our waahi tapu (sacred places). That's all we were looking for" (O'Sullivan, 2017). For Mutu, attention to cultural values and sensitivity to locale, are of primary importance when making business decisions that impact on local people.

In sum, the February 2017 Dragon Taniwha Summit highlighted that productive partnerships can develop and be sustained between small localized tribes in places like the South Pacific, and businesses from a large country that has a global reach through its Belt and Road Initiative. There was a sense of goodwill and perhaps mutual back-patting demonstrated at the Dragon Taniwha Summit with commentary generated from the talkfest using the language and niceties of diplomatic engagement. Beyond these general affirmations of goodwill, however, what issues might businesses across the globe attend to, that would help them work with Chinese companies? Business leaders can do serious damage when operating in cultures outside of their own experiences and expertise, by trampling on local customs and mores. Therefore, it is important for businesses to attend to core competencies in order that the deleterious effects of colonization and the inappropriate behaviors of investors from one country seeking a foothold in another, may be avoided.

Lessons from the Dragon Taniwha relationship

There are several issues that arise out of my working with Chinese leaders in New Zealand. Exploring the long-standing Free Trade Agreement between China and New Zealand prompted my research, especially examining how partnerships are developed and sustained over time. I was interested in exploring beyond immediate instrumental concerns towards the ground from which business partnerships might develop. It soon became apparent that poly-dexterity was at work as leaders dealt with the many paradoxes and ambiguities of their parentships. Indeed, these constructs helped identify both continuities and discontinuities between Māori and Chinese people,

Business partnerships between firms that cross national boundaries can go terribly wrong, with investors standing to lose substantial sums of money because of inadequate cultural preparation. The ideas that I explore in what follows, penetrate beyond the cursory and overly optimistic summary of holding common values. Shared histories and similar ideologies do not necessarily tend toward sustainable business partnerships. What is required is an acute awareness of and desire to know the world of the partner and to encounter them as an equal.

Cultural antecedents

There is some evidence that Māori and the indigenous people of Taiwan share a common ancestry. Some genetic markers in traditional Taiwanese people, that are also found in the Māori population, are not observed in

Han Chinese (Lin et al., 2000); and both indigenous Taiwanese and Māori people have held a common practice of decorating the body and face with tattoo (Johnson et al., 2009), but neither of these phenomena guarantee successful business partnerships.

However, there are cultural commonalities between Chinese and Māori people, and these can be observed in the Māori welcome ceremony, the *pōwhiri*. Visitors (*manuhiri*) to a local *marae* (meeting grounds) are afforded an official welcome by the local people (*tangata whenua*), whether they be indigenous Māori from another area, tourists, or people on official business. The newcomers wait outside the marae's boundaries until they are called in by a chant (*karanga*) sung by a woman. A representative of the visiting group responds with their chant which carries on until the newcomers are all inside the meeting house (*wharenui*). Once inside, with the tangata whenua on one side facing the manuhiri on the other, speeches of welcome are given. Each speech concludes with a song (*waiata*), and once the tangata whenua have concluded, the manuhiri respond with speeches and song.

This part of the ceremony concludes with the manuhiri offering a gift (*koha*), which is placed on the ground. One member from the tangata whenua picks up the gift and this signals the end of the speeches and songs. Once the gift has been given and received, each visitor is acknowledged by the tangata whenua through making physical contact by pressing noses (*hongi*) or kissing cheeks. This final act lifts the ceremonial tapu in place, and immediately following this, visitors are ushered into a dining room area where they have food and drink, thus returning everyone to the natural world (*noa*).

The interplay between tapu and noa are important because they help participants acknowledge that the business world is more than just a series of economic transactions. When people from various backgrounds come together, there must be something other than a quest for reciprocal give-and-take. The pōwhiri ceremony brings people together in emotional and physical ways that a normal business negotiation and transaction can never replicate. It is impossible to participate in a pōwhiri and not be moved at a deep, visceral level. It is a highly-charged and dignified way of bringing people of difference together.

The attention to ceremony through speeches and musicmaking resonates with Confucian ideas that have underpinned Chinese culture for several thousands of years. Confucius was a politician-philosopher who lived 551–479 BCE. Confucianism underpins Sinitic cultures, including China, Korea, Japan, and many parts of Southeast Asia. Although sometimes Confucianism is held as a religious code, it is non-theistic and deals more with human behaviors at both the family and State levels.

In 20th-Century Maoist China, Confucianism was rejected because of the nation's secularizing agenda. However, it has made a comeback in recent years because of the idea of filial piety. Respect for parents, elders, and deceased ancestors is a fundamental Confucian tenet, and Chinese leaders have used that core ideology to promote loyalty to the State, mediated by the story of the heroic People's Liberation Army soldier Lei Feng (Roberts, 2014). However, to use Confucius and his writings to boost contemporary State power is a corruption, if not misreading of his ideas.

Confucius valued ceremonial ritual and music making, the same two elements that underpin the pōwhiri in Māori rituals. Thus, *li* (禮 carrying out rituals) and *yue* (樂 making music) were crucial to a well-functioning society, and these were qualities, claim Bathurst and Chen (2018), were valued more by Confucius than managing the affairs of State, or maintaining a functioning bureaucracy

For Confucius, observing li was fundamental to exercising leadership at both family and State levels, and that rulers need to be "governed by observing ritual propriety and custom (*li*) rather than by law and force" (Ames & Rosemont, 1998, p. 3). Therefore, by attending to proper behavior in formal settings, leaders would create a context where creative dialogue could occur.

Young people were instructed in ritual observances from early childhood, and as they learned the social rules, and practiced them, the rules became less of a straitjacket until they were embodied and natural. Lai (2006) notes that observing li enabled trust to grow, because morality was judged by outward behaviors, and not on an individual's verbal claims to trustworthiness.

The complementary element to *li* is *yue*, music making. Finding the right strategy, path, or direction, known to the Chinese as the "way" (*dào*) was crucial for social solidarity. The Confucian scholar Tzu Hsün, also known as Xunzi, (c. 310 BCE–c. 220 BCE) believed that when people made music together, they bonded with each other and would overcome the negative effects of self-interest and competition. He wrote that "the former Kings who hated disorder, and therefore they created the musical forms of the odes and hymns in order to guide [behaviour towards the Way]" (Tzu, 3rd C BCE/1969, p. 112). Making music together built social solidarity and harmony.

Observing ritual and making music were designed to place limits on human behaviors, and thereby ensured the smooth running of the State. Thus, says Kim (2011):

> In his [Xunzi's] view, the anarchic state of his time arose from human nature which is self-interested and passion driven, and this amoral state had to be rectified artificially by means of the Kingly Way consisting of 'Ritual (*li* 禮), Music (*yue* 樂), Penal Codes (*xing* 刑), and Royal Ordinances (*zheng* 政)' (p. 375).

These cultural antecedents are important for us to recognize in a 21st Century world of hardnosed business negotiations. Attention to ritual and music making that underpin both traditional Māori and Chinese cultures are a precursor to sustainable business partnerships.

Curiosity

Learning another's cultural symbols and rituals, and then feeling comfortable to take part in them, requires an ability to go beyond self-absorbed reticence and to develop a curious attitude. One Māori leader I interviewed (Arapeta, a pseudonym) talked of his relationship with his Chinese business partner. They have been working together for several decades, importing and exporting products between countries.

Arapeta expressed his insatiable curiosity to know and understand Chinese cultural values, and of his willingness to be known. His company hires local Chinese to staff the administration office and hosts Chinese travellers seeking to imbibe the Māori culture. Tikanga (social norms) expectations mean that visitors are welcomed with a pōwhiri, explored above, is a routine practice for Māori communities but exceptional for visitors. The sense of welcome and inclusion that the pōwhiri brings in its wake, invites inquisitiveness, a willingness to step out of the comfortable and known, into a new world rich in cultural expressions.

This willingness to be known also flips to its obverse, a desire to know. Arapeta spoke of his fascination with Chinese cultural values and his desire to understand them beyond a cursory knowledge. To that end he spent several months living in Qufu, an ancient city in China's west.

Qufu, is located 130 km south of the Shandong Province's capital, Jinan. The city was founded in 11th-century BCE and is the spiritual and cultural center of Confucianism. As the hometown of Confucius, it has much of historical and cultural significance with its there are three main Confucian tourist sites (*san Kǒng* 三孔), including the Temple (*Kǒngmiào* 孔廟), Cemetery (*Kǒnglín* 孔林), and Family Mansion (*Kǒngfǔ* 孔府).

It was not so much that he gained knowledge of Confucianism, rather, Arapeta described the deep spiritual connections he felt with the place itself, the land. It was the Cemetery of Confucius that made the most profound impact on him. He spoke of the sense of connection he had with the Chinese people, both with his friends and business partners, and the spirits of the deceased. For Arapeta the living and the dead are present to him.

Curiosity about and knowledge of the physical and metaphysical are fundamental to *te ao Māori* (the Māori worldview) because cultural expressions are located in time and place, and in the presence of tupuna (ancestors). A person's *turangawaewae* (home base, literally "a place to stand") is core to identity. Therefore, the *wharenui* (the central meeting house on a marae and the focal point of Māori life) is significant in providing a place for people to dialogue and to recollect stories of the past through the exterior and interior carvings, and woven flax panels on the interior. For, according to Best (2016) the physical and spiritual worlds are contiguous.

Arapeta visiting Qufu and spending time at the Confucian sites enabled him to know is Chinese business partners beyond instrumental, transactional concerns. The thin separation of the physical and spiritual, the worlds of the living and ever-present deceased, are a normal part of Arapeta's life, so finding resonances with the living and dead in Qufu was an outcome of his desire to know and experience Chinese life in its totality.

This, then, is the value of curiosity because it helps move us beyond attending perfunctory meetings towards a deep understanding of the other's life-world. Symbols, historical artefacts, texts, ancient buildings, language, and cultural anecdotes form the warp and weft of the fabric from which business partnerships are woven. Commercial success comes from paying attention to these elements and becoming curious about them. This is necessary for both parties if they are going to survive the inevitable conflicts which will arise and achieve longevity in their partnership.

Poly-dexterity

Earlier I discussed Professor Margaret Mutu's experience of a US investor stepping on cultural sensitivities in the Northland region of New Zealand. She noted that Shanghai Cred understood the importance of waahi tapu; that some places are sacred which have spiritual and mythological importance. To ignore the sacredness of a piece of land by excavating and then erecting buildings on it is sacrilegious and offensive. To tread on waahi tapu is as abusive as physical violence on another person because the land is the source of life. Land is *Papatūānuku*, the mother who nurtures and sustains all life.

To protect the integrity and vitality of a place while doing business requires a fleet-of-foot often seen is professional football players who are equally comfortable kicking with the right and left boots. Such agility enables leaders to play in different positions while holding multiple perspectives.

Ambidexterity, the precursor to poly-dexterity as I describe it here, entered the business lexicon through Duncan (1976) in his proposal that it is necessary for leaders to attend to several different elements at the same time. March (1991) extended this approach by studying the two competing elements of exploration and exploitation. He notes that exploitation refers to "refinement, efficiency, selection and implementation" and exploration refers to "search, variation, experimentation and innovation" (p. 71). In other words, exploitation draws on existing knowledge in well-understood ways, while exploration opens the possibility for new and creative ideas to emerge. Although the two may be conflicting, leaders sensitized to the potential contributions of both can work on multiple planes to achieve success.

The environment in which Māori leaders operate in their home country is complex. Businesses are founded and developed within a liberal, sometimes neo-colonial context where dominant business rationalities spring from North America and Europe. The indigenous ethos is often at odds with this capitalist focus where their economic drivers are more communitarian and participatory. Thus, the situation is both individualistic and collective; they draw on ancient values and forms of knowledge while innovating in an environment now driven by digital technologies.

Contemporary Māori business leaders, therefore, go beyond the exploitation-exploration binary, exemplifying a poly-dexterity that attends to multiple, sometimes paradoxical, elements to fulfil their work. This 21st-century leader is like a Taniwha with many eyes and limbs guarding traditional knowledge while seeking new and creative forms of engagement.

In the same way, Chinese partners, inspired by the Dragon of this age, are of the same kind, called to operate in multiple worlds with differing legal, political, and cultural frameworks. Its eyes, ears, and limbs must attend to multiple interests without being consumed by a singular instrumental focus where economic return is the sole arbiter of partnerships.

Sustaining connections

My foray into Māori and Chinese business partnerships and the leadership insights from this study circles back to where I began this discussion, with the Belt and Road Initiative and the influence of the trade war between the USA and China under the tutelage of then President Donald Trump, which offered a foil to this exploration. The Taniwha-Dragon rubric uncovers viable alternatives to politicians' bellicosity.

Sadly, international divisions have become even more entrenched due to Russia's invasion of Ukraine on February 24, 2022. Business partnerships that have developed over time and have been tempered through agreement and disagreement, conflict, and resolution, will be tested as supply chains contract and loyalties are questioned.

The discussion I have offered here of lessons characterized by the Taniwha-Dragon may offer guidance to businesses seeking to operate in this more constrained environment across the globe. Understanding cultures and nurturing curiosity about each other will help rebuild the world following this current and future crises. But it will take leadership of another kind, leadership that follows different paths from the traditions that encourage strength and determination that then develop into intransigent isolation. The Chinese Ambassador to the USA in 2019 declared a similar position in his advocacy for living partnerships facilitated by the Belt and Road Initiative.

> Traditional Chinese wisdom states that a man of virtue will seek to establish others while establishing himself. In this sense, as we are currently moving China's economy from a phase of rapid growth to a stage of high-quality development, we also pursue quality development in BRI [Belt and Road Initiative] cooperation. The projects are designed to conform with international laws and norms governing international relations and meet international business practices and operating models.
>
> (Cui, 2019)

Several ideas are salient in this statement. First, by considering how to support partners and seeking their benefit is fundamental to ensuring a future of cooperation and prosperity. Second, adhering international customs and rules of business conduct helps give confidence that all parties are operating in good faith. The life-full relations between Māori and Chinese business leaders will show the way to a future where all can participate and benefit.

References

Ames, R. T., & Rosemont, H. (1998). *The analects of confucius: A philosophical translation*. Ballantine Books.

Bathurst, R. J., & Chen, M. S. (2018). A smile and a sigh: Leadership insights from the East. In C. Neesham & S. Segal (Eds.), *Handbook of philosophy of management* (pp. 1–18). Springer. 10.1007/978-3-319-48352-8_21-1

Best, E. (2016). *Spiritual concepts of the Māori*. New Zealand Electronic Text Collection. Retrieved January 13 from http://nzetc.victoria.ac.nz/tm/scholarly/tei-BesMaor-c4-3.html

Breuninger, K., & Schoen, J. W. (2019, August 7). *US-China trade war is hurting farmers, but they're sticking with Trump*. Retrieved August 9 from https://www.cnbc.com/2019/08/07/us-china-trade-war-is-hurting-farmers-but-theyre-sticking-with-trump.html

Cui, T. (2019, April 23). *Why the U.S. shouldn't sit out the belt and road initiative*. Retrieved May 6 from http://fortune.com/2019/04/23/us-china-belt-and-road-initiative/

Dudding, A. (2015, March 15). *New Zealand's long-lost Taiwanese cuzzies*. Retrieved May 6 from https://www.stuff.co.nz/travel/destinations/asia/67390585/null

Duncan, R. B. (1976). The ambidextrous organization: Designing dual structures for innovation. In R. H. Kilman, L. R. Pondy, & D. P. Slevin (Eds.), *The management of organizational design* (pp. 167–188). North Holland (It is an imprint of Elsevier).

Fink, J. (2021, 14 July). *Mike pence says China seizing on Biden admin 'weakness' to become 'evil empire'*. Retrieved November 3 from https://www.newsweek.com/mike-pence-says-china-seizing-biden-admin-weakness-become-evil-empire-1609794

HKTDC. (2019). *What is Belt and Road Initiative?* Retrieved May 6 from https://web.archive.org/web/20170203222847/http://beltandroad.hktdc.com/en/about the-belt-and-road-initiative/about-the-belt-and-road-initiative.aspx

Ip, M. (2009). Introduction. In M. Ip (Ed.), *The Dragon & the Taniwha: Māori & Chinese in New Zealand* (pp. 1–9). University of Auckland.

Johnson, D., Tseng, Y.-J., & Her, J.-H. (2009). The tradition of facial tattoo in Taiwan: The case of the Truku people. *He Puna Korero: Journal of Māori & Pacific Development, 10*(1), 3–16.

Jullien, F. (1995). *The propensity of things: Toward a history of efficacy in China* (J. Lloyd, Trans.). Zone Books.

Kim, S. (2011). Confucian constitutionalism: Mencius and Xunzi on virtue, ritual, and royal transmission. *Review of Politics, 73*, 371–399. 10.1017/S003467051100341X

Lai, K. (2006). Li in the Analects: Training in moral competence and the question of flexibility. *Project Muse, 56*(1), 69–83. 10.1353/pew.2006.0001

Lin, M., Chu, C. C., Lee, H. L., Chang, S. L., Ohashi, J., Tokunaga, K., Akaza, T., & Juji, T. (2000). Heterogeneity of Taiwan's indigenous population: Possible relation to prehistoric Mongoloid dispersals. *Tissue Antigens, 55*(1), 1–9. 0.1034/j.1399-0039.2000.550101.x

Lobosco, K. (2019, August 29). *This one business shows exactly how Trump's China tariffs are hurting the economy*. Retrieved 4 September from https://edition.cnn.com/2019/08/29/politics/tariffs-trump-economy-business-uncertainty/

March, J. G. (1991). Exploration and exploitation in organizational learning. *Organization Science, 2*(1), 71–87.

MFAT. (2018, June 30). *New Zealand-China FTA overview*. Retrieved May 6 from https://www.mfat.govt.nz/en/trade/free-trade-agreements/free-trade-agreements-in-force/china-fta/nz-china-fta-overview/

Mutu, M. (2009). Foreword. In M. Ip (Ed.), *The Dragon & the Taniwha: Māori & Chinese in New Zealand* (pp. vii–viii). Auckland University Press.

Nelson, E. S. (2009). Levinas and early Confucian ethics: Religion, rituality, and the sources of morality. *Levinas Studies, 4*, 177–207. 10.5840/levinas2009411

NZH. (2016, April 8). *Captain and the crayfish: Former All Black Taine Randell chases big money in China*. Retrieved April 24 from https://www.nzherald.co.nz/index.cfm?objectid=11618598&ref=twitter

NZH. (2017, February 22). *Future dividends for Taniwha and Dragon*. Retrieved April 16 from https://www.nzherald.co.nz/business/news/article.cfm?c_id=3&objectid=11804928

O'Sullivan, P. (2017, February 25). *Benefits of befriending the dragon*. Retrieved May 6 from https://www.nzherald.co.nz/the-country/news/article.cfm?c_id=16&objectid=11807082

Pless, N. M., & Maak, T. (2004). Building an inclusive diversity culture: Principles, processes and practice. *Journal of Business Ethics, 54*(2), 129–147.

Roberts, R. (2014). The Confucian moral foundations of socialist model man: Lei Feng and the twenty four exemplars of filial behaviour. *New Zealand Journal of Asian Studies, 16*(1), 23–38.

Semones, E. (2019, August 30). *Trump blames companies impacted by his trade war*. Retrieved September 4 from https://www.politico.com/story/2019/08/30/donald-trump-china-trade-war-1479012

Singman, B. (2021, 15 October). *Pompeo says world is 'very concerned' America is 'leaving the international stage' under Biden foreign policy*. Retrieved November 3 from https://www.foxnews.com/politics/pompeo-world-concerned-america-leaving-international-stage-biden

Strauss, D. (2019, August 7). *China's economy faces currency devaluation drag*. Retrieved August 9 from https://www.ft.com/content/fb97c5fa-b853-11e9–96bd-8e884d3ea203

Tzu, H. (3rd C BCE/1969). *Hsün Tzu: Basic writings* (B. Watson, Trans.). Columbia University Press.

Wiseman, P., & D'innocenzio, A. (2019, September 1). *'They're on,' Trump says of tariffs set to kick in on Sunday*. Retrieved September 4 from https://apnews.com/758dbf03f541481db7982cfa8de43064

7 Confucian leadership in the age of Xi Jinping

Simon Burgess

Introduction

The Chinese Communist Party's official storyline suggests that Xi Jinping is a beacon of hope, and that his leadership is restoring national pride (Nikkei Asia, 2021). But his critics point to widespread repression, allege that he has not genuinely addressed the problems of corruption, and describe his leadership as being reminiscent of Stalin's (Pei, 2017). While bearing these divergent perspectives in mind, my aim in this chapter is to consider what a Confucian style of leadership might look like in today's China. I also seek to suggest ways in which to approach some of the challenges faced by contemporary business leaders in China.

Confucius as a liberal

Confucius (551–479 BCE) was not a leadership scholar of the kind that contributes to mainstream business journals like the *Harvard Business Review*. The study of his work does not yield any specific insights into the importance of being authentic, the development of trust, or the communication of shared goals, for example. Yet there is, I suggest, a liberal outlook inherent in his way of thinking, much of which remains pertinent to 21st-century leaders.

With good reason, some scholars may be inclined to trace the philosophical basis for liberalism in China back to the poetic mysticism of Lao Tzu:

> The world is won by refraining.
> How do I know this is so?

By this:

> As taboos increase, people grow poorer;
> When weapons abound, the state grows chaotic;
> Where skills multiply, novelties flourish;
> As statutes increase, more criminals start.

DOI: 10.4324/9781003213604-7

So the Wise Man will say:

> As I refrain, the people will reform;
> Since I like quiet, they will keep order;
> When I forebear, the people will prosper;
> When I want nothing, they will be honest.
> (Lao Tzu, 600 BCE/1962, p. 110)

As a statement of liberal conviction and the wisdom of leaving the people alone, Lao Tzu's words are clear. If we are seeking insights of relevance to liberalism, leadership, and the needs of China today; however, the works of Confucius are much more detailed. Moreover, President Xi Jinping has often emphasized the abiding relevance of Confucius (China Daily, 2018; Gardels, 2014). In November 2013, he sought to "send a signal that we must vigorously promote China's traditional culture" (Buckley, 2014), and he did so by visiting Qufu in Shandong Province, Confucius's hometown.

Drawing upon Confucius, there are three basic leadership ideas that I explore here, namely, that leadership is accountable, responsible, and decentralized. I do not suggest that these ideas are unique to Confucianism, but, rather, that they are ideas for which Confucius, among others, shows respect. Each of them is apt to meet with support both in China and the West; in my efforts to articulate them in greater detail, I draw upon a range of Confucian and Western sources.

Accountability

In business, the need for leadership accountability is obvious. We expect to see it, for example, in regular meetings, performance reviews, audits, and annual reports, practices that are familiar to organizational leaders around the world. Developing and maintaining a culture of leadership accountability requires consistent attention and effort. And so, the advice of someone like Patrick Lencioni (2012), for example, a consultant who specializes in such challenges, may always be in demand. But in broad terms, expectations about leadership accountability in the world of business do not appear to differ greatly between China and the West.

Regarding accountability for political leaders, however, there are stark differences between contemporary China and the West. In the West, political leaders are kept accountable through the institutions of constitutional democracy, the legality of oppositional political parties, regular elections, the rule of law, a free press, and the recognized legitimacy of religious institutions, professional associations, lobby groups, and other freely formed civil associations. By contrast, the Communist Party of China has rejected many such forms of accountability. The rule of law, such as it is, remains firmly subordinate to the Party's "centralized and unified leadership" (China Daily, 2021). Moreover, the Party has sought to delegitimize constitutional democracy, universal values, civil society, and freedom of the press by casting them as mere "Western" notions (Chinese Communist Party, 2013).

Although the Communist Party of China's stance is clear, Confucius was insistent that political leaders need to be accountable to others. For example, when Zhong You asked him how to serve a prince, Confucius's response was simply to say: "Tell him the truth even it if offends him" (Confucius, 1997, 14.22, p. 70). When asked whether there is "one single maxim that could ruin a country," Confucius replied:

> Mere words could not achieve this. There is this saying, however: 'The only pleasure of being a prince is never having to suffer contradiction.' If you are right and no one contradicts you, that's fine; but if you are wrong and no one contradicts you – is this not almost a case of 'one single maxim that could ruin a country?'
>
> (Confucius, 1997, 13.15, pp. 62–63)

Such thoughts express what translator and commentator, Simon Leys, described as:

> one of the noblest and most heroic aspects of Confucianism: its tradition of bold speech, political criticism, and moral disobedience. It was a duty for statesmen and scholars to stand up to the ruler, even at the risk of their lives, whenever higher principles commanded them to do so.
>
> (Leys, in Confucius, 1997, p. 136)

Responsibility

In essence, responsibility involves an acceptance, by leaders, that success or failure rests with them. As explained by former military commander and Secretary of State for the United States of America, Colin Powell, "Real leaders take that responsibility, willingly and unquestionably." And while "Failures are their own, successes belong to their colleagues" (Harari, 2002, p. 98). By contrast, those who shirk responsibility for their failures prefer to make excuses, blame others, shoot messengers, identify scapegoats, or diabolize those who are more successful.

Confucius had no trouble recognizing such tendencies, and it can be interesting to think about what his perspective would be on the way in which the Communist Party of China's leaders have handled affairs in Tibet, Taiwan, Hong Kong, and Xinjiang. Consider, for example, his reflections in the *Analects* on Ji Kangzi's contemplation of an attack on Zhuanyu, an autonomous domain within the larger state of Lu. Lord Ji sends Ran Qui and Zilu to Confucius to consult his opinion, and the resulting exchange between the men is compelling for several reasons. Confucius forces Ran Qui to think about whether he is fulfilling his responsibilities as a minister, and whether he should have resigned. He then also raises questions about Lord Ji's motivation and candour, suggesting that the problems that Lord Ji needs to confront are not caused by Zhuanyu, but instead by his own inept rule. As Confucius explains:

> If there is equality, there will be no poverty, and where there is peace, there is no lack of population. And then, if people who live in far-off lands still resist your attraction, you must draw them to you by the moral power of civilization; and then, having attracted them, make them enjoy your peace. But now, with you two as his ministers, your master is incapable of attracting people from far away, his land is racked with divisions and unrest, he cannot hold it together any longer – and yet he wants to wage war against one of his own provinces! For Lord Ji, I am afraid, the real menace does not come from Zhuanyu, it lies within the walls of his own palace.
>
> (Confucius, 1997, 16.1, p. 81)

Such passages remind us of the Confucian expectation that leaders take responsibility for their errors and learn from them, rather than try to deny them and to overcome opposition through sheer force.

None of this is to suggest that Confucius was a proto-democrat. He saw little reason to welcome the civic engagement of ordinary people: "He who holds no official position discusses no official policies" (Confucius, 1997, 14.26, p. 70).[1] Nor did he anticipate the conventions of modern cabinet government: "Do not discuss the policies of an office that is not yours" (Confucius, 1997, 8.14, p. 37). But Confucius did appreciate that ordinary people can vote with their feet (see, for example: Confucius, 1997, 13.4, p. 61; 13.16, p. 63). As neatly summarized by Leys: "the virtue and political wisdom of a prince could be measured by the number of subjects he managed to attract and retain on his lands" (Confucius, 1997, p. 182). So, from a Confucian perspective, there is good reason to think that the democratic administration of Hong Kong is one that the Communist Party of China ought to respect.

Decentralization

The idea that leadership can be decentralized is liberal in character and consonant with Lao Tzu's thinking. In the West, thinkers such as de Tocqueville (1981), von Hayek (1967), and Nisbet (2010) are prominent among those whose work could be drawn upon for elaboration.

Implicit in this idea is a vision of a thriving and diverse society in which there are innumerable businesses and civil associations, each of which may be established and led independently. The idea also carries with it certain suggestions about managing work within a business. It suggests, for example, that as human beings we are most likely to be productive, innovative, engaged, and fulfilled when we are not stifled by bureaucratic procedures or "micromanaging" supervisors, and are able to resolve most of our work-related problems for ourselves.

The appeal that decentralization has is further nourished by a conviction about the ways in which knowledge, wisdom, experience, and skills are developed and shared in society. That conviction, simply put, is that such things are widely distributed; there is no central repository for them, and there is no family, political party, university, or corporation who can claim to be their progenitor or exclusive guardian. It stands to reason, then, that if our sources of knowledge, wisdom, experience, and skills are so widely dispersed, we have little choice but to accept that leadership, along with all the authority, decision-making power, and responsibility that it carries, needs to be decentralized.

A plain and undisputed fact about Xi Jinping's leadership of the Communist Party of China is that he has been interested in neither liberalization nor decentralization. Quite to contrary, he places great faith in the idea that the leadership of China, as represented by the Party and his own role within it, should be centralized.

During Xi's time at the helm, the Communist Party of China has stressed the need for "Unwavering adherence to the principle of the Party's control of media" (Chinese Communist Party, 2013), and Xi has instructed the various state-run media organizations (such as China Central Television, Xinhua News Agency, and the *People's Daily*) to "love the party, protect the party, and closely align themselves with the party leadership in thought, politics and action" (Phillips, 2016). The scholar Zhang Lifan thus observed: "They are not journalists anymore. They are the party's mouthpiece. They wait on the party" (Phillips, 2016).

In 2017, both "Xi Jinping Thought" and the leadership of "Comrade Xi Jinping" were written into the Constitution of the Party (Chinese Communist Party, 2017). More recently, it was announced that "Xi Jinping Thought" will be taught in schools as part of the national curriculum (BBC, 2021).

Increasingly, the ideology of the Party has been making its presence felt within what were once thought of as private companies. Even major foreign companies such as L'Oréal, Disney, and Dow Chemicals have Party committees or "cells" embedded in them (McGregor, 2019). At Disney, for example, the staff members who belong to the Party are said to "adorn their work sites with hammer-and-sickle insignia and spend several hours a week attending lectures and study sessions in the park's 'party activity center'" (Bayles, 2017). In the words of Samantha Hoffman, a senior analyst at the Australian Strategic Policy Institute, those Party committees remind the companies "that the Party ultimately has power … Not only is a company responsible to do what the party demands, but they also can't admit to doing that if they're asked" (Peach, 2021).

As noted by Richard McGregor, wealthy entrepreneurs and CEOs in China "go to abject lengths to praise the party" (2019), and Party directives continue to be concerned with the need to "lead private economic persons to unceasingly enhance a sense of political identification with the Chinese Communist Party and Socialism with Chinese Characteristics" (Dotson, 2020). In 2018, the Civil Aviation Administration of China demanded that international airlines operating in China show Taiwan as part of China on their maps, lest a record of their "dishonesty" be made, and disciplinary action taken (Kobie, 2019; Perryer, 2019). And Hollywood insiders acknowledge that there is now no way that the major studios would make films like *Kundun, Seven Years in Tibet*, or *Red Corner* anymore; nothing so unflattering to Chinese officialdom would be acceptable (Tager, 2020).

The experience of Chinese billionaire Jack Ma is also instructive. In late 2020, Ma addressed some high-profile figures with a speech in which he called for reforms to China's financial system. In what appears to be retaliatory action, he was summoned by the regulators, the planned initial public offering for his latest venture was halted, US$76 billion was wiped off the value of shares in his companies, and he disappeared from public view for several months. In the words of Christina Boutrup, a journalist and seasoned China analyst, "he apparently crossed the invisible red line for what can be said and done in Xi Jinping's China" (Peach, 2021).

It would be easy enough to provide further illustrative examples of Xi's moves to centralize the leadership of China and to thereby enforce ideological conformity. But the crucial question to consider is how such moves can be reconciled with Confucian thinking. Confucius observed that: "A gentleman seeks harmony, but not conformity. A vulgar man seeks conformity, but not harmony" (Confucius, 1997, 13.23, p. 64). It would be absurd to suggest that Xi is, indeed, vulgar. And the rationale behind his desire for ideological conformity is well known. As Minxin Pei has observed, since the Tiananmen Square massacre in 1989, "no nightmare has obsessed the [Communist Party of China] leadership more than the collapse of the Soviet Union" (Pei, 2016, p. 17). Xi's explanation for its collapse is simple:

> An important reason was that the struggle in the field of ideology was extremely intense, completely negating the history of the Soviet Union, negating the history of the Soviet Communist Party, negating Lenin, negating Stalin, creating historical nihilism and confused thinking. Party organs at all levels had lost their functions, the military was no longer under Party leadership. In the end, the Soviet Communist Party, a great party, was scattered, the Soviet Union, a great socialist country, disintegrated. This is a cautionary tale!
>
> (Tiffert, 2019, p. 43)

It would seem that in Xi's mind the maintenance of national leadership through the centralized power of the Party is of paramount importance, even if such thinking cannot be reconciled with Confucian (or Taoist) concepts.

The challenges of leadership, as the twain meet

For both Chinese and Western business leaders, operations in China over the past decade have become fraught with even more challenges. The fact that Xi has taken China down a centralizing path of repressive, authoritarian, and confrontational rule has given rise to a range of profound difficulties, some ethical, others prudential or strategic.

In the West, the economic arrangement with China over the past few decades has been beneficial. China's manufacturing sector remains the world's largest, and few political or business leaders – whether they are from China or the West – are enthusiastic about Western businesses "decoupling" their economic activities from those of China (Black & Morrison, 2021; Ignatius, 2021). Some senior Chinese political figures do face travel restrictions,[2] and bills are being drafted to prevent the importation of goods produced through forced labour in Xinjiang.[3] But people like Elizabeth Braw (2021) who call on Western companies to leave China are in the minority.

In seeking to make sense of these challenges, it is worth remembering that not all of them can be attributed solely to Xi or the Communist Party. It is arguable that at least some of the underlying problems involved are best understood as a kind of cultural clash. After all, few people are fluent in both Chinese and Western modes of thought, and it is easy to allow thinking about these issues to be dominated by blinkered assumptions, simplistic arguments, or jingoistic feelings of cultural pride.

Roy Chua (2012) has conducted several studies into trust, cultural psychology, and business relationships in China. Admittedly, his work is not particularly focused on the ethical challenges associated with doing business there, and much of it was carried out before Xi became president. Nonetheless, when he explains the importance of deep cultural knowledge, for example, his insights are of abiding relevance. Chua's research participants included both North American and Chinese business managers and executives, as well as some European expatriates who had worked in China. He found that in some respects, China's ways of doing business were becoming more Westernized. When describing the network of personal relationships on which business activities in China commonly rely, the notion of *guanxi* (关系) is routinely invoked. As he observed "Experts line up to sell Western executive courses, websites, books and articles that promise to help them build *guanxi*" (2012, p. 28). Yet the advice that such experts provide is not necessarily helpful. As Chua explained, while Western executives were often being told to give gifts and to spend on entertainment:

> An increasing number of Chinese companies now actually frown on gift giving and other such gestures and are focusing instead on the business value that a potential partner brings … In that sense, developing *guanxi* is

> starting to parallel the more pragmatic networking that Western executives are used to; there is now a much stronger emphasis on what you know and what you can do than on whom you know. (2012, p. 28)

Chua's research stresses the contrast between two kinds of trust. First there is *cognitive trust*, or what Chua and his colleagues call "trust from the head." It is the kind of trust that results from the confidence that one can have in a person's accomplishments, skills, and reliability. Second, there is *affective trust*, or trust from the heart. This second kind of trust results from feelings of emotional closeness, empathy, and rapport, and it is the basis for most friendships and personal relationships.

Chua found that North American executives are more inclined than their Chinese counterparts to distinguish these two kinds of trust, and he makes sense of this as follows.

> The West has a long tradition of separating the practical and the emotional. Mixing the two is perceived as unprofessional and risks conflicts of interest. Among Chinese executives, however, there is a much stronger interplay between trust from the head and trust from the heart. (2012, p. 29)

So, while affective trust is the basis for most friendships and personal relationships, Westerners can be somewhat ambivalent about it in the context of business given that it can appear unprofessional and can give rise to conflicts of interest.

Some of the practical lessons to draw from such work are that Chinese businesspeople value cognitive trust. They may be less inclined than Westerners to distinguish it from affective trust, but it should never be assumed that they are ambivalent about it. Indeed, it appears that they are as interested as Westerners in the kind of competence, skills, and reliability that generates it. Therefore, instead of starting with lavish gifts and free entertainment, "Western executives need to start by developing the other person's trust in their capability" (Chua, 2012, p. 31).

Chua and his colleagues also found that Westerners commonly fail to develop the kind of heart-felt trust that their Chinese counterparts would like to have in them. It is not that gifts, entertainment, or respectful observances of etiquette are always a bad idea. But rather, Chua believes that this "trust deficit" will almost always exist, except in cases where Westerners have bridged it through "deep cultural knowledge and experience" (2012, p. 30). As he explains:

> Western executives who have mastered the art of building affective trust do so by developing a deep cultural knowledge – one that goes far beyond the mastery of social customs and etiquette. This deep

> knowledge can help bridge the trust deficit by approximating the basis of common ties and values that individuals from the same culture enjoy. (2012, p. 32)

Furthermore, as Chua notes, "Speaking the language can be a powerful tool for navigating the culture" (2012, p. 33), although he also outlines several specific suggestions that require far less commitment. As he explains, executives who have mastered "cultural metacognition" are aware of their cultural assumptions, and revise those assumptions in the light of their experiences. This helps ensure that their Chinese counterparts feel understood, instead of stereotyped.

It is arguable that the main insights to be drawn from Chua's research will be of practical value for a long time to come. His work suggests that through the development of deep cultural knowledge about China it is possible for Westerners to bridge the trust deficit, to do so with heart-felt trust, and to find something like the common ties and values that individuals from the same culture enjoy. Moreover, we may well expect the development of deep cultural knowledge, trust, and common values to be of genuine assistance when seeking to address important ethical issues. But we should never deceive ourselves about the problems that remain. When a company has Communist Party committees or "cells" embedded within it, serious and probing discussions can become very difficult. How, for example, do Western business executives in China get together with their Chinese counterparts and have full and frank discussions about the reliance or otherwise of their company upon forced labour in Xinjiang? What about discussions relating to the use of the company's intellectual property or to the sharing of customer details and data?

As Chinese regulatory requirements have become more restrictive, Western social media companies have withdrawn from China (Subin, 2021). And as Elizabeth Braw has noted, aside from the ethical and regulatory reasons to leave, in certain industries such as manufacturing, technology, and pharmaceuticals, there are now good business reasons to favor Vietnam, Thailand, or India (2021, p. 9). Yet there are still around one million foreign companies registered in China (RegistrationChina, 2021), and Western political leaders appear reluctant to impose sweeping trade or investment restrictions on business there.

While various criticisms and concerns about the role of Western businesses in China can be considered, it is also worth remembering that businesses can be expected to make the world a better place in one way or another. They serve customers, provide employment, transfer knowledge and skills, contribute to economic development, and return profits to their investors; such are the standard elements of their moral justification. Even when business owners decide to close an operation for ethical reasons, some people will suffer, and so the decision to be made is momentous.

Indeed, it may be that a great many Western businesses that continue to operate in China are able to do so in good conscience. While there are many possible ways to be complicit in the wrongs of the Communist Party of China, profiting from the forced labor in Xinjiang is not one of which all foreign business leaders are guilty. Similarly, many companies presumably have no reason to collect personal data relating to their customers, to participate in the theft of intellectual property, or to feign support for Party claims in relation to Taiwan, for example. In sum, to call for the withdrawal from China of all Western companies for these infractions would be, in effect, a call for collective corporate punishment. Innocent companies, workers, consumers, and shareholders would suffer, and it is very doubtful that anything worthwhile would be achieved.

For Western companies that continue to operate in China, serious challenges of leadership remain. Consistent with Chua's work, one can expect that the development of deep cultural knowledge, trust, and common values will be vital. Fluency in another culture is perhaps the most effective way to gain a congenial and sophisticated sense of humility, to liberate oneself from blinkered assumptions and simplistic arguments, and to transcend any facile or jingoistic feelings of cultural pride. And as Western leaders develop that cultural knowledge, a basic understanding of Confucian ideas should also be expected. Accordingly, they should come to recognise that enforced ideological conformity is contrary to Confucian teaching, and that leadership, in its best form, is accountable, responsible, and decentralized.

In the Western corporate world, some of the more influential trends in leadership thinking are in harmony with Chua's suggestions. Talk of "authentic" or "values-based" leadership has been ascendant in recent decades, and it is part of a more general trend in which leaders are prompted to think about their company's purpose and social contribution. By cultivating a shared understanding of that purpose, leaders are better able to justify the activities of the firm, and to motivate their teams. Bill George, one of the chief proponents of authentic leadership, notes:

> Authentic leaders have a deep sense of purpose for their leadership and are true to their core values. They are people of the highest integrity who are committed to building enduring organizations.
>
> (George, 2003, p. 5)

Such integrity requires us to be truthful and transparent:

> Values begin with telling the truth, internally and externally. Integrity must run deep in the fabric of an organization's culture. It guides the everyday actions of employees and is central to its business conduct. Transparency is an integral part of integrity.
>
> (George, 2003, p. 71)

Moreover, our words need to match our actions:

> The trust of leadership is earned through practicing the company's values every day, not just by espousing them. But when leaders preach one thing and practice another, commitment is quickly lost and employees become doubly cynical.
>
> (George, 2003, p. 75)

Being such a leader is not always easy, but it does help to create the kind of trust and confidence that successful leadership requires:

> Most authentic leaders … build their networks over time, as the experiences, shared histories, and openness with people close to them create the trust and confidence they need in times of trial and uncertainty.
>
> (George, Sims, McLean, & Mayer, 2007, p. 136)

In the literature on authentic leadership, talk of values and integrity is prominent. There is no suggestion, however, that all those within the firm need to adopt the same set of beliefs and values in all respects, that there is any need for ideological conformity, that they all need to behave or dress the same way, or that they all need to be of the one personality type. Indeed, the opposite is the case. Robert Goffee and Gareth Jones are keen proponents of authentic leadership, and they are insistent that "the organisation of your dreams" is one in which – among other things – individual differences are nurtured. As they say, such an organization is one in which employees can be themselves, more than one type of person fits in, and all of them are encouraged to be passionate and to express their differences even when it leads to conflict (Goffee & Jones, 2006, p. 102). In simple terms, we serve our organizations in the same noble way that Confucius believed in serving a prince: we tell the truth, even if it offends.

In some contexts, especially in today's China, authenticity in leadership may seem provocative and risky. Again, George's line is that "Values begin with telling the truth, internally and externally" (2003, p. 71). Given that speaking candidly against the Communist Party of China can result in the loss of one's livelihood or worse, the concern involved here is an important one.

In considering how best to respond to this concern, we need to remember that George was not writing with the current Chinese context in mind. A more nuanced perspective is provided by Aleksandr Solzhenitsyn (1974), a Soviet dissident imprisoned for sharing truths deemed by the authorities to be unacceptable. While Solzhenitsyn famously urged his fellow citizens to live not by lies, he was not calling for martyrs. His expectations were more-or-less realistic:

> We are not called upon to step out onto the square and shout out the truth, to say out loud what we think – this is scary, we are not ready. But let us at least refuse to say what we do not think!

Solzhenitsyn reminds us that there are times when discretion is prudent. While there is something heroic in those who would tell the truth boldly in all circumstances, silence does not always amount to cowardice. It is difficult to say how many business leaders – whether Western or Chinese – are working behind the scenes, holding their tongues in public while trying to bring about reform in private. But in any case, only the most strident of moralists could criticize such people for their lack of transparency.

Yet there is a further concern to raise here, and it relates to those who prefer to not even think about the truth. Václav Havel, the playwright, dissident, and later President of Czechoslovakia, acknowledged that for those living under a repressive regime, the official ideology has a kind of "hypnotic charm" (1985, p. 25). As he explains:

> To wandering humankind it offers an immediately available home: all one has to do is accept it and suddenly everything becomes clear once more, life takes on new meaning, and all mysteries, unanswered questions, anxiety, and loneliness vanish. Of course, one pays dearly for this low-rent home: the price is abdication of one's own reason, conscience, and responsibility, for an essential aspect of this ideology is the consignment of reason and conscience to a higher authority. (1985, p. 25)

So, regimes in which ideology plays this role are regimes that ask us to debase ourselves. Havel illustrates this most memorably through his discussion of the greengrocer:

> The manager of a fruit and vegetable shop places in his window, among the onions and carrots, the slogan: 'Workers of the World, Unite!' Why does he do it? What is he trying to communicate to the world? Is he genuinely enthusiastic about the idea of unity among the workers of the world?... I think it can safely be assumed that the overwhelming majority of shopkeepers never think about the slogans they put in their windows, nor do they use them to express their real opinions. That poster was delivered to our greengrocer from the enterprise headquarters along with the onions and carrots. He put them all into the window simply because it has been done that way for years, because everyone does it, and because that is the way it has to be. If he were to refuse, there could be trouble. He could be reproached for not having the proper 'decoration' in his window; someone might even accuse him of disloyalty. He does it because these things must be done if one is to get along in life. It is one of the thousands of details that

> guarantee him a relatively tranquil life 'in harmony with society', as they say. (1985, pp. 27–28).

We would hardly expect the greengrocer to display a sign that reads: "I am afraid and therefore unquestioningly obedient," even though such a statement would have at least been true. As Havel recognizes:

> The greengrocer would be embarrassed and ashamed to put such an unequivocal statement of his own degradation in the shop window, and quite naturally so, for he is a human being and thus has a sense of his own dignity. (1985, p. 28).

Instead of a sign that is truthful but shameful, the greengrocer understandably puts up a display that is of doubtful sincerity. The ideological performance helps him to conceal from himself both "the low foundations of his obedience," and "the low foundations of power" (1985, p. 28). In other words, ideology enables him to hide his self-abasement and fear behind the façade of something noble. As Havel so summarizes: "Ideology is a specious way of relating to the world. It offers human beings the illusion of an identity, of dignity, and of morality, while making it easier for them to part with them" (1985, p. 28).

Conclusion

President Xi Jinping's leadership has taken China down a centralizing path of repressive and authoritarian rule, and this has given rise to a range of profound difficulties, both for Chinese people and for Westerners. A Confucian approach to leadership, by contrast, would accept that leadership should be accountable, responsible, and decentralized.

While a Confucian form of leadership would be preferable, it is not something that Xi Jinping or the Communist Party of China is about to embrace. This being so, it is important to think about some practical steps that business leaders in China may take to mitigate the challenges that they face.

In search of such steps, it is worth remembering that not all of the problems faced by those business leaders – whether they be Chinese or Western – can be attributed solely to Xi or the Party, and some may be understood as a kind of cultural clash. The work of Roy Chua, however, is informative, serving to suggest that through the development of deep cultural knowledge about China it is possible for Westerners to bridge the trust deficit, and to find something like the basis of common ties and values that individuals from the same culture enjoy.

Yet even if all Western business leaders in China were to develop such deep cultural knowledge, problems would remain. When a company has Communist Party of China "cells" embedded within it, leaders within that business are bound to face difficulties if they need to have full and frank discussions about sharing customer details and data, for example.

In the Western corporate world, authentic leadership has been ascendant in recent decades. In today's China, however, the idea that leaders should simply tell the truth, internally and externally, is one that is best taken under advisement. Consistent with Aleksandr Solzhenitsyn's wisdom, a more realistic expectation may be that such leaders simply refrain from telling falsehoods. And calling to mind Václav Havel's reflections: To participate in an ideological performance is to indulge in a kind of self-abasement.

Notes

1 Or again: Lord Ji Kang asked Confucius about government, saying: "Suppose I were to kill the bad to help the good: how about that?" Confucius replied: "You are here to govern; what need is there to kill? If you desire what is good, the people will be good. The moral power of the gentleman is wind, the moral power of the common man is grass. Under the wind, the grass must bend." (Confucius, 1997, 12.19, p. 58)
2 For example, in March 2021 the United States of America, the European Union, the United Kingdom, and Canada all imposed sanctions on individual Chinese officials due to the alleged human rights abuses in Xinjiang.
3 At the time of writing, the "Uyghur Forced Labor Prevention Act" had been passed by the US Senate but not by Congress.

References

Australian Strategic Policy Institute (N.D.). *The Xinjiang data project*. Australian Strategic Policy Institute, retrieved from https://xjdp.aspi.org.au/

Bayles, M. (2017, 6 November). The not-so-magic kingdom. Retrieved from: https://www.the-american-interest.com/2017/11/06/not-magic-kingdom/

BBC. (2021, 25 August). China schools: 'Xi Jinping Thought' introduced into curriculum. *BBC News*. Retrieved from: https://www.bbc.com/news/world-asia-58301575

BBC Monitoring. (2017, 24 October). His own words: The 14 principles of 'Xi Jinping Thought'. *BBC Monitoring*. Retrieved from: https://monitoring.bbc.co.uk/product/c1dmwn4r

Black, J. S., & Morrison, A. J. (2021). The strategic challenges of decoupling. *Harvard Business Review, 99*(3), 49–54.

Braw, E. (2021, 17 February). Why Western companies should leave China. *Foreign Policy*. Retrieved from https://foreignpolicy.com/2021/02/17/why-western-companies-should-leave-china/

Buckley, C. (2014, 11 October). Leader taps into Chinese classics in seeking to cement power. *New York Times*. Retrieved from https://www.nytimes.com/2014/10/12/world/leader-taps-into-chinese-classics-in-seeking-to-cement-power.html

Buckley, C., Wang, V., & Ramzy, A. (2021, 28 June). Crossing the red line: Behind China's takeover of Hong Kong. *New York Times*. Retrieved from https://www.nytimes.com/2021/06/28/world/asia/china-hong-kong-security-law.html

China Daily. (2018, 23 April). Understanding China: 10 books from Xi's bookshelves. *China Daily*. Retrieved from: http://www.chinadaily.com.cn/a/201804/23/WS5add2c69a3105cdcf6519c80_1.html

China Daily. (2021, 10 January). China issues plan on building rule of law. *China Daily*. Retrieved from http://www.chinadaily.com.cn/a/202101/10/WS5ffaf586a31024ad0baa196f.html

Chinese Communist Party. (2013, 22 April). *Communiqué on the current state of the ideological sphere (Document No. 9)*. Retrieved from: https://www.chinafile.com/document-9-chinafile-translation

Chinese Communist Party. (2017, October 24). Constitution of the Communist Party of China, revised and adopted at the 19th National Congress of the Communist Party of China on October 24, 2017. Retrieved from: http://www.xinhuanet.com//english/download/Constitution_of_the_Communist_Party_of_China.pdf

Chua, R. Y. J. (2012). Building effective business relationships in China. *MIT Sloan Management Review*, *53*(4), 27–33.

Confucius. (1997). *The Analects of Confucius*. Translation and notes by Simon Leys. W.W. Norton & Company.

de Tocqueville, A. (1981). *Democracy in America (De la démocratie en Amérique)* (H. Reeve, Trans.). Random House.

Dotson, J. (2020, 28 September). The CCP's new directives for united front work in private enterprises. Retrieved from: https://jamestown.org/program/the-ccps-new-directives-for-united-front-work-in-private-enterprises/

Gardels, N. (2014, 29 September). Xi launches cultural counter-revolution to restore Confucianism as China's ideology. *Huffington Post*, blog entry. Retrieved from: https://www.huffpost.com/entry/xi-jinping-confucianism_b_5897680

George, B. (2003). *Authentic leadership: Rediscovering the secrets to creating lasting value*. Jossey-Bass.

George, B., Sims, P., McLean, A. N., & Mayer, D. (2007). Discovering your authentic leadership. *Harvard Business Review*, *85*(2), 129–138.

Goffee, R., & Jones, G. (2006). *Why should anyone be led by you? What it takes to be an authentic leader*. Harvard Business School Press.

Havel, V. (1985). The power of the powerless. *International Journal of Politics*, *15*(3/4), 23–96.

Harari, O. (2002). *The Powell principles: 24 lessons from Colin Powell, a legendary leader*. McGraw-Hill.

Ignatius, A. (2021). Americans don't know how capitalist China is. *Harvard Business Review*, *99*(3), 61–63.

Kobie, N. (2019, 7 June). The complicated truth about China's social credit system. Wired. Retrieved from: https://www.wired.co.uk/article/china-social-credit-system-explained

Lao Tzu. (600 BCE/1962). *The way of life* (R. B. Blakney, Trans.). Penguin Books.

Lencioni, P. (2012). *The advantage: Why organizational health trumps everything else in business*. Josey-Bass.

Leys, S. (1999). *The angel and the octopus*. Duffy & Snellgrove.

McGregor, R. (2019, 25 July). How the state runs business in China. *The Guardian*. Retrieved from: https://www.theguardian.com/world/2019/jul/25/china-business-xi-jinping-communist-party-state-private-enterprise-huawei

Nikkei Asia. (2021, 1 July). Full text of Xi Jinping's speech on the CCP's 100th anniversary. Nikkei Asia. Retrieved from: https://asia.nikkei.com/Politics/Full-text-of-Xi-Jinping-s-speech-on-the-CCP-s-100th-anniversary

Nisbet, R. (2010). *The quest for community*. ISI Books.

Peach, S. (2021, 20 March). Why did Alibaba's Jack Ma disappear for three months? *BBC News*. Retrieved from: https://www.bbc.com/news/technology-56448688

Pei, M. (2016). Transition in China? More likely than you think. *Journal of Democracy*, *27*(4), 5–20.

Pei, M. (2017). *China's crony capitalism: The Dynamics of Regime Decay*. Harvard University Press.

Perryer, S. (2019, 22 May). China's social credit system awards points to citizens who conform. The New Economy. Retrieved from: https://www.theneweconomy.com/strategy/116498

Phillips, T. (2016, 28 February). Love the party, protect the party: How Xi Jinping is bringing China's media to heel. The Guardian. Retrieved from: https://www.theguardian.com/world/2016/feb/28/absolute-loyalty-how-xi-jinping-is-bringing-chinas-media-to-heel

RegistrationChina. (2021, 2 November). How many foreign companies in China. Retrieved from: https://www.registrationchina.com/articles/how-many-foreign-companies-in-china/

Solzhenitsyn, A. (1974, 12 February). *Live not by lies*. Translated by Y. Solzhenitsyn. The Aleksandr Solzhenitsyn Centre. Retrieved from: https://www.solzhenitsyncenter.org/live-not-by-lies

Subin, S. (2021, 14 October). Microsoft to shut down LinkedIn website in China as internet censorship increases in the country. *CNBC*. Retrieved from: https://www.cnbc.com/2021/10/14/microsoft-to-shut-down-linkedin-in-china.html

Tager, J. (2020, 5 August). Made in Hollywood, censored by Beijing: The U.S. film industry and Chinese government influence. *PEN America*. Retrieved from: https://pen.org/report/made-in-hollywood-censored-by-beijing/

Tiffert, G. (2019). Memory in the era of Xi Jinping. *Journal of Democracy*, *30*(2), 38–49.

von Hayek, F. A. (1967). *Studies in philosophy, politics and economics*. University of Chicago Press.

Index